Pro-Social Language:
A Way to Think
about Behavior

Ellyn Lucas Arwood, Ed.D.

Mabel M. Brown, M.A.

Carole Kaulitz, M.Ed.

APRICOT, Inc., P.O. Box 230138, Tigard, OR 97281-0138

www.apricotclinic.com

P.O. Box 230138
Tigard, OR 97281-0138
www.apricotclinic.com

Arwood, Ellyn Lucas.

Pro-Social Language: A Way to Think about Behavior / Ellyn Lucas Arwood, Mabel M. Brown, Carole Kaulitz. – 1st ed. – Tigard, Oregon: APRICOT, Inc. © 2015

ISBN: 978-0-9679720-1-5

Key words:
1 Behavior
2 Language
3 Children on the autism spectrum
4 Teachers of children with learning, language and behavior difficulties
5 Metacognition in children
6 Pro-social behavior
7 Pro-social language

Sold and published by **APRICOT, Inc.**

Printed in the United States of America.

POD through Lightning Source, Inc.

Table of Contents

Dedication

We would like to dedicate this work to our families and friends.

Acknowledgements

We would like to acknowledge Tom Slavin's technology assistance in producing the many figures and works of students; and, David Kaulitz's and Robert Rostamizadeh's technology skills and patience during the process of publishing this book. And, to the many families with whom we have had the honor to work, we say "thank you." We understand that learning to behave is often a difficult task and we appreciate the time that our clients' families have spent learning to provide better options for their children with the hopes that their children will become productive citizens.

-Ellyn Lucas Arwood

-Mabel M. Brown

-Carole Kaulitz

Preface

The process of publishing this book has been both an arduous and rewarding task that has taken place over the past five years. From the very beginning, the authors found attempting to publish this material daunting; most likely because we are using a different cultural lens and interpretation of the most current literature that intersects cognitive psychology, neuroscience, and language together into what we call Neuro-Viconic Education, as the basis for our interventions.

Our strategies look and sound very different (relational language, whole to part, visual thinking) from what is currently considered to be best practice in education. Instead of emphasizing behavior as a unit of study, separate from people; we approach behavior as a form of communication. We interpret the behavior based on knowledge about how people learn to think (neuroscience and cognitive psychology), use language (cognitive psychology and language), and become socially competent (cognitive psychology, neuroscience, and language). Then we plan an approach to help the learner acquire pro-social ways to be able to make choices for behavior.

We sincerely hope that when reading this material, readers enjoy the book's emphasis on the learner's development of higher order, more pro-social development.

All children learn to behave. Children's behavior is a composite outcome of the way their neurobiological systems interact with their environments, the influence the environments have on the children's neurobiological systems, and the way that people within the children's environments assign meaning to their behaviors. From these experiences, all children learn to think about how to behave. The purpose of this book is to describe the connections among learning to behave, the use of language to help a child learn to think, in order to behave in pro-social ways, and how to foster higher order thinking for improved pro-social behavior.

It should be noted that "how" children learn to behave is not a philosophically agreed upon science. But, these authors have more than 100 years of combined work experience with children, schools, families, and educators around issues of behavior. It is our agreed belief set, and perception that many educators and families are often left feeling frustrated with programs designed to emphasize changing behavior without consideration for increasing a child's language or thinking. Therefore, these authors will emphasize the connections between learning to behave using language to help individuals learn how to think. The authors will show how to use language to increase a child's thinking so that a child has a language-based choice on how to behave. In turn, as the language improves the way children think, their social behavior also becomes more acceptable.

In this book, the authors view language as more than a set of structures or grammatical parts. Language is more than word order or syntax, word endings or morphology, word vocabulary or limited semantics. Language is more than the way it is used to get immediate tasks completed or pragmatics.

Language is more than an oral form of expression or the study of sounds or phonology. Language names a person's thinking and in turn represents the way the speaker values others, the speaker's own self, and the speaker's value of the relationship between the speaker and others. Language functions to help a child learn how to think about self and others. Language shows how a child thinks and learns to think. Language is a dynamic system of thinking that helps connect the child with his cognitive and social development.

These authors will make the connection between how people within society treat each other and how thinking about others increases the process by which children learn to behave or treat others. Learning how to treat others is part of the cognitive process of how to learn to be social and to be civil. Behavior is not the goal but the outcome of learning. How educators and parents assign meaning with language makes a difference in how children treat others; and, ultimately on how children behave. Behavior that works to support healthy interactions is pro-social in nature; while behavior that works to support unhealthy relationships is considered anti-social in nature. In order for parents and educators to assist children in developing pro-social behavior, adults must also be able to "know" what healthy relationships "look like" and how to assign meaning through supportive, rich language in order to promote healthy, pro-social behavior.

Even though pro-social healthy behavior is the goal for today's children; not all environments create opportunities for children to develop pro-social development. In fact, unfortunately, many children grow up in an environment of incivility (Walker, Ramsey, & Gresham, 2004). Incivility takes many forms; and, incivility is a form of anti-social behavior. Anti-social behavior is often assigned meanings such as "rude", "mean", "inconsiderate", "unpleasant", or "disturbing". Since incivility is prevalent, parents and educators often have difficulty understanding what behavior is acceptable as pro-social in nature. Therefore adults struggle in deciding what meaning to assign to behavior. This difficulty in assigning meaning to behavior is further complicated in families where the children's behavior does not match with what the adults expect as in the case of children with Autism Spectrum Disorders (ASD).

To determine whether a behavior is acceptable, parents and educators must decide what meaning they must assign to a given behavior. After educators or parents decide if a behavior is acceptable or unacceptable, they assign meaning. Then, educators and parents must decide what consequences or discipline is subsequently appropriate. Therefore, parents and educators often walk a tight rope between accepting a behavior based on popular "norms", and not accepting the behavior which may risk marginalizing the child. So, parents and educators must first decide if the behavior is okay, then decide what meaning to assign to the behavior, and finally how to follow up with the child's behavioral response to the assigned meaning. The following case provides an example of how difficult deciding what meaning to assign to a behavior might be.

This example comes from a 7-year-old child who is crying loudly and uncontrollably in a restaurant. The child's cry is loud enough to impact other people's social interactions. From the parents' perspective, they are doing the best they can to redirect the child so that he stops crying. Some restaurant patrons feel that the crying is disturbing their dinner. The owner of the restaurant feels responsible for making the restaurant a positive experience for all patrons; but the owner is unsure of whether it is okay to ask the parents to remove the child from the restaurant. Each person in this setting has an individual perception of why crying behavior is acceptable or unacceptable. And, if these adults experience difficulty in setting limits for what behavior is okay or not okay, imagine what it is like for a child growing up in this society to decide how to socially behave. If adults have difficulty deciding whether or not it is appropriate to allow a child to cry in a restaurant, then the process for a child to decide how to behave is even more difficult.

The adults in the restaurant must think through their actions and decide how to assign meaning to the child who is crying. Likewise the child is learning to behave based on what meaning the adults assign. This balance between what is acceptable, what is not acceptable, and making sure the child grows up being able to think about his own behavior is part of a learning process. The child brings his own neurobiological learning system to the setting and so the parents must not only decide what is okay, they must be able to assign meaning in the way the child's learning system is able to process the meaning.

The purpose of this book is to describe the learning processes and relationships among thinking, language, and learning to behave. These relationships are based on several principles that the authors will explain throughout the book. The first principle is in *Chapter One*: *All behavior is a form of communication*. Behavior tells the adults what the child knows, needs, wants, and is able to produce. Furthermore, this same behavior is used to diagnose. For example, two pre-school children are filling containers with pennies. One child picks up a handful of pennies and with a lot of effort puts each of those pennies into a cylindrical, small mouth container. This child is viewed as "patient", "inquisitive", and a good learner. Another preschool child is also filling a container with pennies. This child repeats the task for hundreds and hundreds of pennies. The child cannot be redirected verbally. Finally, the child's parent steps in and picks up the child to physically redirect the child; but the child begins to scream and tantrum. It is not long before this second child is referred to professionals, evaluated and diagnosed with an autism spectrum disorder.

Both children showed the same behavior, putting pennies into a container. But, it was the behavior in context of the environment and what each child was communicating with the behavior that resulted in different meanings being assigned by the adults in the children's environments. The first child was learning about how the pennies went into the jar. When the child had gained that concept, then the child went and found something else to do. The second child continued to see the patterns of the pennies as new input; and, so the second child did not stop the repetitive task.

Therefore, more than the children's behaviors must be examined – the place, extent, time, and situation of the behavior must be considered. Furthermore, many diagnostic labels such as autism spectrum disorders (ASD) often occur in co-morbidity with other diagnoses such as attention deficit-hyperactivity disorder (ADHD), conduct disorder, oppositional defiant disorder (ODD), obsessive/compulsive disorder (OCD), and/or bipolar disorders, to mention a few. Therefore, it is important to consider behavior independent of the disability label as well as consider the behavior within a context or cluster that determines the disability diagnosis. Even though the diagnosis may be important for eligibility of services or additional types of support, the child's behavior is separate from the disability or cause of the disability. *The adults must interpret the behavior (Chapters One and Two)* based on their experiences and beliefs. The second principle is that *all behavior is interpreted*.

Behavior is not the child; behavior is a result of what the child is learning. Children learn to behave. Therefore, *all behavior is acceptable*[1] (*Chapter Three*); but there are conditions surrounding whether or not the behavior is acceptable. The issues about behavior are: When does the behavior occur, under what conditions, where, and why? Two more principles are important for assisting children in learning to behave: *Children learn to behave through their own neurobiological learning systems.* These systems consist of neurosemantic processes of input, feedback, interpretation, and change. The principle that *children show what they mean through their behavior* is explained in *Chapters Three through Five.*

Therefore, learning to behave is a social development process that occurs as a parallel process of learning to think. The tools in this book include not only these principles but also how to use the principles as part of the way we assign meaning to how children behave (*Chapters Six through Eight*). The principle that *all behavior is assigned meaning* is important for establishing pro-social programs for behavior. The assignment of meaning to behavior is a language process that must occur in the way that children learn to behave so there is an emphasis on how to use language (*Chapters Nine through Eleven*) as well as how to identify the misuse of language (*Chapter Twelve*). Therefore, the principle that *language names the meaning of the behavior* is important to understand. Since the approach in this book on how to help children learn to be pro-social in their behavior, the authors also suggest that the emphasis should be on thinking and learning or preventing unwanted behavior, not on intervention based on eliminating unwanted behavior (*Chapter Thirteen*). The principle that *all children learn to behave through assigned meaning* helps establish strategies for providing children with pro-social opportunities.

The book is divided into two sections: The first section discusses the principles behind learning to behave. The second section emphasizes the tools for helping children learn pro-social behavior. Each of the chapters in **Section II** highlights a specific child or youth learning to behave while providing the readers with practical tools for helping children and adults learn to behave. Prior to each section, there is a description of the chapters in that section and what each chapter will provide the reader. It is the authors' beliefs that emphasizing pro-social development will result in more children learning to think about themselves in relationship to others' needs, thereby increasing civility among society's members. Parents and educators will find the use of the suggested language strategies as an effective and positive approach to helping individuals learn to choose pro-social behavior. The authors will provide many examples of what pro-social, rich language used to assigned pro-social meaning sounds like and looks like; so, parents and educators have the tools to determine which behaviors are acceptable and how to assign a pro-social meaning to children's behaviors. Furthermore, this book is loaded with real examples from children, most of who are diagnosed with ASD. And, the examples include all levels of children, from those who are non-verbal as well as from young adults with lots of language.

The authors believe that individuals diagnosed with autism spectrum disorders (ASD) struggle with the same issues of learning to pro-socially behave as do many individuals in society. There are many individuals with social challenges or what these authors will call anti-social ways of behaving that are not diagnosed under a specific disability. The methods in this book are aimed for all individuals who are learning to develop social competence….thinking about others in a way that

---

[1] Principle of behavior.

initiates and maintains healthy relationships. However, in addition to having to learn to behave, individuals with ASD often learn to behave with meaning assigned to their behavior in different ways than typically expected. This book will provide the reader with many ways to assign pro-social meaning to behavior in the way that individuals with ASD learn to think and behave.

Section I

Thinking about Behavior

This section of the book provides the reader with knowledge about behavior, a product of a child's learning system; how children learn to pro-socially think and therefore behave the way society expects. *Chapter One* overviews the principles about learning to think in order to pro-socially behave. In order for a child to learn to behave, those around the child must be able to assign meaning. So, the authors explain how all behavior is a form of communication in *Chapter Two*. The authors provide many examples of the same behavior interpreted in different ways based on adults' beliefs. These authors believe that a child's behavior is not the child, and that children must learn what behavior is acceptable from the child's environment. So, in *Chapter Three* the authors explain how all behavior is okay but where and when a specific behavior occurs is a choice dependent on thinking. Children must learn to think about their choices of behavior and how they all behaviors affect others. This thinking means that helping children learn to think improves the expected behavior, even for the lowest functioning children. Therefore adults must learn how to set limits and establish boundaries through pro-social use of language. So, *Chapter Four* provides the reader with an understanding of how we acquire or learn to think. By knowing how we think, adults are able to understand how to help assign meaning to children's behavior so children learn to choose behavior that matches others' expectations. In *Chapter Five*, the authors explain how thinking about others, which leads to behavior that will initiate and maintain healthy relationships, is pro-social in behavior. So, that the meaning assigned to children's behavior helps the child learn to pro-socially think. **Section One** (*Chapters One-Five*) *help the reader think about behavior, how it is learned, how to assign pro-social meaning for higher order thinking and improved social development.*

Important Concepts in *Chapter One*

Readers should be able to explain each of these behavior principles upon completion of this chapter:

1. All behavior is a form of communication.

2. All behavior means something.

3. All behavior means what others interpret.

4. All behavior is okay.

5. All behavior is learned.

6. All behavior has multiple interpretations

7. All behavior is either socially acceptable or socially unacceptable.

8. All behavior results in social development.

9. All behavior is subject to limits of what is "okay" as established by others.

10. All behavior means what verbal behavior, language, or nonverbal behavior interprets.

11. All behavior affects others.

12. All behavior has consequences.

CHAPTER ONE
What is Behavior?

Everything we do and say,
Everything we see and touch,
Communicates who we are
And why we act the way we do.

What do you think or do when you see a behavior you don't like? Maybe you see a child who hits or kicks, bites, or scratches, and you don't like kicking, scratching, or biting. So what do you do? Maybe you interpret what you see as a child who is angry or frustrated, anxious or curious. Maybe you see the child as troubled, irritated or needing some attention? Maybe you see the child's behavior as a product of learning? There are endless ways to interpret the child's behavior as communication.

The purpose of this chapter is to define behavior as a form of communication and then overview all of the elements of what defines behavior. When considering behavior as a form of communication, the true questions are "What does the behavior mean?" "What does the behavior communicate?" "What meanings do adults assign to the behavior?" In order to address the aforementioned questions, definitions for communication and behavior will be provided. And, how individual's backgrounds or philosophical beliefs affect the interpretation of behavior will also be addressed. Finally, this chapter will address the various conditions that change the meaning of behavior.

All Behavior is a Form of Communication

All behavior and the resulting interpretations tell a story. The story is a narrative about the child's behavior and the adult's interpretation of the behavior. In this way, *all behavior is a form of communication!* The adult[2] interprets the behavior, so the behavior means what the adult interprets. For example, if the adult sees the child's arm move through space, the adult might see the child "stretching." However, the child might move his arm in the same way but toward someone, in which case the adult interprets the arm movement as trying to "hit" another person. Thus, **the same behavior may have multiple meanings and, therefore, different stories.**

What the behavior means, depends on the observer's interpretation. If a child "looks like" she is running and the adult says the child is running, and then the behavior is running. But, if the child is

---

[2] Adult refers to the person who assigns meaning. This person could be an educator, a parent, a sibling, or another person in the child's environment. Typically adults decide the meaning children will receive. Child refers to the learner. The learner could be a child or an adult. In most educational settings, the child is the learner.

standing on her tip toes and moves toward a wall, a door, anything that stops her; then the same behavior that looked like running may mean that she is vertical but falling through space. In other words, the behavior is a form of communication, and the meaning of the behavior depends on the person who is observing. For example, some of the students with special needs are called "runners" because every time they are in a large open space, they start moving. These same students are communicating about the space they are in. In fact, they may just be filling the big space with their bodies, not running at all.

All behavior is a form of communication and what the behavior means is dependent on what language the observer, parent or educator, assigns to the behavior.

All Behavior Means Something

A newborn baby cries, and the mother rocks and comforts the baby. The baby continues to cry and the mother tries to feed the baby, change the baby's diaper, and swaddle the baby. Each time the baby cries, the mother tries to "understand" what the behavior of crying means. The mother is interpreting the baby's cry. The baby is using no words, no formal communication system, yet the mother responds as if the baby were talking. The baby's behavior is communicating because the mother assigns meaning to the baby's cry.

The baby's behavior of making a face and noise that the mother calls "crying" means to the mother that the baby needs or wants something that the mother can provide. The mother's interpretation of the baby's actions or behavior is what the behavior means. The mother assigns meaning to the baby's behavior, as if the baby is telling its own story. The baby cries. The mother tells the story. *All behavior means what someone else assigns.*

Activity: Who provides the meaning to a baby's cry?

When the baby cries, the baby's mother labels the baby's facial and vocal acts as crying. She interprets the behavior further. In response to the crying, she might say, "Oh, she is so cute; she is hungry." Now the crying means that the mother thinks the baby is hungry. If the mother feeds the baby and the baby stops crying, the mother says the crying meant the baby was hungry.

This type of interaction between the mother and the baby creates the agreed-upon meaning of the behavior: "When a newborn baby cries, the baby may be hungry." The behavior of the acts that make up crying (scrunched face and recognizable noise) becomes known as "crying," and the meaning of crying is that the baby might be hungry. In this way, behavior holds the meaning of those who **assign meaning**.

Activity: How does behavior acquire societal meaning?

All Behavior Means what Others Interpret

The previous example of the baby who cries and the mother interprets the cry is now a five-year-old kindergartener. The five-year-old drops to the floor, kicking and screaming, and with tears associated with crying. When the newborn baby did these same behaviors, the mother saw the baby as cute and wanting to be fed. But now these same movements in a five-year-old are seen as a "tantrum." That is, the societal meaning for the same behavior associated with "crying of the newborn" is different for the five-year-old. Mother smiled at the newborn baby who had a scrunched-up face and loud vocalization with legs and arms moving rapidly. But, when the five-year-old "tantrums," the same behaviors are seen as "inappropriate" and the mother's facial responses express disapproval, unhappiness, unpleasantness, and even anger.

The meaning of the same behaviors in a different setting, at a different time, is different. All behavior is meaningful. The people observing the behavior assign meaning to the behavior. This interpretation that the observers assign to the baby or child, tells the learner what the behavior means. *All behavior means what others interpret.*

All Behavior is Okay

When the baby cried, the mother thought the baby was cute. But when the same child used the same behaviors as a five-year-old, the mother named the behavior as a tantrum and responded differently. The reality about behavior is that *all behavior is okay; it is just where and when the behavior occurs that makes a difference in how the behavior is interpreted.* So, the meaning of behavior is not within the behavior but is dependent on the setting of the person, the age and, the agreed-upon interpretation by others. This principle about behavior places a lot of responsibility on the adults in a child's environment to provide the type of learning that is expected.

More examples of behavior that is okay in one place or in one culture, but is not okay in other places or cultures will be provided in later chapters. The point here is that *all behavior is okay*; but when the behavior occurs can have serious negative effects on others or on the child doing the behavior. Therefore, it is important for adults to provide clear explanations of when and why behavior occurs so that the children learning to behave are not confused. More about how to provide this clear language will be provided later in the book.

Activity: Why is all behavior okay?

All Behavior is Learned

If all behavior communicates, but the meaning of behavior is dependent on the setting, the situation, the person's age, and the agreed-upon interpretation, then how is behavior learned? When a person moves any part of the body, an observer may assign meaning to the movement. For example, a newborn baby's body will move to specific types of stimulation. For example, a touch to the area around the mouth will result in a primitive sucking response also known as a "reflex."

These *acts* combine into large movements. By the time the baby is between 4 and 6 months old, the baby reaches out for a toy, a bottle, or a bright object, and as he pulls the object toward his face, he begins to suck. There are numerous linked acts: hand moving out away from body, hand touching objecting, hand closing to pressure of object, arm moving with grasp of object toward the face, mouth beginning to suck as object moves toward face, object now in mouth, baby is drooling and mother is reaching to take the object out of the baby's mouth. This series of acts is seen as behavior. *A behavior is made up of a series of recognizable movements or acts.* For the acts to be a specific behavior, then someone must recognize the movements and name the movements with language. So, children learn "to behave" according to what others assign meaning.

Not all researchers or educators agree in how this learning takes places, but neuroscientists are providing a window into how the neurobiological learning system acquires meaning. This neurobiological learning system will be briefly explained later in this chapter and then multiple examples will be provided throughout the book for how the learning system provides children with necessary input for learning to behave.

Activity: What is the definition of behavior?

All Behavior has Multiple Interpretations

As children perform many of the same movements, adults assign different meanings. For example, parents and educators want children to be able to stand, move their feet forward in an alternate way, and therefore "walk." But, teachers don't want children to "walk" around the room during discussion and so teachers will tell students to "not distract" the other students. So, are these behaviors a "distraction" or "walking?" And, sometimes children who "are in trouble" will even tell the teacher "I was just walking."

All behavior lacks meaning until someone else, like the parent or an observer, decides to interpret it: "She wants her bottle; she must be hungry." But if the object were an earring that the baby pulls off the table and pulls toward her mouth, the meaning might be, "She is reaching to see why it is so shiny." or "We have to be sure that bright, shiny objects are out of her grasp so she doesn't pick them up and put them in her mouth and swallow them." Or, when the crying baby performs the same behaviors as a kindergartener that falls to the floor kicking and crying, the teacher may call the behavior as a "tantrum." *Individual acts combine into a whole behavior such as "reaching," "tasting," or "tantruming."* Over, a child's lifetime, there are many, many different interpretations to the same behaviors.

In order for children to learn what meanings go with what behavior and when such behavior is okay and when the behavior is not okay, children must receive a lot of language so that they are able to think about their choices of behavior. When is it okay to walk around the room? When is it not okay to walk around the room? The connection between behavior, thinking, and language is huge.

Activity: How do acts define a behavior?

All Behavior is either Socially Acceptable or Socially Unacceptable

Acts combine to form a behavior. Behaviors combine to tell a story. The people, in the learner's setting, tell the story. The baby or child shows a series of acts or behavior and the educators, parents, and others assign meaning to the behaviors. In this way, the meaning of the behavior belongs to those in the setting, not to the behaviors. This assigned meaning by those in the setting is a function of the human brain. Humans have the one commonality; a human brain. This commonality is what makes people social. How humans are different are the cultural components. Therefore, the human brain learns how to be social. In other words, we all have a human brain that is the foundation for how we all learn to behave and become literate (talking, reading, writing, thinking, viewing, speaking, and calculating). Deciding what meaning to assign to the behavior is cultural in nature. So, how does the human brain function to learn the meanings assigned?

Since initially all behavior or motor acts are (in newborn babies) responses to sensory (eyes, ears, nose, mouth, skin) input, all behavior represents the way the baby responds to a given sensory input, and the responses are judged, and then assigned a meaning, by those in the baby's environment. *The interpreters may judge the behavior as acceptable or unacceptable.* If the behavior is judged as acceptable, the baby fits into the norm of society's expectations. If the behavior is judged as unacceptable, the baby or child does not fit into the norm.

Since all behaviors are okay, such judgment is critical to the baby or child growing up and "feeling okay" about his or her responses or behaviors. Fitting into society depends on the behaviors that the child learns. For example, if a baby cries but the mother abuses alcohol and cannot consistently respond to the baby's crying, the baby may not be able to learn what socially acceptable behavior is. That is, the mother's inconsistency interrupts the learning cycle of figuring out what behavior is okay. This learning cycle is a consistent interaction among the child doing something, the parent assigning meaning to what the child does, and the child responding to what the parent did and so forth.

Because the mother is not always capable of assigning meaning, the mother's inconsistency might look like this: Sometimes the mother is drunk, and sometimes she is not drunk. So this mother does not always respond to the baby's attempt to communicate. Sometimes, when the baby cries, the mother responds and sometimes the mother is too drunk to respond. The baby is not learning what behavior to use to be socially appropriate. In other words, the baby does not know when to use what behaviors. The baby's meaning for behavior is unclear. So the baby grows up, unsure of the relationships between herself and what others do in relationship to her. The child learns that sometimes people are there to assign meaning and respond to her needs and sometimes people are not there to assign meaning and to respond to her needs.

Because the baby grows into a child with an uncertain meaning for behavior, she may grow up with behavior that reflects her knowledge of how others (the child's mother) will or will not be there to assign meaning for the child's development. For example, the child may grow up unable to intimately trust that others will care. So, how others interpret the baby's behavior determines the meaning that the baby learns about her, and about her relationship with others. The meaning of behavior is dependent on what meaning is consistently assigned. The baby depends on others to assign meaning to behavior so that the child is able to develop a healthy, pro-social (positive) development.

Activity: How does consistently assigning meaning to behavior help a child develop?

All Behavior Results in Social Development

Acts may look the same, but when combined to form behavior, they may be judged as having different purposes or meaning. For example, a child learns to reach for a shiny bottle to drink milk, but when the child reaches for mother's shiny earrings, Mother says, "Stop! Don't touch." To distinguish the difference between the shiny bottle and the shiny earrings, the baby must be able to discern the differences in input. And, the baby must be able to gain more information about each object, earrings or bottle. This additional information about the differences in the objects comes from those who assign meaning as well as the child's own experiences with those objects. So, babies grow up learning how to behave based on how the people around them assign meaning to the way the babies respond. This communication between the baby and others continues through childhood and into adulthood. In response to what and how meaning is assigned to the child's acts and behaviors, the child is learning how to think about the meaning of behavior. The child does something and the environment assigns meaning. The environment assigns meaning in a cyclic manner. The cycle of learning the meaning about behavior occurs in four neurosemantic stages. These stages are as follows: Sensory input, perceptual patterns, concepts, and language.

The first stage is sensory input to which the child moves in response to sensory input: Eyes blink to light or change in focus, skin twitches to change in the temperature of the air, heads turn to sound, and so forth. Those who observe or see these movements assign meaning as if the child were talking to them, "Oh, Suzie needs her bottle." or "Jack wants his binky." These behaviors become meaningful because the people in the child's environment give meaning to the behaviors.

The meaning given to the behavior helps the child determine what movements have what meanings, so the child begins to use those behaviors that are given the most meaning. For example, if the parent always laughs when the baby kicks someone, the baby will increase that movement because the laughing (face changes, vocalization changes, body moves toward the child) gives the baby a lot more input than a parent who does nothing when the child kicks. In this way, *the child learns what behavior means, how to use behavior to communicate or create changes, and when to use behavior for what type of communication effect.*

These responses to sensory input create a second stage of meaning or perception. All perceptions or recognition of sensory experiences are valid. This means that all behavior is a form of communication to which someone assigns meaning so that the learner acquires the meaning of behaviors. These patterns allow individuals to imitate what they have learned to see, touch, taste, smell, and/or hear. Imitation of patterns occurs at a sub-cortical level of the brain; and, therefore occurs without thinking.

As these perceptions for what behavior means occur over time, the meanings of the patterns begin to overlap, provided the learner's neurobiological system is able to overlap the patterns. When the meaningful patterns overlap, they form concepts or thoughts, the third stage. The child is beginning to think about how he or she is acting within the expectations and context of the setting. The child is learning to be an "agent," a social being, capable of choosing actions. These social meanings or concepts develop a social cycle between the child's behavior and what meaning that others consistently assign to the child's behaviors. This social cycle between the child and those around him helps the child learn what society considers is appropriate behavior. In this fourth stage, the parents or adults and others in the child's environment assign meaning with language. The parents might say, "Oh, I see you like spinach" in response to seeing the child eat the spinach. The child is learning how to behave according to the meaning of what others in his social environment assign. It is through this cycle of learning to behave that the child is developing a social being. The child may hear the parent's tone of voice and recognize that the parent does not usually say this comment so does the parent not like spinach? Did the parent expect the child to not like the spinach? Is there something wrong with eating spinach? Or, maybe the parent is thrilled that the child eats the spinach? Any meaning that is assigned with language will require more explanation, more language to explain all of the intricacy of the meaning. The bottom-line is that all behavior will result in social development, which can be positive or negative.

Activity: What are the four stages of learning the social meaning to how to behave?

All Behavior is Subject to Limits of what is "Okay" as Established by Others

This cycle of communication between the child and others helps the child learn how to behave, which in turn teaches the child how to "socialize," as defined by society. If the child learns the social meaning of behavior from those who are not part of the dominant culture, he will often not see how to fit into the dominant culture. Conversely, if the child learns how to behave according to dominant cultural expectations, the child will typically learn how to fit into society. Of course, this predicted social development is contingent on the child possessing a learning system that fits with the way that the people around him assign meaning (more about how to adjust the input for learning to behave will be provided in subsequent chapters).

If the child's behavior fits into society's expectations, the behavior is believed to be pro-social. If the behavior does not match society's expectations, the behavior is considered anti-social in nature. In other words, when a child learns to behave, he learns to be pro-social or anti-social in terms of the behavior he uses. *Pro-social behavior* refers to the way that people initiate and maintain healthy relationships with others. *Anti-social behavior* refers to the way that a child moves away from initiating and maintaining healthy relationships toward more societally unacceptable behavior.

Activity: What is pro-social behavior? What is anti-social behavior?

If a child learns the socially acceptable way to behave, then the child has more of an opportunity to become socially competent as a youth or an adult. *Social competence* refers to the ability to initiate and maintain healthy positive relationships. On the other hand, if the child is not able to behave in the way that society accepts, she becomes a child who is not able to initiate and maintain healthy positive relationships. This cycle between learning to behave based on how others assign meaning is important to the positive social development of all children as well as the basis to developing effective intervention practices for children who struggle to develop pro-social behavior or who struggle in interpreting what is socially acceptable behavior. Learning to behave reflects the social process of initiating and maintaining healthy relationships. Learning to behave is more than about discipline. Learning to behave is about social development. Later chapters will provide strategies for how to establish intervention that develops healthy pro-social development.

Activity: How does a child learn to be pro-social or anti-social?

Learning to behave is as simple as learning to communicate. If a child is alive, his body is responding to sensory input and the child is moving. If a child is moving, he is communicating, as long as someone is interpreting the behavior or movements. In this way, all children learn to communicate. All children behave. And, all behaviors are okay. The problem is that not all behavior is acceptable for specific situations and not all behavior leads to higher order thinking or better literacy for all children.

The biggest concern for educators and parents is that not all children learn to behave in a way that is pro-social. In other words, it is not whether or not the child can behave; it is whether or not the child's behavior matches the expectations of those in the child's environment. Therefore, those who work with children must decide what acceptable or unacceptable behavior is. That is, the adults in a child's environment must decide what behavior is okay or not okay. In this way, the adult knows what constitutes the behavioral limits. Once the adult understands the limits of what behavior is okay, then the adult is able to begin to assign meaning in ways that allow children to learn socially acceptable behavior.

Limits *are the behaviors that the adult interprets as okay or not okay within the expectations of others in that context.* When an adult sees a behavior, what does the adult think? Look at the list of interpreted acts as "behavior judgments" and decide what behavior is okay or not okay:

A 2-year old is waiting for a parade to start. He and his parents are sitting alongside the street. The two-year old begins to play in the street. *Is this okay or not okay?*

A 3-year-old is happily playing with sticks by pushing the sticks through the rails of a fence. *Is this okay or not okay?*

A 4-year-old is standing on the seat of a booth in a restaurant. He is staring at the people eating dinner in the next booth. Is this okay or not okay?

A 5-year-old is walking around a restaurant touching tables and talking to the people at the tables. *Is this okay or not okay?*

A 6-year-old is attempting to climb the magazine racks at the grocery store. *Is this okay or not okay?*

A 7-year-old is hiding under clothing racks and then running after another child in a department store. *Is this okay or not okay?*

An 8-year-old walks up to a stranger and then points his index finger in her face before saying, "Bang." *Is this okay or not okay?*

A 9-year-old walks through the grocery store touching a lot of the fresh fruits and vegetables at eye level. *Is this okay or not okay?*

A 10-year-old sees his friend across the common area of an indoor mall and yells a greeting to his friend. *Is this okay or not okay?*

An 11-year-old sees a younger sibling with a bigger cookie and snatches it out of her hands. *Is this okay or not okay?*

A 12-year-old asks a neighbor to buy some cookies; and then, when the neighbor says she can't, the twelve-year-old rolls her eyes. *Is this okay or not okay?*

Your interpretation of what behavior is okay and what behavior is not okay determines the meaning that a child will learn from a given behavior. Now, let's go back through these behavioral acts and put some limits to the behaviors.

A 2-year old is waiting for a parade to start.

He and his parents are sitting alongside the street. The 2-year-old begins to play in the street. One parent sees the child playing and thinks that there is nothing wrong. The other parent quickly redirects the child back to the sidewalk and says, "It is not safe to play in the street because people who drive cars and bicycles in the street may not be able to see you and you may get hit by the cars and bicycles, and if you get hit you will be hurt." This second parent realizes that a 2-year-old cannot determine when it is okay to play in the street. So, the parent decides that until the child is old enough to decide when it is okay to play in the street, the child is better off never to play in the street. Later chapters will explain how much language a child would need to have to be able to make a decision about when it is okay to play in the street. *A 2-year-old does not have the language to make that decision.*

A 3-year-old is very happily playing with sticks by pushing the sticks through the slats (vertical boards) of a fence.

One parent thinks nothing about the action and actually helps the child push some sticks between the slats as a game. The other parent explains how the owner of the house on the other side of the fence will have to pick up the sticks, how some sticks get stuck and push the boards apart, and how we might want to make our own woodworking project to learn how to push wood or pick up wood sticks as kindling for the fire in the fireplace. Again, one parent did not see anything but the immediate act of pushing sticks while the other parent was helping the child learn about when it is okay to push sticks and when it is not okay to push wood sticks. *Setting the limits here helps the child learn about other people (the neighbors) that the child does not see.*

A 4-year-old is standing on the seat of a booth in a restaurant.

The four-year old is staring at the people eating dinner in the next booth. The child's parent sees nothing wrong with the child standing on the seat and says nothing until the people in the next booth begin to stare back at the child. Then the parent says, "Sit down." At a third booth sits a different family. The family, in this third booth, also has a four-year old child, Jonathan. As soon as Jonathan begins to climb up to stand on the seat (and before the child can stare), the parent says, "Jonathan, sit on your bottom so you can eat your dinner. If you stand on the seat, you won't be able to eat your dinner. Also, you have dirt on the bottom of your shoes because you have been walking outside. When you stand on the seat, the dirt on your shoes will get on the seat and then the next person who comes to sit down will get dirt on the seat of his pants when he sits down." The second parent is setting limits – this parent explains why it is not okay to stand on the seat at a restaurant. *By learning the limits, the child is not given the opportunity to stare or engage in other anti-social behavior.*

A 5-year-old, Jonathan, is walking around in a restaurant touching tables and talking to the people at these tables.

The child's parent sees Jonathan's behavior as staying busy and doing what children do. At another table, a second child, Rachel, sees this behavior and asks her parent if she can get down and walk around, too. Rachel's parent thinks about the other people at those tables and recognizes that the child may be interrupting those people's dinners, conversations, evening out, and so forth. So, Rachel's parent explains to Rachel why she should not walk around – Rachel might interrupt others who are eating by touching their table or standing by them while they are having a personal conversation, and so forth. Jonathan's parent hears the explanation given to Rachel, so Jonathan's parent physically redirects her child away from the other tables and tells Jonathan to say, "I am sorry" or "Excuse me." *Rachel is learning the limits because her parent is explaining why she cannot walk around, while Jonathan is learning to say "I am sorry" but not understand why.*

A 6-year-old is attempting to climb the magazine racks at the grocery store.

The child's parent smiles and sees the child as staying busy, not making noise, and staying out of trouble. But a parent of another child sees this behavior as inappropriate, so when his child puts her hands on the racks, this parent immediately says, "Sammy, that rack is for magazines. It is not a climbing toy. When we get home, you can go outside and climb the climber in the yard. This rack is for magazines, not a toy for you to climb on." The second parent is setting limits. To the child, the magazine rack has rungs just like a climber, so the magazine rack can be climbed. The child does not know the rack might tip over; the magazines might get soiled and could not be sold, that the rack might not hold the child's weight and so forth. The child learns this information from those around, just like the child learns what behavior is okay and not okay according to this information. *The more information the parent gives about why the child should not climb the rack, the more information the child has for making choices during later situations.*

A 7-year-old is hiding under clothing racks and then running after another child in a department store.

The child's dad is tired of waiting for Mom so he begins to play hide-and-seek with the child. The child is learning to play with the clothes and clothing racks. Mom comes out of the dressing room and sees the child running. She immediately says, "Charley, you must make your feet walk because you cannot see around the racks and you might run into a lady who has a lot of clothes. When you hit her, she might drop the clothes and the clothes will get dirty, or she might fall over and get hurt. When you hit her, she is bigger than you are and you also might get hurt. When you run, you might also trip on the carpet and fall and hurt yourself. I don't want you to get hurt, or someone else to get hurt, or the clothes to get dirty. So, you can walk around or sit down." Of course, the child is looking at Dad who allowed this behavior. *The child is not only learning about behavior, he is learning that not all people set the same limits.*

An 8-year-old walks up to a stranger who is trying on some shoes at the shoe store.

The stranger is looking down at the shoes. The child points his index finger in the stranger's face and says, "Bang." The child scares the stranger. The stranger tells the child that he scared her because he pointed a toy gun, his finger, in her face and the rule is that he should never threaten another person with any type of weapon, gun or make-believe gun, because threatening another person means he wants to hurt the person. And, hurting someone else is not nice and that she does not want to be hurt. Meanwhile, the child's parent is in a corner of the store laughing. The laughing parent does not like to see the stranger set limits, so the parent tells the stranger that she should not talk to her child.

Basically, the parent is telling the child that he doesn't need to show regard for a stranger's well-being or safety and that hurting someone is okay – and, that the child does not have to attend to another adult's words. *This child is learning how to engage in anti-social behavior that is a form of bullying* (Chapter 12 addresses bullying).

A 9-year-old walks through the grocery store touching a lot fresh fruits and vegetables at eye level and then begins to pick up apples and drop them one-by-one onto the other apples.

The child's parent watches the child's acts and says. "Well, we don't need apples today." A near-by shopper tells the child, "When you drop apples onto the other apples, the apples bruise each other. You can't see the bruises, but when another shopper buys the apples and takes them home, the bruises will begin to show and eventually rot the apples." *The shopper was setting limits that the parent did not.*

A 10-year-old sees his friend across the common area of an indoor mall and yells to his friend.

Most of the adults around are annoyed but say nothing. One adult says to another adult, "He must think he is outside." *No limits are placed on the youth's yelling behavior, which means that the behavior is acceptable.*

An 11-year-old sees a younger sibling with a bigger cookie than hers. She snatches it out of her hands and gives the younger child the smaller cookie.

When her mom asked her why she did that, she says, "Well I am older so I get the bigger cookie," and the mom says, "All right." The mother is saying that it is okay to take objects without asking as long as the reason is okay. But what about the younger child's worth? Since the younger child had the cookie, wouldn't it have been appropriate to ask her to trade cookies? Does the mother value situational logic, or respectful behavior towards all people? *Values are important to consider in setting limits.*

A 12-year-old is selling cookies for a group at school.

She asks a neighbor to buy some cookies, and when the neighbor says she can't, the 12-year-old rolls her eyes. Most readers can identify with the rolling of the eyes. What does that mean? That behavior, rolling the eyes, is often interpreted as meaning, "I don't respect who you are." The youth meant that she did not respect the neighbor's decision. *The neighbor feels bullied and buys some cookies even though the neighbor cannot really afford the cookies.*

Notice that in these examples, there is a lot of language to explain the thinking perspectives of what is okay or not okay. The above examples demonstrate the following:

1. Children learn what is okay by others assigning meaning.

2. Learning to think about others, or being social, is a result of what meaning others assign to behavior in given situations.

3. *Setting limits* on behavior establishes what meaning a child learns about societal expectations. Such limits are established with language.

Activity: Why are setting limits an important part of teaching children to learn to behave?

All Behavior has Non-Verbal and Verbal Meaning

All behavior has consequences. What meanings does a child gain from the behaviors the adult interprets? And what happens when other children and youth assign meaning to adults' behaviors. If the behaviors and the interpretations do not match the rules of the society, the meaning of the behaviors is confusing. Such confusing messages, or mixed messages, do not provide limits for what is acceptable or unacceptable behavior. Without limits being placed, the behavior of the adult may teach an unwanted message or even multiple messages. The following are some simple examples of mixed messages.

- The students in a third-grade classroom are not allowed to climb on top of a stool to hang their work on a cord that is strung across the ceiling of the classroom. Yet, the teacher climbs on top of the stool to hang the pictures. When the teacher is not looking, students do the same climbing. *The students have not learned that this type of climbing is dangerous. Why?*

- An adult has to change a light bulb, so he stands on the seats in the restaurant to change it. The teens from a nearby high school are coming into the restaurant for lunch and see the manager standing on the seat. The students want to tell others in the group their ideas; so, they stand on top of the tables and seats to get others' attention. The manager asks the students to leave because they are standing on the seats and tables. *The students think that the manager is unfair to ask them to leave. Why?*

- A teacher does not allow students to doodle or draw while they are listening to the teacher. Yet, the same teacher knits through all staff and faculty meetings. She says she has to knit to listen, but she does not allow her students to do something with their hands when they are listening. *Why does her message seem confusing?*

Activity: How does assigning meaning to behavior set limits for how to behave?

All Behavior Affects Others

Why do we set behavioral limits? Is it for the child's safety? Is it for the parent's peace of mind? Or, is it so the child will learn to have acceptable behavior? Ideally, we set limits on behavior for all three reasons. *Limits are rules that we impose on a child so that the child will eventually learn how to govern his or her own behavior.* Limits require a lot of language. When a child acquires the language that goes with the limits, the child will have enough information to make decisions on how society expects the child to behave. *These rules or limits are given through the story that is told with language about the child's behavior as well as the meaning that the child assigns using the child's own language.* It is important to understand that all children need limits especially those diagnosed with social development issues, such as those with autism spectrum disorders. Remember that all behavior means what it is interpreted. So, even those who are significantly impacted with very little spoken language or those who are non-verbal need limits. And, the authors would say that those with little language need even more non-verbal limits to be able to learn to think about others. Through the use of language to assign meaning to behavior, the children learn what socially acceptable behavior looks like, under what conditions, and why.

Activity: How does language affect how a child behaves?

Adults use language to tell the story of the behavior. And, adults use their own behavior to show a child what the story means in different settings or situations. This cyclic learning –between the child's behavior and meaning the child assigns to others' behaviors – affects how the child learns to behave. The cycle is often perpetuated through generations because most adults rely on how they were raised to assign meaning to their own children's behavior. Parents, like teachers, often provide the same limits or lack of limits, the same stories, the same interpretations as they received as children. Therefore, the same behavior receives the same assigned meaning as the adult received as a child. If these behaviors are pro-social, the children are more likely to demonstrate pro-social behavior. On the other hand, if the parents and educators do not provide pro-social limits, the children are more apt to engage in anti-social behavior. Developing more pro-social behavior means that the adults must provide the language of behavior. The adults assign meaning with language about behavior—why the behavior is socially acceptable or not, when the behavior is socially acceptable and why. In this way, different adults use language to assign meaning, even different meanings to behavior. Overlapping the assigned meanings through different experiences results in children receiving multiple meanings about how language assigns meaning, their thinking about the meanings given to behavior, and how behavior interconnects with social development occurs.

The language of behavior helps children learn the limits of their behavior—what behavior is pro-social or anti-social. Adults must consider the following perspectives when using language to assign meaning to behavior: 1) the child's perspective: the child's developmental level of understanding of language about how to behave, 2) the parents or family's perspective: their values; and 3) the societal perspective: others' expectations for what is acceptable behavior.

Activity: What are some of the perspectives that children and adult need to consider when using language about how to behave?

Using the 3-year-old who was putting sticks in between the fence slats as an example, let's examine these three points of view. From the child's perspective, he appears to be happy, busy, and playing! From the parent's perspective, the parent is delighted because the child isn't making any demands on his time; that is, the child isn't crying, is not in danger, and is not causing damage to anything. If we stop analyzing the behavior at this point, the child will continue to put sticks through the fence because the adult allows the child to put sticks through the fence.

But let's consider this child's behavior from the point of view of others outside the child and the adult. Will this child's play behavior impact anyone else? For example, who is going to pick up all of the sticks on the other side of the fence? If the sticks are landing in a flowerbed, the owner of the flowerbed will have to pick up the sticks so that the flowerbed looks nice and the plants will be able to grow. It is also possible that the sticks are damaging flower leaves and petals. If the sticks are landing on the sidewalk on the other side of the fence, an elderly person could walk by and step on the sticks, resulting in a twisted ankle or a bad fall. If a young child learning to ride a bicycle drives over the sticks and loses control of her bike, she could crash her bike and skin her knees or elbows. If someone roller skates over the sticks, it could cause him to lose balance and fall down, perhaps getting hurt. Without the parent providing the language of the behavior of how putting sticks through the openings between slats in the fence affects others, the child will not learn others' perspectives.

Behavior does not occur in isolation. For children to learn how to behave, they must have social settings in which to learn the perspectives of others through lots of language that is presented in the way the children are learning to think.

Activity: How does language provide knowledge about others' perspectives?

Consider the example of the three-year-old child again: Most children at age three are thinking only about themselves, as most children are at an egocentric age. Therefore, it is appropriate for a three-year old child to only think about what he is doing. No one else is in the child's picture. But, adults are supposed to be able to think about others. Others should be in the adult's mental pictures. But, this parent in this example is egocentric, thinking just like the child. From the parent's perspective, dropping sticks doesn't hurt the parent and the behavior isn't hurting others right now. However, it is up to the parent to think about others, a higher developmental level. The parent must use language to assign meaning to the child's behavior so that the child learns about others. A parent's role in assigning meaning to a child's behavior begins at the birth of the child. To think about others means that the parent is helping the child learn about how behavior affects others. This book will provide lots of examples for how to assign meaning to children who do not learn from modeling or the sound of the voice. In this way, parents and educators will have tools for assigning meaning to the three-year-old child's behavior that the child will be able to understand.

All behavior has an effect on others at some level. Sometimes the effect is obvious such as when a child hits someone or sometimes the effect is not obvious such as when the sticks disappear onto someone else's property. Learning the language of behavior not only provides knowledge about others' perspectives but also helps a child learn how behavior affects others. Learning to think about others is part of learning the language of how to behave.

Activity: Why do all behaviors have an effect on others?

All Behavior has Consequences

A child moves. The adult assigns meaning. The child moves again, and the adult once again assigns meaning. As the child learns how to behave from these interactions between the child and others in the child's environment, the child also learns about the effects of behavior. For some behaviors, the child learns that there is a positive payoff. For example, the eight-year-old in a shoe store who used his finger as a pretend gun learns that adults sometimes like the behavior since his mother laughs; and, the child learns that other adults do not like the behavior, since the stranger set limits about the behavior.

The difference in meaning assigned by the two adults results in several meanings for the child: (a) The child is dependent on Mom, so Mom's meaning must be the one that counts; (b) Other adults are not reasonable as they do not assign meaning like Mom; (c) The child's behavior needs to occur again to clarify what the real meaning is; (d) Maybe Mom doesn't care as much as others so she needs to be tested in other settings; (e) whatever meaning an authority figure assigns, only Mom's meaning counts, and so forth. The number of meanings is limitless, the expected behavior is unclear, and the consequences of the child's behavior hold multiple interpretations.

Adults and others assign meaning and, therefore, give meaning to the child's behavior. Sometimes, the meaning of a child's behavior comes as a natural result of the behavior itself. For example, the child touches a hot stove, and the natural response is to quickly withdraw the hand since the stove's heat provides an unpleasant sensation. *Natural consequences* are responses to sensation without language or thought about the meaning of the behavior. Most natural consequences are to environmental sensations such as shivering to cold, sneezing in response to dust in the air, sweating in response to heat or anxious feelings, or jerking the knee in response to the doctor's physical mallet tap. However, learning conceptually about the outcomes of behaviors that do not have immediate natural consequences requires someone else to assign the language of the behavior.

Activity: What are natural consequences?

Even though natural consequences are responses to sensory input, there are also consequences to all behavior. For example, if a child understands a parent's words, "Be quiet," the child may close her mouth and not say anything for a while. One of the authors, Arwood, worked with a child who was told "Don't talk in school." The child literally would not talk in school for months. When she came to the school to consult, Arwood was told that they were not sure what had happened to the child. The child talked at home, according to the mom, but was selectively mute at school.

Arwood assigned verbal meaning to the child's nonverbal behavior. "I see your eyes look at my paper so you must have some ideas. Draw your ideas." As the child drew, Arwood continued assigning meaning: "I see you have lots of ideas to draw about. I can tell from your eyes and hand that you know about school because I see you looking at your paper. Your eyes are talking to me. Your eyes are telling me about what you are thinking." After about 20 minutes of Arwood assigning meaning to the girl's nonverbal behavior, the girl walked over to her mom and whispered loudly enough for everyone to hear, "Why does she think I am talking?" Her mom told her to ask me.

That was the end of the girl's selective mutism. When Arwood asked her why she had not been talking, she told Arwood that her mom told her not to talk at school. Mom's words provided a behavior consequence that did not match with what Mom expected. *Behavioral consequences* occur when a behavior is a result of some type of input. These types of consequences are a result of interpreting the meaning of what is expected; but these behaviors are not natural consequences. Natural consequences do not need language for thinking and responding with an interpreted behavior.

Activity: What is a behavioral consequence?

Behavioral consequences and natural consequences always occur as a result of a behavior or others' behaviors. In other words, all behavior has an effect. *Something always occurs as a result of a behavior.* This is an important principle of behavior, because sometimes people think that their behavior goes unnoticed and that, therefore, there are no consequences. Even in the most private environment, there is a consequence. For example, an adult sings in the shower. There is no one else in earshot. Therefore, the adult does not think there is a consequence; but there is! For example, the adult's singing may change the stress levels of hormones or neurotransmitters, resulting in a more relaxed feeling. This neurotransmitter change is also an effect, even if only at the cellular level of the peripheral or central nervous system. Some behaviors increase "calm sensations;" others do not. For example, running increases the response of the autonomic nervous system resulting in increased heart rate, perspiration, and beta-endorphins (positive feeling endorphins). Even though "running" does not calm the physical systems, the after-effect is positive.

When adults realize that all behavior has consequences, they begin to "think" about what a child's behavior is telling about the child. And, more importantly, adults begin to think about their behavior and what their behavior, verbal or non-verbal is telling the child. Thinking about behavior and its effects, on the child as well as the effects of behavior on others, helps the adult assign meaning that matches with what society expects. If the adult expects the child's behavior to promote healthy, positive (pro-social) relationships, the adult will want to assign meaning to the behaviors that promote pro-social behavior.

Activity: Do all behaviors have a consequence?

For an adult to be able to assign the meaning she expects from the child, the following conditions must exist in the adult who assigns meaning:

- The adult knows that all behavior results in a consequence.

- The adult realizes that the consequence of a child's behavior assigns meaning to the behavior.

- The adult knows that children learn the meaning of their behavior from the consequences.

- The adult knows that the meaning of the consequences could be verbal language or non- verbal behavior such as the child seeing the adult's behavior.

- The adult is aware of the social acceptability or meaning of the adult's own behavior.

- The adult is aware of the effect the adult's behavior has on others.

- The adult is aware of developmental levels of thinking about the behavior and the behavior effects.

- The adult understands that behavior has developmental levels of acceptability.

- The adult wants the child to be socially acceptable as part of becoming socially competent.

If these conditions exist, the adult is able to choose what meanings to assign to a child's behavior. For example, two parents decided to bring a 2-year old to an adult party. The purpose of the party was for colleagues to celebrate work-related activities. The success of having a 2-year old at this party was mixed. The house was decorated with many Christmas-related ornaments at the child's hand and eye level, and the parents did not redirect the child from playing with these decorations, from chasing the pet birds, from tasting others' alcoholic beverages, or from climbing on the furniture and playing with the blinds. These parents were lacking knowledge about behavior:

- These parents do not know that all behavior results in a consequence. If they had understood this, then when (or before) the 2-year-old put a glass nativity figurine in her mouth, the parents would have explained to her that the figurines were for looking at, not tasting; and, that they might break in her mouth (glass). Other adults did assign such meaning.

- These parents do not realize that the consequences of their behavior or lack of behavior assign meaning to the child's behavior. When the child "chased" the birds, the parents said nothing, even though the two birds were chirping and flying past the adults. The lack of the parents saying anything told the child that this was the behavior they expected when the child sees a bird or other animal. The person having the party immediately grabbed the birds and put them in their cages and explained how the birds were scared.

- These parents did not know that children learn the meaning of their behavior from the consequences. After many instances of other adults explaining, redirecting, and changing the environment to assign meaning for this 2-year-old, the mother said, "I am sorry that you cannot play here. I know that you are only 2." She had not said much of anything to the child and said this loudly enough for others to hear. Her message to some of the adults was that the child was just playing with the decorations, the birds, the blinds, and so on, and that if the party guests understood children, they would allow such behavior. Unfortunately, this mother did not understand that she was teaching a child how to behave for life. The mother's comments are telling the child that in some way, the child is "special" and that the child does not have to attend to other's assignment of meaning to her behavior. This lack of "respect" for others' assignment of meaning results in the child not seeking to develop pro-social behavior with others. Instead, the child is learning to scoff at others' opinions, a form of anti-social behavior. There is a great deal of anti-social behavior in today's dominant culture. More about anti-social behavior will be found in later chapters, especially *Chapter Twelve*, which discusses bullying.

- The parents do not understand that the meaning of the consequences to the child's behavior could be verbal or nonverbal, such as the child seeing the adult's behavior. Even though the child is only 2 years old, she will learn from the parents using language or not using language. Language is a form of input that has patterns as well as functions. The child is able to hear differences in the language patterns as well as see how the words match what the child sees. So, taking a decoration out of the child's hands after the child has been chewing on it says nothing about why this consequence occurred. For the child to understand why the figurine was not to be chewed on would require some oral language. As the reader will discover in later chapters, assigning meaning can occur with oral language, written language, pictures, drawing, and signing. The child needs the parents to set behavioral limits with lots of language so the child learns why she is not to chew on class decorations. Knowing why the child should not chew on the figurines is more important than stopping the behavior.

- The parents are not aware of the social acceptability or meaning of their own behavior in this situation. The fact that the adult was a guest at an adult party means that any deviation from the expected norm must be carefully weighed and considered. For example, asking the person throwing the party if he thought that bringing a 2-year-old would be appropriate would be a good start. And, then the parents should bring child-appropriate entertainment and maintain appropriate social behavior with the child and other adults; it is not the responsibility of the other adults to entertain or assign meaning to the child's actions.

- The parents are not aware of the effect their behavior of not setting limits has on others. When the 2-year-old tasted the nativity ornaments, chased the birds, or played with the blinds, many of the adults began watching the child and eventually redirected the child's behavior. This meant that they were no longer actively socializing with the other adults at the party, which changed the dynamics of the interactions. The adults' behaviors changed the celebration. After the party, the host commented that the adults had not been able to celebrate the year's activities as he thought they might. In fact, many adults left early in response to the child taking up most of the couch space, running through most of the living room space, and so forth.

- The parents are not fully aware of children's developmental levels. They are aware that their child is in a sensory level of response to input (tasting, touching, handling, and seeing), but the child is learning only her own meaning of those sensory inputs: The child sees an animal fly and the child runs. The child sees a figurine and the child tastes it. The child will not learn about the effect of the child's behaviors on the birds or figurines if the adults in the child's environment do not assign meaning for the child to learn. To be developmentally appropriate later in life, the child must learn what behavior is acceptable or not.

- The parents do not understand that there are some behaviors that are not okay in some situations, even by a 2-year-old. The behavior of tasting such as tasting different foods is acceptable; but, tasting the glass ornaments, which are not food, is not okay. Running outside through the grass is okay, but running after birds is not okay. (Birds, like other animals, are stressed physically by such aggression as part of their fight or flight system.) Just because a child is only 2 years old, these behaviors in these contexts are not acceptable. For example, decorations are for looking at with the eyes, not the mouth. Furthermore, the 2-year-old cried when she was redirected by other adults who did not want her to bend the venetian blind slats or break the turner of the blinds. Her crying is not okay at the party. Crying is not developmentally appropriate behavior for an adult celebration party where adults want to talk.

- Parents want their children to be socially acceptable, but this means that the children have to learn how to be part of an environment, how to fit in. To fit in at this party meant that the parents had to spend time helping the child belong. Accepting the child as a 2-year-old engaged in behavior that does not fit the party means that the child is not learning how to learn others' perspectives so as to initiate and maintain healthy relationships. If the parents want this child to develop pro-social behavior so that the child will be able to initiate and maintain healthy social relationships, then helping the child fit into the situation is an important meaning for the child to gain. Learning to fit into this situation allows the child to learn others' perspectives and develop appropriate social behavior in a variety of settings. The child's ability to fit into a variety of settings, as well as to understand others' perspectives, provides the child with meaning about how to initiate and maintain healthy relationships. In this way, the child is learning to be social.

Activity: What is the purpose of assigning meaning to helping a child learn to be pro-social?

Summary

Learning to behave is the result of interactions between the movements of a child and those who assign meaning to what the child shows. Language as well as nonverbal behavior is used to assign meaning to behavior. All behavior is okay, and all behavior communicates. The exact meaning of behavior is dependent on others' interpretations of the behavior as well as the outcomes or consequences of the behavior. The meaning given to behavior is the result of how others interpret or judge behavior as acceptable or not acceptable. Since behavior is social development, then all behavior has meaning that is learned by the human brain in context with others in the child's environment. For children to have positive or pro-social development, limits of what is okay or not okay behavior must be provided in ways that children learn best. Learning to set limits in ways that children learn to think through the *use of language provides children with better thinking choices of how to behave to be socially competent.* Examples of how to assign meaning to behavior so that children become socially competent will be provided throughout this book.

Important Concepts in *Chapter Two*

Readers should be able to explain each of these behavior principles upon completion of this chapter:

1. The meaning assigned to behavior comes from the adult's perspective or view

2. Adults determine the value of a child's behavior

3. Adults' values and beliefs come from the adults' past experiences

4. Adults assign meaning according to their past social experiences

5. Adult's interpretations as well as the learner's experiences contribute to the meaning of the learner's behavior

6. The meaning of values, beliefs or philosophies, and subsequent interpretations develop a child's social development.

CHAPTER TWO
All Behavior is a Form of Communication

I see what you believe.
I see your actions.
I see the way you see me.
I know I am a mirror of you.

A third-grader throws a toy across the room. The child's mother explains to the teacher that the child is "just tired and needs more sleep." The teacher sees the child's behavior as unsafe: The toy could hit someone and, therefore, the child's actions could hurt someone. The teacher interprets the child's behavior as destructive and potentially harmful to others. The parent sees the child's actions from an intentional perspective: The child does not intend to hurt anyone; therefore, the child is okay. If the child is okay, the behavior is okay. Both the parent and the teacher are correct in their interpretations: The parent is correct; the child is okay. The child is a "good" person. But the teacher is also correct. The behavior in this situation is unacceptable.

How a person interprets behavior is based on several factors: 1) the adult's perspective in assigning meaning; 2) the connection between the child's learning system and experiences; 3) the adults' values and beliefs based on their past experiences; 4) how the adults assign meaning based on their past social experiences, 5); the way adults assign meaning how the adult values the child's behavior; and 6) the values and beliefs of all the persons involved. This chapter will address each of these factors to provide the reader with an understanding of how thinking and behavior connect to others' language-based perspective, philosophies or beliefs, and assigned interpretations of behavior.

Perspective

The way a person assigns meaning or value to behavior is based in part on the person's own perspective. *Perspective* refers to a person's mental view of relationships, ideas, and facts. In literacy, perspective is also called *viewing* (Cooper, 2006). So, how a person views a behavior, determines how that person will assign meaning. In the previous example, the parent's perspective was that her child did not intend to hurt anyone and that the behavior of throwing the toy was the result of being tired. In other words, the parent viewed the behavior as a result of being tired. The parent did not see the behavior as a choice. The teacher must consider the perspective of all students. Therefore, when the child throws the toy, some other child could be hurt. Throwing the toy in the classroom is not okay, under any conditions. The parent has learned that behavior is not always a choice and that the child cannot help but throw the toy when the child is tired. And, the teacher has training to help her know that throwing a toy is a safety issue. The teacher and parent have learned to consider the behavior from their own perspectives. The teacher's and the parent's perspective is a product of each person's learning.

In learning to be literate, perspective is also referred to as "view." So, in order for children to become literate, they must be able to view the world in the way that the majority of people think. Otherwise, the safety of the majority is not considered and the child runs the risk of not being included or developing the feelings that go with marginalization. Viewing or being able to take perspective to think about others means that the learner has to acquire meaning about others. If a child or adult is only thinking about him- or herself, then the thinker is not going to engage in behavior that includes viewing other's needs. If adults help children increase their understanding of others' needs, then their ability to understand others' perspectives increases. This ability to think at a higher level is acquired through the neurobiological learning system.

Activity: What is perspective?

Learning System

Learning is the process of acquiring meaning (Arwood, 2011). Whether a person is learning to make choices about behavior or learning how to assign meaning to behavior, the process by which a person assigns meaning to behavior is an acquisition process. The acquisition process (Arwood, 2011) occurs in the following way. 1) The senses provide sensory input. 2) Each sensory system creates specific meaningful patterns that overlap. 3) These overlapping patterns form circuits in the brain. These circuits represent thinking or cognition. Thinking or conceptualization is the way children or adults socially connect to their world. 4) This thinking is named by language. Language forms from the cortical brain networks.

Because learning involves the neurobiological system, it is neurologically meaningful or neurosemantic. Through this learning process, a child learns to think and a child learns to behave the way a child thinks. When the child moves, the adult assigns meaning. The child learns to acquire the meaning of behavior in the same way that the adult learns to assign meaning to behavior. In this way, the child is learning to think the way the child is able to learn from the meaning being assigned by the adults.

Activity: How does a child learn to think?

The Meaning of Adult's Experiences

The adult's thinking or perspective is a learned product from the adult's past learning experiences just like the child is learning based on the child's own experiences. So, how adults view themselves also affects the way that they assign meaning to what children do. The adults in a learner's environment assign meaning to the child's behavior based on the adult's own thinking or perspective.

Viewing refers to how a person sees others based on his or her own thinking or past learning about the person's self. A person's "self" is the person's ability to be an agent, someone who is capable of doing something meaningful. So, how adults think about their own development of being capable as an agent affects the way they assign meaning to a child's behavior. For example, if an adult believes that he was not capable of making choices as a child, then the adult will not expect his own children to make choices. The response might mean the adult would see that a child is not capable of choices and therefore look to excuses to explain why the child threw a toy: The child is tired; he is only a year-old; he has autism; and so forth.

How adults view themselves as agents affects the way adults assign meaning to children's behaviors.

Activity: How does an adult's perspective about him or her "self" affect the way a child learns to think about perspective?

Adults Assign Meaning Based on Past Social Experiences

Since perspective or viewing relates to how a child is learning about others and others' inputs, a child learns to "view" his world according to what others value, which ultimately results in what the child thinks about "who" he or "she" is. For example, if the teacher values the safety of the other children, she will stop the child's throwing of toys even if it means removing the child from the classroom through suspension, in school detention, and so on. However, if the teacher views the child's throwing of a toy as a failure of the child to understand the consequences of his behavior, the teacher will spend time explaining to the child why he cannot throw, toss, hurl, or bounce objects that might hit someone else.

"Who" is the child. The child learns the meaning by how the adult handles the situation. This meaning will contribute – in either a positive or negative way – to the child's self-worth. Any element of "self" has to do with learning about "who" the child is in relationship to others in the child's environment. "Who" the child is refers to the child's development of self. What the child does represents the child's thinking and learning but the behavior does not define the child's "who."

For example, if the child's actions (throwing toys) are stopped; but, the child does not understand "why," he stops the actions; then the child may not learn the desired message. The desired message would have something to do with others…how others might get hit by a toy and be hurt or how others might fear being hit and therefore be afraid to be in the classroom. Or, how being afraid to be in the classroom would affect other's thinking or learning and their schoolwork is important to them. These types of meanings about others' views or perspectives suggest that other people are important, how other people think is important, how other people feel is important, how the child acts in terms of others' needs is important and so forth. People or agents are meaningful! In order for the child to learn that the child is important, the child must be able to view others in the child's thinking.

These messages about the meaning of behavior help develop the concept of "agency" or self—how people learn to be in a community with other people. These are messages about "who" people are, who the learner is, how the people within the learner's environment think, and so forth. Messages aimed at developing the self of a person or "who" messages help promote social development. The child is learning to think about being social and being in the community with others.

Activity: Why are messages about a person's "who" important to develop?

"What" is the behavior. But, when children stop an undesired behavior without understanding how that behavior relates to others in the child's world, then the child is learning about the objects and how to value things. The child learns that the adults value "what's" – what happens, what he did, what others do, what will happen. Value for the "what's" result in the child's self or "who" not being as valued. As a result, the child, as a person, values the "what" portion of his behavior but not necessarily his own personhood, an ***agent***, someone who consciously or intentionally does something. Too much emphasis on the behavior or the child's products, the child's "what's" will result in the child not growing as an agent. Learning to be an agent is the foundation to learning to be social in learning to behave.

Activity: How does an adult's perspective about the "who" or "what" affect learning to behave?

Adults Assign Meaning Based on their Values

Each learner values what others have pointed out or indicated is meaningful. For example, in some cultures, there are no words for color, because those cultures have color as part of the function of the object. But, in our culture, we categorize color so we see color as a value. With the development of learning to behave, what we value as a culture, a family, a parent, a school helps determine how a child learns to think about making behavioral choices. Or, in the case of children who are severely impacted, even learning to think affects how the child will function in the child's immediate environment. Learning to think about what is socially acceptable means that a child has to learn to think about the other people or "who's" in the child's environment.

Who vs. What. A person's "who" (Arwood & Young, 2000) refers to his or her development of ***self***. The various aspects of self-such as self-esteem, self-concept, self-awareness, and so forth, come from learning to be an agent. So when a newborn cries, the newborn is trying to become a person who can do something to get his or her needs met. When children are born with conditions such as Autism Spectrum Disorders (ASD), they have difficulty developing the concept of agency because they cannot communicate the way others around them expect. So, people around children with ASD have difficulty assigning meaning. And, when adults do assign meaning, individuals with ASD often have difficulty processing the input.

The development of "who" is social development. For example, some children with ASD cry, but the typical parent soothing, which is done with the parent's voice (sound), does not comfort them. Typically, a parent would follow the child's actions and meet the child's needs based on the child's behavior, but since the child cannot produce the expected behavior in response to the parent's voice, touch, and so on; the parent cannot assign meaning that the child is able to receive. Therefore, the parent is not able to meet the needs communicated by the child. Likewise, some babies do not cry a lot and so the parent has difficulty figuring out the baby's needs. Therefore, the parent struggles with finding appropriate behavior to assign meaning. And, the baby is also not learning to be an agent.

Figure 2.1 (also *Figure 10.1*) shows how most neurotypical learning systems develop concepts. Since social development is about acquiring the meaning related to the concept "self" or agency, the learning system must provide for learning of these concepts.

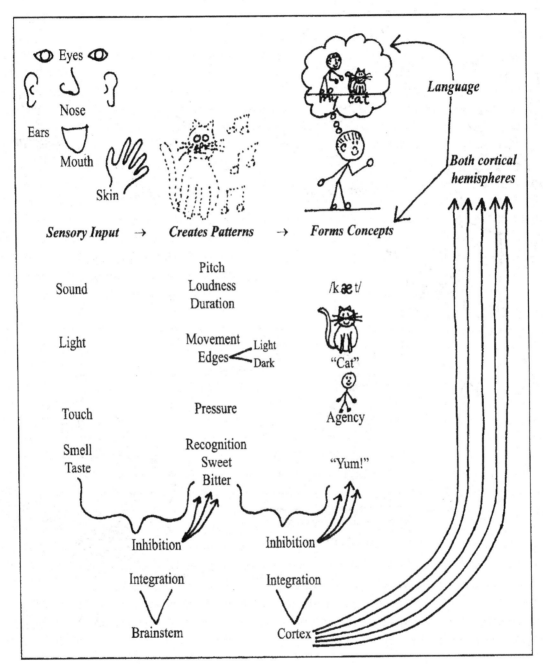

Figure 2.1. Arwood, E., & Kaulitz, C. (2007). *Learning with a visual brain in an auditory world: Language strategies for individuals with autism spectrum disorders.* Shawnee Mission KS: AAPC Publishing. Permission granted.

Figure 2.2 (also *Figure 10.2*) shows the difference in the learning system of a child with ASD. Notice that the sensory patterns do not become concepts. Therefore, individuals with ASD struggle with concepts of self or agency.

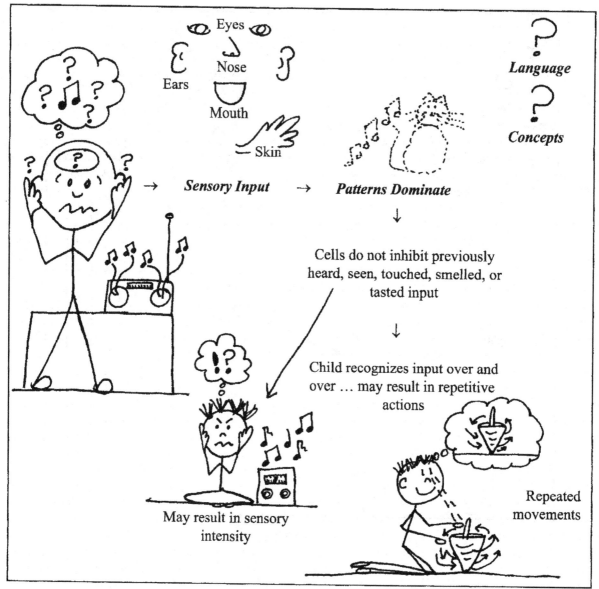

Figure 2.2. Arwood, E., & Kaulitz, C. (2007). *Learning with a visual brain in an auditory world: Language strategies for individuals with autism spectrum disorders.* Shawnee Mission KS: AAPC Publishing. Permission granted.

Not being able to form those concepts related to being an agent who communicates with others in a typical learning environment results in children with ASD having a lack of social development. On one hand, the environment expects the child to learn to become an agent but the child with ASD cannot learn to become social from "typical environmental input." The child's lack of social development and therefore "lack of learning to be social" is based on not being able to process typical environmental input. This lack of social development contributes to the child's behavior looking as though the child is impacted by ASD. The result is that the behavior is used to diagnose the child with ASD. This mismatch between expectations and helping a child with ASD learn to be social can be affected by thinking about how a child with ASD learns to be social and then changing the input of assigned meaning to match the way a child with ASD learns.

Activity: Why do children with ASD have difficulty developing social communication?

Most educators realize that the input for children with ASD must be visual (e.g., Arwood, 2011; Arwood & Kaulitz, 2007; Arwood, Kaulitz, &Brown, 2009). However, visuals are not all the same (Arwood et al.), and all visuals have a developmental level (Arwood et al., 2009). (More about the types of visuals used with behavior issues and the developmental levels will be presented in *Section II* of this book.) But providing a visual input is only one factor in the process of learning to be social. Learning to be social means that the child develops appropriate behaviors to initiate and maintain healthy relationships. Learning to be social necessitates that the adults are able to assign meaning to the child's "who," not the child's "what's." Therefore, how the adults' value or think about the child's behavior as well as the adults' use of language also makes a difference in what meaning is assigned to a child's behavior. For example, one of the authors, Kaulitz, worked with a 12 year-old non-verbal, non-reader, non-writer, non-signer, non-toilet trained individual. This youth was large for her age and her behavior had become very aggressive. Even with nine years of behavioral training, speech-language therapy, occupational therapy, and special education supported by medications; this 12 year-old was no longer capable of staying in the same room as other children or adults. The adults (with legal counsel representing the family and the school) sat down and agreed to a six-week program where the adults would provide lots of language in the way the 12 year-old learned (hand-over-hand[3]) so that she could learn to think about how to behave. They drew, wrote, and performed activities of daily living (e.g., meals) with lots of rich oral language, lots of rich cartooned pictures, as well as lots of writing. The change in her performance was amazing. She no longer hit, kick, bit, screamed; but, she did point, walk independently, have non-vocal conversations using her picture book, and intently watched others' faces move, how their hands moved, and tried to make her hands sign or indicate meanings. She was learning to think and more importantly learning to be an agent because the people working with her treated her as an agent, someone they valued. The adults assigned meaning in a way to make the girl's behavior function in a way that she acted as an agent, someone who does something that is pro-social.

The value of the child as a person "who" is able to do something comes from learning to be a competent agent, someone who is able to carry out an action that others respond to as meaningful or acceptable. However, not all adults believe or adhere to a set of beliefs about behavior that emphasize the development of agency. Some people place an emphasis on the behavior alone, not the person. The emphasis on the person's "what" and not the person's "who" will not always develop a person into a social being.

---

[3] More about how to use hand over hand will be provided in later chapters.

Activity: What is the difference between learning to be an agent (self or who's) and learning to be associated with "what" a person does?

Values and Beliefs of Society

There are many philosophies or theories (e.g., see Webber and Plotts, 2008) that have been promoted as ways to understand where behavior comes from, what to do with undesired behavior, and how to help children or adults who exhibit such undesired behavior. In many of these philosophies, behavior is not a form of communication. Therefore, when someone talks about behavior, behavior means discipline. The meaning assigned to behavior makes the child and the behavior the same. The authors do not see these beliefs helpful in assigning meaning so that children learn to think about their actions; and therefore, learn to be social. When behavior is thought about only in terms of controlling behavior and disciplining children for unwanted behavior, then negative meanings are being assigned to the child.

The authors believe that all behavior is a form of communication. Therefore, behavior is not a 'four letter word'! Behavior is the result of what a child has learned, wants to show, what others believe who have assigned meaning, and the interaction between children's learning systems and others' assigned meanings. This section will highlight some of the tenets that the authors believe help us focus on developing pro-social development, how to help children view themselves and the people around them as valuable.

Pro-Social Development. The authors do believe that all behavior is a form of communication. Adults will assign meaning to the behavior. And, how a child is able to learn from those around the child does make a difference in how the child learns to think about the child's "self" or about others. This thinking could result in becoming an agent who is capable of initiating and maintaining social relations (pro-social development) or the meaning could result in the child not being able to learn how to initiate or maintain social relationships with others.

Pro-social thinking means that the learner exhibits behavior that contributes to the development or initiation of *positive* relationships as well as the maintenance of healthy relationships. These authors believe that the goal of all work on behavior is to improve the pro-social development of a child through better conceptual thinking. There are several considerations in the interaction between the child and others in the child's environment.

The first consideration is that the family does contribute a history (*e.g., Freud, 1957); but the family does not determine who the child is or will become.* The family provides the meaning that the family believes or values. Some of these meanings may result in thinking that is rational, irrational or misconceived. These meanings help form the child's thinking about "self" and others. For example, if a male treats females differently at work; there might be some family history that explains the difference in treatment between males and females. The authors see this influence of the family as one set of meanings. The adults in the child's educational environment can provide additional meaning to help the child fit into other settings such as the school. Examples of how to draw out these meanings will be found in later chapters.

A second consideration in helping a child develop pro-social behavior is to realize that *behavior is a result of thinking, but not all of us learn to think in the same way.* Cognitive Behavior Therapy or CBT is a way to examine the thinking behind behavior (e.g., Kelly, 1955; Briers, 2009). For example, Adam is a nine-year-old who does not want to go to school. Mom assigns the following meaning, "Adam does not like P.E. and today is a P.E. day." So, she tries to give Adam a different perspective, "Adam, you will like P.E. today. Sam, your friend, will be in P.E. today." The more Mom talks, the more the Adam seems to be out of control. Mom is trying to help Adam see the situation from a different perspective, but Adam does not learn like Mom thinks. Adam learns best when he can see what her words mean. She needs to draw and write about where Adam is going, what he will be doing, when he will be doing what, and with whom. Furthermore, he needs mental thought bubbles to be able to see what others think under these same conditions.

Adam needs some help learning to think. Just talking to him using oral language about his behavior is not helping him learn to socially think about appropriate ways to situationally behave. Later chapters will provide lots of cartoons and examples of how to help children see the thinking behind their behavior and others' beliefs. A learner acquires the meaning behind behavior so as to think or self-regulate. The authors believe that being able to talk about self-regulation is something adults are able to do; but children must learn the thinking first. Furthermore, since most of the CBT strategies involve the use of oral language, for many with ASD who not have a fully developed language systems or who cannot use the sound of oral language, changing the way a child or youth or adult learns to socially function will depend on using lots of language to assign meaning to what others believe.

A third consideration for developing pro-social behavior is that language names what we know; *but children do not know what adults know. So, children must be given the language for what adults expect.* For example, a four-year-old child, Jimmy, with ASD is told to sit down like his brothers are sitting. Jimmy is not able to understand that input, so he starts jumping up and down and screaming. Young children, below age seven, value what others request because they want to be like those who take care of them, that is a known element of social development. Therefore, if Jimmy could sit and remain seated, then he would. Talking with the child through a rational explanation such as "you need to sit like your brothers so you can get a happy face" does not help Jimmy. Jimmy has a lot of borrowed language and imitates a lot of others' phrases but he does not possess a lot of natural, shared, conversational language. So, giving him the adult words of sitting to obtain a happy face does not help Jimmy know that when he sits, his job is to make mental pictures of what the teacher is saying with the movements of her mouth. So, children, like Jimmy, will only socially develop as well as their language has been given meaning for through ways that Jimmy learns. Jimmy needs to see what the adults are saying with sound. Jimmy needs the written patterns or words that go with the pictures.

A fourth consideration about pro-social thinking is that the people in a child's environment assign a lot of meaning, *but not all inputs are the same in meaning.* In other words, many belief systems consider the environment influences on social development. For example, Bronfenbrenner's ecological systems (1979) or bio-ecological model (Bronfenbrenner, 1993), explains how a person's behavior is influenced by the external elements of the surrounding world. Most educators know that the environment makes a difference in behavior. For example, a child may not exhibit unwanted behavior in one setting like P.E.; but that same child may always demonstrate unwanted behavior in reading. So, obviously the environment has some contributing effect on the child. But what is the effect? Is the environment causing the behavior or does the child not have enough information about how to be successful in reading to be able to behave like everyone else?

These authors suggest that it is important to consider "how" the child learns and how the child is being given input in the two situations, P.E. and reading. Certainly, the environment affects the child's learning, but how the child learns must also be considered. If the child is able to make meaning from watching what others do in P.E. and imitate what they do, then the child can do what others do. So, in P.E., the child can act as an agent, a person is able to fit into what is expected. But, if the child is asked to produce the sounds of what the child sees on the page in reading, and the child cannot process those sounds into mental pictures, then the child may not be able to do what others do. The child in reading is no longer able to act as an agent. The child will find some other behavior to communicate what the child can do...cry, hit, walk around the room, rock back and forth, repeat the class rules and so forth. The child's difference in behavior between the two settings has little to do with the setting as much as it has to do with what the learner is able to make meaningful.

The environment does not cause behavior, but what meaning the child or learner is able to create from the environment does make a difference in how the child is able to function in relationship to others. In this way, the child learns to be as pro-social as the environment is meaningful to the child.

Activity: What are the primary beliefs of an ecological approach toward behavior?

A fifth consideration about becoming pro-social connects to how well children are able to use their language to name their thinking. In other words, not all words are equal in level of difficulty or in understandability. For example, students who have sufficient language and cognitive development to understand the school's rules are able to choose to follow the rules. But, a child who does not learn concepts the way the school rules are taught may not learn the meaning behind the rules. Or a child who lacks conversational levels of language may not be able to understand the school rules from the adult's perspective. If the child or learner does not have the language to name his thinking or enough conceptual learning to understand social rules, then the learner is limited to making choices based on what the learner does understand.

So, the environment cannot provide all of the learning. The child's neuro-semantic language learning system must also play a role (see Neuro-Semantic Language Learning Theory in Chapter 2 or NLLT). The relationship between nature (neurobiological system) and nurture (environment) has been a long time consideration regarding behavior. Today the relationship between the environment and the genetic makeup (epigenetic studies) points to the relationship between genes and the environment affecting one's learning, thinking, and subsequent behavior. In turn, one's learning, thinking, and subsequent behavior may have an effect on the person's gene regulation. The University of Utah offers an excellent explanation of this process (http://learn.genetics.utah.edu/content/epigenetics/).

There are methods for dealing with the environment of children. For example, family education or community school programs attempt to deal with the interaction between the child and the child's environment. In order for a child to learn to fit within an environment, the child must be able to engage in behavior that the members of the environment accept. And, members must be able to assign meaning about the environment in ways that the child is able to make meaningful. Children must be giving opportunities to be agents if they will develop pro-socially.

Activity: What are some connections between the way meaning is assigned and the way children learn meaning?

The sixth consideration in pro-social development is to consider how a child constructs meaning. Historically, children were observed to develop their social ability within a context (Bandura, 1968; Bruner, 1983; Vygotsky, 1962). The child learns to be social because those around him provide the opportunity to develop socially through modeling and through interactions between the child's construction of meaning and the development of the child.

Using this belief system about neurotypical development, social development seems to "unfold" (Piaget, 1952). A child who is surrounded by other people constructs meaning from those others' actions. According to Vygotsky, this type of development as it relates to language and thinking is reciprocal: Language increases with development and, therefore, so does cognition. But, cognition or thinking must first develop before language can be used to name the thinking. Language represents thinking, but thinking is acquired through learning to think. When a child constructs enough meaning to create language; then, language may become a tool to mediate thinking and learning. A child's language level will determine how well a child is able to think about being social.

Activity: What is the reciprocal role between constructing meaning for cognition and language?

Most interpretations of how atypical learners construct their social concepts from the environment do not explain what happens when a child cannot "unfold" like others. For example, a child with ASD can be surrounded by healthy, loving families that provide a lot of directed opportunities for learning; yet, the child with ASD still not is able to construct the expected level of social meaning. Therefore, it is apparent that not all individuals learn to be social by the modeling of socially acceptable behavior.

This brings us to the seventh consideration in helping children pro-socially develop. *Constructing meaning about social development must come from the way the child's learning system can make use of the input.* In other words, attention must be paid to the way the learning system develops the thinking and the language (see NLLT). Unfortunately, modeling the appropriate social constructions does not create an explicit approach to guiding the child's construction of meaning in a way that all children are able to learn. Therefore, not all children are able to construct meaning without intervention. So, then there exists the question, "What intervention do we choose to help children become pro-social?"

For example, if you believe that a child is learning to behave based on modeling behavior, then you will want to put the child into lots of role plays and intervention scenarios to practice the social roles and social sayings from models. These authors recognize the importance of social roles modeling the language and/or asking the children to imitate the language will not increase the thinking for natural applications of language. Children must learn the concepts of pro-social thinking therefore their learning systems, developmental levels, and ways in which they learn to be pro-social must be considered.

Activity: How does the environment play a role in children learning to construct pro- social meaning?

An eighth consideration in pro-social development is that all behavior is the result of the physical neurobiological system, *but not everyone has the same neurobiological way of learning concepts.* All behavior comes from the human body. All behavior reflects the way the human body functions. Studies show that diet, exercise, meditation, relaxation therapy, and medications are possible ways to treat behavior problems and have an effect on behavior. For example, children with ASD might be put on a special diet, enroll in special exercise programs, participate in relaxation therapies, and/or receive medication for their behavior. And, for many students, positive results are found with each of these treatments.

However, the relationship between thinking and physical behavior in the human relates (Osgood, 1956) to the way the learner is able to use language to mediate thinking and doing (Arwood, 2011). For example, a child with ASD no longer wanted to touch paper, draw on paper, write on paper, or have anything to do with paper in any form. The educator explained to the boy that the paper is made of trees. She then explained how the tree is chopped down and ground into fiber, like the fiber on celery or snap peas (the boy likes snap peas). She then had the boy rub the surface of the smooth desk and had him feel the fiber in the yellow paper. She explained to him that he could feel the fiber of the trees on the yellow paper but not on the desk since the desk was not made up of trees.

Once the student had the cognitive knowledge that the roughness in the paper was fiber, he had no problem handling paper. The mind (cognition) can have a huge influence on the physical processes of the biological system. The biological system may also be influenced by medical interventions. On the other hand, medication may help the learner tolerate the environment or, even better, process new information, but it will not provide for a lack of past thinking and learning. And, medication will not help a learner use language better for learning information that the learner has missed. A child will develop pro-socially only if both the child's mind and body are considered.

Activity: What is the relationship between the child's body and mind in learning to be pro-social?

The ninth consideration in the process of becoming pro-social is that learning to be social involves the acquisition of concepts (Arwood, 2011). People acquire social concepts through the neurobiological learning system. At each neurobiological level, whether or not the cells receive and transmit the information is dependent on whether the input is meaningful or neurosemantic. As previously mentioned, the Neuro-Semantic Language Learning Theory (NLLT) explains the process of social concept acquisition as follows: First, the sensory receptors like the eyes and ears input the features of the visual wave (light and movement) and of the sound wave (loudness, pitch, duration). Then these features become electrical messages through chemicals that send patterns of these features through the nerves to the cerebrum or brain. Along the pathway from the receptors to the brain are cellular structures that recognize the patterns. At the brain level, recognition occurs in large sets of patterns from several different inputs, past and present, as part of neuronal circuits. These circuits of overlapping layers of input, past and present, are thoughts or ideas called concepts. So, in this model, children learn to be social by creating meaningful overlapping patterns of physical input that will form social concepts. (See *Figure 2.1.*) These neural circuits or social concepts represent thinking. If these concepts are positive, the child learns to initiate and promote the maintenance of healthy relationships, and those in the child's environment view the child's behavior as pro-social. The child's language will then name this pro-social development.

Activity: What are the four levels of the Neurosemantic Language Learning Theory?

Summary of Pro-Social Development. The early social concepts are about the agent who develops his or her "who" into various components of "self" over time. In order to acquire these social concepts, the authors suggest that parents and educators deal with behavior in the following ways: 1) match the input to the way the learner is able to construct concepts; 2) assign meaning to the learner's development of self in order to offer the learner with multiple sets of patterns about how to act like an agent; 3) match the developmental levels of language, materials, and programs to the developmental level of the learner's concept development; and 4) set clear limits and boundaries to establish social expectations based on societal norms. Emphasis is on the child's development as a person or agent in relationship to others. Thinking is a product of the neurobiological learning system. In other words, children learn to behave through the neurosemantic processes of language acquisition and then use language to name the child's thinking. As the interaction between language and thought increases over time, the child becomes more and more able to demonstrate more social skills and concepts so as to develop social competence, the ability to initiate and maintain healthy relationships.

Activity: How does learning and pro-social development interrelate?

Beliefs about Children

All behavior is a form of communication. What meaning is assigned by others coupled with the child's own learning system determines the meaning of the child's behavior. The meaning of behavior comes in part from the meaning others assign; from what others believe about pro-social development, and even from how beliefs about social development assign meaning. Different cultures, families, communities, and individuals develop different beliefs about how adults "should" treat children. And, therefore, how to assign meaning as well as what meaning to assign to a child's behavior becomes relevant in helping set up programs for children to learn to be social. Some of these beliefs may be tied back to general camps of philosophy or even training. For example, some people believe that all behavior is learned from the imitation or copying of what others say and do. So, when a child produces behavior that others in school do not produce, rather than seeing the child as unskilled and, therefore, needing more conceptual learning about "how to behave," the educator believes that the child is living in an environment that does not provide the correct models. As a result, the school attempts to target the "correct behaviors" and set up programs for the child to learn to "behave" from models that are imitated, shaped, and reinforced. But imitation has to work for both unwanted and targeted behaviors. If a child learns "target behaviors" by imitation, the child must also have learned unwanted behaviors by imitation.

The authors have worked with plenty of children who demonstrate behavior that the families, schools, and communities do not present. In fact, many children with unwanted behavior have siblings raised in the same family who do not show the unwanted behavior. For example, one child repeatedly banged her head and chewed on her digits, but no one else did this in her environment. So, if she used this behavior – having never seen it – the child had not learned it from imitation. Perhaps the original behavior was "typical," and the unwanted behavior was a product of someone shaping the typical behavior into something unwanted? If this were the case, the child would show some "typical" response to self-injurious behavior such as the child would flinch because it hurts to chew on a finger or bang one's head. Obviously, the child does not produce behavior that has typical natural consequences of "pain." The child is able to move the hand or fingers to her face like others do, but the thinking behind the chewing of the fingers, the cognitive pain, is language-based and this must be considered in setting up meaning for behavior.

So, children do not learn to behave based solely on imitation. This means that children are not learning to socially understand their world only by imitating good models of the world around them. Furthermore, imitation cannot account for children's differences in learning. Therefore, the methods that assume all behavior is the result of imitation do not match the evidence. *Only when thinking is included in helping children learn to behave does the child learn to be social at a higher level than just imitation occurs. These authors suggest that thinking must be included in interpreting the meaning of behavior. Social development is the acquisition of learning to think.*

Activity: So, what does it mean when a child produces a behavior that no one else in the child's environment exhibits?

The authors believe that children do not imitate behaviors but learn to become "who" they are, not what they do. According to this view, children learn to behave based on how well their neurobiological learning system (brain and spinal cord of the central nervous system) functions in coordination with the way the environment assigns meaning. Therefore, a child who chews his fingers or bangs his head is demonstrating differences in his learning system. These differences suggest that the child will need different types of input from the adults than usual for the child's neurobiological learning system to recognize the meaning of a chewed finger – it bleeds, it hurts, it looks bad, and so on. Furthermore, the child who is hurting his body does not have the language to name what the child sees, smells or feels.

For example, one non-vocal child diagnosed with ASD could write the patterns of any words she ever saw. Often she chewed her cuticles until they bled and got infected. One day, one of the authors, Brown, used oral language to help the child see the relationships between bleeding and pulling the skin of the cuticle. The author made sure Bekka could see the author's face and mouth movements. The author said something like this, "Bekka, when you bite your fingers, you pull the skin off. When your skin comes off, your fingers bleed. When your fingers bleed, they get infected. When your fingers bleed and get infected, they hurt. When your fingers bleed and get infected, then your fingers will hurt. When your fingers hurt, you will not like it. So, Bekka, do not put your fingers in your mouth. Do not chew on your fingers. Do not pull the skin with your teeth. Do not make your fingers bleed. Do you understand?" The child nodded her head and even though she had no oral language, she recognized the patterns of the concepts and did not chew on the skin around her fingers again. Even more important, it was probably not the behavior that made a difference; it was the meaning assigned to the concept "hurt."

This child did not have enough language to "feel" the sensation as "hurting." Once the educator assigned the meaning of "hurt" to the behavior, the child no longer engaged in the behavior. She "knew" one meaning of "hurt." This author's belief system is one that assumes that all behavior is the result of learning concepts. Concepts are a product of learning to think through the changes of the neurosemantic language learning system as a result of input that the child is able to understand. Since children with ASD think using visual cognition, providing the language within the context of a story or event so the child could see the movement of the educator's mouth provided sufficient meaning for the child's neurobiological system to recognize it as meaningful.

If adults believe that children are able to learn to behave, and if adults have an understanding of how that learning takes place, they provide more opportunities for children to learn the thinking behind their behavior. On the other hand, if adults believe that children learn behavior based on what children see, then they will look for ways to change the behavior because the behavior represents "bad or incorrect" learning. To correct faulty learning of behavior, most adults want to structure the classroom and family with rewards (punishers alike) to change behavior. These external controls will not improve the child's thinking or language development to become pro-social.

Activity: What is the difference between learning to behave through imitation and learning to think about how to behave?

Providing children and adults with opportunities to learn the cognition or thinking behind behavior results in development of social concepts, pro-social behavior, and an emphasis on the pro-social development. Providing children and adults with programs designed to correct faulty learning of behavior that results in a focus on the behavior places an emphasis on "what" the child does, not on "who" the child is. Such programs do not develop the child's social conceptualization (e.g., self-esteem, self-concept, self-awareness) and may objectify some low-functioning children over time, resulting in more aggressive, anti-social behavior.

These two paradigms, providing pro-social opportunities to become an agent who is capable and programs designed to correct faulty learning, have a different focus: The former emphasizes the child's learning strengths in that the emphasis is on how the child acquires meaning. The latter emphasizes the child's deficits – what the child doesn't do correctly. The authors of this book suggest that most of us want to place meaning on how to pro-socially develop the child, so methods center on ways to help the child learn to socially think in the way the child acquires concepts.

Activity: How do people's views of children's behavior affect how they think about how a child learns to behave?

Values

Philosophies affect beliefs, and beliefs affect the way we deal with behavior. Everyone with language has a set of values. *Values* refer to the positive or negative judgments or interpretations about beliefs, interests, desires, and needs. These value sets exist within groups – families, communities, cultures, and societies. For example, one family believes that children are possessions – "that is my child." That particular family also values parenting as all-inclusive; meaning that all behavior stops with what the parent does, says, acts, thinks, and so forth. When a child within that family produces unwanted behavior, the family believes the child's behavior is a personal affront to them. As a result, they may try to control the child's behavior at all costs. This may result in verbal and physical forms of abuse. Abuse is the process of imposing another person's will on a child in such a way as to objectify the child rather than empowering a child's development. Furthermore, because the family values children as possessions, it is reluctant to ask for help and even rebukes others' attempts at helping them learn how to handle the child's unwanted behavior. Such control reflects the personal family values.

On the other hand, some families value children as people who do not have the skills or wisdom of older youth or adults and believe (or value) that it is the family's responsibility to help the child learn the skills and gain the knowledge. Such families seek out all sorts of help for a child who demonstrates unwanted or unskilled behavior with the idea that it is the family's responsibility to find methods and strategies to help the child. Furthermore, these families often see their role as part of a bigger community so that they encourage their children to consider all adults as helpful citizens.

These are just two examples of how values impact the way families view children. There is an entire continuum of values in families, and these values do reach into norms of what cultural groups such as schools expect. In fact, many professional development programs are designed to teach the faculty and staff to be consistent – adopt one set of values for how to treat behavior across the entire school. For example, with Positive Behavior Supports (PBS, 2008), adults expect teachers to educate the students on specific behaviors in the school such as "Be Kind" through explicit principles of applied behavior analysis where behaviors are targeted and rewarded. But, how does "Be Kind" look to a child who can say the words but does not have mental pictures of what "be kind" means. Or, is the teacher being kind when the teacher keeps telling the child he can read, but the child cannot make meaning out of the sounds for oral fluency? Maybe seeing the child's behavior as valid and assigning meaning to the child's behavior will help provide a shared value that meets both the learner and the adult educator or parent.

Values come from philosophical beliefs about how to treat behavior as well as from training in those beliefs. For example, one school may foster the belief that all students can succeed (behave, read, write, think, view, speak, listen, and calculate). Therefore, the staff develops a set of methods that they believe will work as a program for all children. The school then places the blame on others such as the family for learners who struggle and don't succeed since the school believes that their program works for all children. When the blame can't be found in the program or the families, then the problem lies with the child; the child's diagnosis keeps the child from learning to read.

All values are perceptions. And all perceptions are valid. The issue of values and behavior is that people don't think or learn alike; therefore, all children or adults are not able to "act" or behave the same way in response to the expectations or values and perceptions of others. Viewing behavior as a product of the learning system allows educators or parents to separate the child's behavior (what's) from the child's (who) and place an emphasis on helping the child "learn to behave" rather than "teaching" a child to behave according to the adults' perceptions and expectations. Learning to behave is a pro-social goal of acquiring meaning, for all children.

Activity: How do values affect the way a person thinks about behavior?

Summary

All behaviors are a form of communication. The meaning communicated rests in the way that adults assign meaning based on their past experiences, values, beliefs, even training. The meaning that the behavior holds is based on others' perspective, philosophy about behavior, philosophy or beliefs about children, and their beliefs about behavior and values. All of these elements contribute to the interpretation of a behavior. And, not all children learn the same way; so how meaning is assigned will determine, in part, what children are able to process for their own ability to learn and think. Therefore, it is important for educators and parents to reflect on their values and beliefs about behavior and how they view the reasons or methods for "handling behavior." When children learn to think in ways that promote the initiation and maintenance of healthy relationships, then a child is learning to think pro-socially. The meaning assigned with language and through actions help children learn to be more social. Since all behavior is either socially acceptable or socially unacceptable, *Chapter Three* discusses the ways in which people determine whether or not a behavior is acceptable.

Important Concepts in *Chapter Three*

Readers should be able to explain each of these behavior principles upon completion of this chapter:

1. All behavior is acceptable; it is the time, place, and situation that determine the meaning.

2. Different people see the same behavior as acceptable or not based on personal limits.

3. Personal limits may or may not align with cultural standards.

4. Developmentally appropriate behavior occurs when personal limits matches cultural standards.

5. Philosophies determine how to assign meaning to a behavior as acceptable or not acceptable.

6. "Disturbing" behavior is personally bothersome, but "disturbed" behavior is a problem in learning social development.

7. Definitions of disturbed behavior relates to thinking as well as learning

CHAPTER THREE
All Behavior Is Okay

I see you spit; spitting into a cup is okay.
I see you hit; hitting a baseball outside is okay.
I see you run; running a marathon is good.
When do I spit, hit or run?

All behavior is okay; it is when a behavior occurs and under what circumstances that determines if the behavior is considered acceptable or not. The question is, "When is a behavior okay or acceptable?" and, "When is the same behavior *not okay* or acceptable?" For example, spitting toothpaste into a sink is okay. So, spitting is okay. But, spitting at a person is never acceptable in the mainstream U.S. culture. Children are told in schools, "Don't run!" but the same children are expected to run when playing ball on the playground. All behavior is okay; behaviors that occur that are okay are judged as acceptable. Behaviors that occur that are judged as not okay are considered unacceptable.

This chapter discusses how to decide what is acceptable behavior based on personal limits and cultural boundaries. Definitions of limits and boundaries will be provided. When educators and parents set limits, they are also defining what behavior is disturbing. And, when society finds that a person's behavior is outside of all personal limits and boundaries of what is acceptable, the individual's behavior is considered "disturbed." The definition for "disturbing" versus "disturbed" behavior will be offered. This chapter also sets up the definition of when and under what condition unwanted and disturbing behavior becomes a behavior disorder.

Personal Limits and Cultural Boundaries

Individuals within a culture may have different personal limits for what they believe are acceptable behaviors. And different cultures establish different norms or boundaries for what a group considers acceptable behavior. For example, a fourth-grade teacher does not have a problem with a child using her hands to drum a rhythm on a desk. Soon, several students are drumming on their desks during literacy. This teacher's personal limits for drumming are flexible. However, a student teacher comes into this classroom and is unable to think when the students are drumming. For this student teacher, the drumming noise takes away her mental pictures. So she must ask the students to not drum during class. Without an explanation for why the drumming worked for the teacher but not for the student teacher, students see this type of change in class rules as arbitrary and not respectful of their needs. The classroom teacher sets one limit and the student teacher sets a different one, providing mixed messages for the learners.

This type of difference between one person allowing the drumming, and another person in the same setting not allowing the drumming, are personal limits. Such personal limits also occur in families. One parent has one set of limits and the other parent has a different set of limits for the same behaviors.

Activity: *What are personal limits with regard to acceptable behavior?*

Cultures represent the aggregate of values for individuals or families and, therefore, establish limits for what is appropriate behavior and not appropriate behavior within society. For example, in some communal cultures, material goods belong to the group. As a result, if a person brings a basket of seafood, any adult is allowed access to the seafood for cooking and eating. If a person brings a basket of seafood to a park for a picnic in the U.S., the basket belongs only to the person who brought it. If an observer sees the basket and takes it, it is stealing.

These personal and cultural limits for what is appropriate behavior under what conditions are learned. A lot of this learning occurs by watching and observing others, by listening to the words of others, and by engaging in behavior to which someone assigns meaning usually with words or nonverbal consequences.

Children diagnosed with ASD and related disorders have difficulty with all of the aforementioned ways to learn to be social. Therefore, it is no wonder that individuals with ASD in the U.S. culture have difficulty with learning social limits. For individuals with ASD, the personal and cultural limits of behavior must be explicitly taught with the developmentally appropriate level of language in the way that individuals with ASD learn. The authors will provide lots of examples of how to provide these limits.

Activity: *How are most personal and cultural limits learned? Does the typical way of learning personal and cultural limits work for individuals diagnosed with ASD and related disorders?*

Learning Limits. Limits are the behaviors that the adult interprets as acceptable or okay or not okay. Limits are often set through rules that we impose on a child so that the child will eventually learn how to govern his behavior according to cultural expectations. For example, "John, sit down! It is time to start class." The assumption behind such a statement is that John is supposed to be able to learn the limits of his culture by what others say with sound, matched against what he sees others do. And, if John is not able to integrate sound with sight, then he is also not able to learn the rules or limits in the way that the teacher assumes.

For John, as well as about 85% of all neurotypical children, the sounds or words alone are not adequate at setting limits. Sound-based words do not tell the listener when to sit, where to sit, why to sit, how to sit, what to do after the child sits. And what do the words "start class" mean? Is the class going somewhere like starting a car or an engine? Do these words mean that the clock is "telling" it's time to create class? The sound of words without the pictures of the meaning of those words leaves children short of what adults expect in setting limits.

To learn the meanings of these types of English phrases designed to set limits, children must be able to hear the sound patterns ("time to start class") and be able to neurologically integrate what they hear with what they see the teacher and the other students are doing (what does it look like to start class). Just watching people does not tell the learner when to sit, why to sit, how long to sit, or what to do when the learner sits. Individuals with ASD (Arwood & Kaulitz, 2007; Arwood et al., 2009) as well as most learners today (Arwood, 2011) are not able to connect the English sound patterns of words with what the words mean in terms of behavior or social limits and expectations.

Activity: Why do the sound of words and the sight of actions not provide enough meaning for learning limits?

To learn behavior limits, the child must be able to connect what he hears with what the behaviors look like. If a child is not able to process this type of input, he will struggle with learning behavior through the sound of others' voices. For example, Gary was the third of five children. His four siblings did well in school and never struggled with behavior at home or at school. Gary was assessed as early as three years of age for social differences and communication differences. He scored well on the tests at that age and was not diagnosed with ASD. Later, because of social differences and academic struggles, he was tested again. This time he was viewed as having a conduct disorder. As a young adult, he was eventually diagnosed with Asperger Syndrome.

For Gary, the diagnostic history is probably not as important as how he learned. As a child, his parents would tell him *not* to do something, but Gary often did what he was told not to do. For example, he was told not to let go (holding) of a calf, but he let go of the calf. The calf immediately ran toward its mother who was on the opposite side of the barbed-wire fence. The family was trying to medicate the calf so to catch the calf again, the family members had to ride their horses for miles and miles to get to the other side of the fence to catch the calf again. One psychologist told the family that they needed to be stricter – set firmer limits. As Dad reported, he could have beaten Gary, but Gary would still not have understood what the parents or teachers were expecting.

For Gary, the sound of typical English words used to set limits did not provide him with a visual metacognition (graphics, pictures, etc.) that showed what he was "supposed to look like." Since most literacy is taught using the sounds of words to read sounds, write sounds, speak with sounds, listen to learn with sounds, view the world through sounds, think with sounds, and calculate with sounds of numbers, Gary also struggled with academics. Gary had lots of language—that is, he talked a lot. So, people assumed he understood what others said.

As Gary aged, his ways to get out of tasks also became more disturbing. Schools, psychologists, parents, support personnel tried lots of different methods to help Gary become social. Behavior contracts based on sounds of words did not work. Behavior classrooms for those who are socially not working within acceptable norms of behavior did not work because the sounds of their voices did not make mental concepts for Gary. In fact, Gary learned a lot more aggressive forms of behavior in those settings. Token economies (reinforcement schedules) at home and in school did not work for Gary except for immediate changes in behavior that did not last. In other words, Gary might be able to do a task to get the tokens and the reward for a short time, but his thinking did not improve so he could apply the meaning of what he was learning to other situations. As an adolescent, he attended military schools and participated in many forms of detention. These military schools and detentions emphasize learning how to avoid punishment and therefore did not help Gary become social. At 17 years of age, this young man was tried in the judicial system as an adult for armed burglary, found guilty, and sentenced to a federal prison. He had followed the structure and orders of an adult who had "befriended him." After sentencing, his family was granted an assessment of Gary's learning. Through language sampling, it was found that Gary did not understand his actions or behaviors. He did what he saw. The other guy went into a house and took material goods, and so did Gary. As Gary argued, "There was nobody home," which meant that his concept of stealing was that a person literally took goods from a person. Because there was no one in the house, Gary was not stealing. Similarly, the other guy took someone else's pickup truck (theft) and asked Gary if he wanted to ride, so Gary went along. Gary thought Jeff was a nice person to ask Gary to ride along. Jeff picked up something in these houses and so Gary did too. Based on the results of a language and thinking assessment, Gary was granted an early release and the family helped him learn limits using other language-based methods for higher order thinking rather than just trying to work on Gary's unwanted behavior through words and the sound of words. (More about these methods will be provided in later chapters.)

Why did Gary have a lot to say but still could not follow what others expected? Gary thought in visuals and he had no mental picture for words like "don't." When he was told not to let go of the calf, the only picture he had was of letting go of the calf. When he was given contracts, he would do what he saw others do or what he could see himself do. If the contract said that he would keep his hands to himself, whenever he saw the contract, he kept his hands to himself. If the contract said for him not to tease others, he would not tease others about the contract, or he would not tease when the contract was visible. He literally was not able to see himself, only his hands and feet move. He could learn from watching the movements, but not learn the higher thinking behind the behavior. In short, Gary could not learn limits through the typical use of sound used to teach children limits. He needed to see the shapes of what others said. He needed to see others draw (shapes) of what medicating the calf looked like; how Gary looked holding the calf; what the family looked like medicating, etc. Gary needed more conceptual development along with the language about the thinking to learn to be socially appropriate.

Activity: How do most people learn limits?

Developmentally Appropriate Behavior. It is the adult who must set the limits. It is the adult who must be the one who decides what is appropriate or not appropriate for children. For example, a parent is with her child at the playground. When the parent says, "It is time to go home," the child begins to cry. In response to the crying child, the parent says, "Okay, we will play for 10 more minutes." The child, not the adult, just set the limit. This is developmentally inappropriate. It is the adult who must set the limit. The reader is encouraged to begin to think about limits – what behavior is acceptable or not acceptable and under what conditions. Adults must be able to set limits according to what is developmentally appropriate for the child as well as what is okay for the setting.

Activity: Who sets the limits in a child-adult relationship?

Limits are not only about what a person thinks is okay or what culture dictates is okay but also about what the child needs to learn. For example, children need to learn that cars cannot see their small bodies so playing in the street is not safe. Allowing a preschool child to play in the street while waiting for a parade to start sends a ***mixed message***; on one hand, the child sees that he can play in the street; on the other hand, the adult has the language to think "he can play because the road is blocked for the parade." The young child does not have the adult language. Therefore, later when the child is playing in the street, the parent tells the child not to play in the street. The child does not know why he could play in the street earlier; but now he cannot play in the street.

Messages that have contradictory meaning are considered "mixed messages." In this case, the two messages are "It is safe for you to play in the street" and "it is not safe to usually play in the street unless the traffic is blocked for parades." These mixed messages require a lot of language to understand the multiple meanings. Therefore mixed messages do not set clear limits for what behavior is okay for most children who struggle learning how to behave. These mixed messages do not provide the meaning for when, where, how, and why specific behaviors are okay. The child will probably have to "test" the limits of playing in the street a lot more times to figure out why he could play in the street on one day but cannot today. Mixed messages tend to increase unwanted behavior.

Limits on behaviors have consistent rules and/or consistent exceptions. For example, walking up a slide is a dangerous behavior, resulting in many serious injuries every year. So, do not put the baby up the slide. Climb the ladder and put the baby on the slide with another adult or older child to ride down the slide. The limit is set by the rule: It is dangerous to climb up a slide. The adult must be able to act consistently with the rules in order for children to learn the limits.

Activity: What are personal and cultural limits?

Here is another example: Standing on chairs at a restaurant is not okay for a 10-year-old; so, to be consistent, it is also not okay for a toddler to stand on a chair. The purpose of the chairs is for someone to sit on, so that is the behavior that is expected and allowed. So, putting a toddler on a chair so he can work at the adult's kitchen counter is not safe and provides a mixed message to the toddler: The multiple messages are that "It is not okay to stand on the chair" and "the adult says it is okay." The toddler does not have enough language to be able to understand the conditions of when it is okay to stand on a chair, if ever. Another example: Grocery store fruit is to eat, but adults often pinch as they check for ripeness. So, to a child, pinching the fruit is okay. Yet, the child is scolded for pinching the fruit. Limits set the rule. But, when is it okay to pinch and why do adults pinch but the child can't? Here is a fourth example of setting limits: Being in someone else's yard is trespassing, so it is never okay to allow children to play in others' yards without permission. If the parents encourage their children to go next door to get a ball or something else that has gone over the fence without asking permission, the children are trespassing. Limits are rules that society sets and expects all to understand and to follow.

Some limits are easier to set than others. For example, most would agree that it is not okay for a child to hit anyone. Therefore, it is not okay to tolerate a toddler's hit, pinch, bite and so forth. Setting limits provides children with rules that children expect to be consistent under all circumstances. Learning how these limits might be conditional to a circumstance or setting requires a lot more cognition and language than offered with rules. Learning limits and how limits might change under different conditions is developmentally dependent on language and cognition.

Activity: Why is it never okay to allow a young child (0-7) to behave in a way that later would be unacceptable?

Children understand limits based on how well they understand the language that defines the rule. Language names thinking or cognition and socializing. So, being able to understand limits; and, under what circumstances limits change, is dependent on the child's level of socio-cognitive learning. The higher the child's social and cognitive development, the better the child's language functions to help the child understand limits. Since learning to behave is based on how well a child is able to think about limits, then language names the child's social and cognitive thinking. *Table 3.1* shows the relationship among language, cognition, and social development.

Table 3.1. *The Relationships among Language, Cognition, and Social Development*

LANGUAGE[4]	SOCIAL DEVELOPMENT	COGNITIVE DEVELOPMENT
Nonverbal/pre-production	Others take care of me ... I am an extension of the world	I see arms and hands do things ... these instruments are not me (sensori-motor thinking)
Verbal/pre-production	I see the world revolve around me ... I am the center of my world	I see myself in my pictures (preoperational thinking) ... but I see my arms and hands do the things in my environment ... I think in the here-and-now
Production of language conversation	I see myself in relationship to others and what they do in relationship to what I do ... I need to fit in (rule-governed behavior)	I see others in my pictures and me in or out of others' pictures(concrete thinking)
Linguistic function – talk with symbols about non-tangible ideas such as democracy, liberty, consideration, or respect	I participate in societal expectations ... work, school, citizenship	I take others' perspectives from ethical and principled position (formal thinking)

---

[4] These stages are further explained in Arwood, 2011.

Table 3.2 shows some relationships between a specific language rule, "Don't run in the hall," and how the typical child at different cognitive or thinking levels is able to interpret the meaning of the rule in order to behave as expected.

Table 3.2. *Language, Interpretation, and Cognition of Rules and Limits*

LANGUAGE Rule: Don't run in the hall.	COGNITION-THINKING	BEHAVIOR INTERPRETATION
No language	Sensori-motor	Child sees the adult and does not interpret the words
Pre-Language Function (lots of verbal language structures but not good use of language for thinking and literacy)	Preoperational	Child hears the words. Child may be able to imitate saying the rule. Child sees self but not the rule. Child stops to voice but then makes a mental picture of the idea "run" and starts to run.
Language function – lots of language used for thinking and learning	Concrete – rule-governed	Child asks or learns that there are many reasons for not running in the hall: Falling down and hurting one's self, running into someone else and hurting them, knocking material out of others' hands, and so forth
Linguistic function – language is a tool for thinking about learning	Formal – ethics/principles	Child or adult does not need a rule to understand that there are safety issues involved in running in a hallway

As noted in *Table 3.2*, there are limits to the rule "Don't run in the hall," which are understood better as a child develops more language to represent higher thinking levels. For children to understand the meaning in order to behave as expected, the language rules must meet the children's needs of different levels of development

---

Activity: What is the relationship between language and thinking for behavior?

Table 3.3 shows how to modify the language of rules for different cognitive levels of understanding.

Table 3.3. *Rule: "Don't Run in the Hallway"*

LEARNING TO BEHAVE	COGNITION	LANGUAGE FOR DEVELOPMENT	SOCIAL BEHAVIOR: CHILD'S NEEDS
Sensory input	Sensori-motor	Show the child the act while talking and drawing … child hears patterns but may not have concepts for patterns	Child needs physical redirection
Perception	Preoperational – self	Cartoon of others in relationship to child's movement in the hall … or could use oral cartoon, "When I see your feet look like this in the hallway, then I know that you will be able to walk safely and quietly down the hall, that you will be able to see others so you don't bump into them and spill their books or hurt them or hurt yourself…"	Lots of language to be able to understand why the child is to not run in the hallway … child is learning the concepts of self in relationship to others and what the child's behavior does to affect others
Conceptual understanding of rule	Concrete – rule governed	Child can say rule and child's behavior will match.	Child is able to teach others the rule about why running in the hallway could hurt the runner or others or their things

From *Table 3.3*, it is clear that acceptable behavior for not running in the hallway appears over time through the use of language that provides meaningful limits for children. The rule for not running may be provided in visual-motor ways such as with drawing a cartoon (Arwood & Brown, 1999), stick-figure pictures, or with oral language that explains all of the reasons for the rule. Rules through the pictures or oral explanations provide the limits, the conditions of change about the limits, and help children understand how limits are consistent. Learning to think about the rule allows the child to possess the language necessary to explain the rule to others. It is not surprising that children who come from environments that lack consistent explanations of why behaviors are acceptable or not acceptable, and under what conditions behaviors are acceptable, tend to engage in more anti-social behavior (e.g., Patterson, DeBaryshe, and Ramsey, 1990). Anti-social behavior is the opposite of pro-social development, and instead of promoting the initiation and maintenance of healthy relationships, anti-social behavior tends to promote unhealthy relationships.

Learners diagnosed with ASD learn social limits best through the visual-motor development of shapes or movements of light on the edges. So, as light hits the edges of the pencil lead moving or a mouth moving, then the learner begins to see shapes or configurations (Arwood & Kaulitz, 2007).

These shapes create visual thoughts for learners with ASD. So teachers who use the sound of their voices to help children learn to socialize or behave will not provide visual concepts or visual thinking for individuals with ASD. For children with ASD to learn about acceptable behavior in lots of settings, they need lots of visual-motor inputs.

Figure 3.1 shows a cartoon of a child thinking about why he should not run down the hall. His thoughts are varied and based on adults assigning meaning to his behavior through words and pictures. *Figures 3.1a and 3.1b* show the language that goes with the cartoons of thinking about running and the consequences of running.

| | When you are inside, people expect you to move your feet and body slowly and carefully. | When you move your feet fast while running, it is hard for you to stop your body quickly and because you can't stop quickly, your body could run into another person's body and make that person fall down. When that person's body hits the floor that person will feel pain in her body. The hurt person will be very upset with you because you chose to run inside and your body hit her body and made her fall down and get hurt. | When you run inside your feet could get caught on the legs of tables and chairs or on the edge of the carpet. When your feet get caught on things while running, you will trip and fall down. When you fall down, your body will hit hard on the floor and that will make your body hurt. |

Figure 3.1a. Cartoon of not running down the hall.

| When you run inside, your feet hit hard on the floor, making the floor, the things on the floor and the things on the walls shake. The things that shake could fall on to the floor and break. The vase of flowers on the table, the picture frames hanging on the wall are just two of the things that could fall and break because you run inside. | When things made out of glass fall on the floor, they break into many, tiny, sharp pieces of glass. These pieces of glass will need to be picked up and thrown away. But, the person who has to pick up these pieces of sharp glass might cut his/her fingers and hands, which will then bleed and hurt. That person will be unhappy that he/she got cut while picking up the glass that because broken because you chose to run making your feet hit hard on the floor | The things that break will have to be repaired or replaced by someone and that will take someone's time and money. No one likes to use their time and money to fix something that broke because your feet ran hard in the house. | Move your feet slowly and carefully—walk—when you are inside so that you keep your body safe, the bodies of others safe and you keep the things in the house safe from shaking, falling and breaking. |

Figure 3.1b. The consequences of running down the hall.

The written language appears to be slightly redundant. Ideas or concepts overlap in a way that explains how the child moves from one frame of the cartoon to another. Children who are at the preoperational level of thinking are able to "see" themselves as part of the limits displayed in the cartoon. Preoperational thinking is about one's Self—me, mine, I, others are to blame and so forth. Most individuals with ASD function at the preoperational social level of development and, therefore, need to be able to see themselves in pictures that show what acceptable behavior looks like. They also need to see the language that goes with the pictures, so writing the words provides the language story that matches the pictures in the cartoon or drawn images. And, they need to see what pictures or concepts the language goes with.

Activity: How does a person with ASD or related disorders need information presented in order to learn the limits of rules?

Sometimes, the context or situation creates an exception to a rule. For example, a cultural limit or rule is that no one stands on the chairs. Some adults might set personal limits to the rule so that they can stand on the chairs as they deem necessary to help decorate higher areas of the room. Since the personal limits do not match the cultural limit, there are conditions or exceptions to the cultural limit. Understanding the conditions or exceptions to the rule requires a lot of language. Since language represents thinking, these exceptions or special conditions mean that the learner has to be able to explain with language the thinking behind whether or not he chooses to stand on a chair.

Many of these "exceptions" are based on the context as well as what is developmentally acceptable. For example, a baby cries to communicate basic needs, but most people who go out to eat at a fancy restaurant for a special occasion like a birthday or anniversary do not want to hear a baby cry. Crying is okay, but not in that context. On the other hand, a five-year-old who cries to get his needs met in a kindergarten is viewed as socially immature. At five years of age, the child is expected to use his words to get his needs met. So, limits are specific to culture, personal acceptance of the behavior, as well as context and developmental issues.

Activity: Are limits ever flexible? If so, under what conditions?

Determining Acceptable Limits

All behavioral limits are subject to conditions and exceptions. Adults set the limits of all behavior of children. Therefore, adults must decide when and where a behavior is acceptable. One of the ways to decide if a behavior or a limit to a behavior is okay is to ask the question: Will this behavior be cute when the child is doing the same behavior under the same conditions, at an older age, for example, eight, 12, or 25 years old? For example, a nine-month-old baby pulls his daddy's beard hard and daddy responds by laughing and allowing the child to repeat the behavior over and over. Would you allow an eight-year-old to pull on your beard? If not, then redirecting the child's hand and not allowing the nine-month-old child to pull the beard is the way for the parent to set consistent limits from the very beginning.

Activity: What question helps an adult set developmentally appropriate limits for behavior?

At what age is it ever okay to hurt another person? Pulling someone's beard (ears, skin, hairs, etc.) hurts. If we want a child to understand that we touch other people gently and softly, for consistency, we never allow the child to touch in a way that could cause someone pain. A nine-month-old child pulling on someone's beard does not cause much pain, so we tend is to accept the behavior. However, when we allow the child to pull on the beard, we send a message to the child that pulling hair is an acceptable behavior.

So when does pulling hair become an unacceptable behavior? Do we wait until there is pain? If we wait until there is pain, we are responding to the pain – our physical discomfort – rather than helping the child develop a clear value system.

At what age is it ever okay to inconvenience another person? A cute little 2-year-old who walks on the top of a table distracting other customers in the restaurant is an inconvenience to those who are busy talking with their families and friends. The inconvenience of a distraction is also a safety issue. What if the child slips or steps off the edge of the table? The distraction then becomes a talking point for others in the restaurant that is taking up the mental pictures and space of those who came to be with their ideas, their families, and their friends, not with a stranger's 2-year-old.

From a value perspective, inconveniences must be excused, which is why we say "pardon" or "excuse me" when we step in front of another person or must move through a blocked area, and so forth. If it seems unnatural to allow a child to stand on a table and then turn to all of the adults in the restaurant who are watching and apologize for the distraction, when the inconvenience was not necessary. Only inconveniences that are necessary and can occur with an apology are acceptable. Other inconveniences are "self-centered" or preoperational, whereby others and their needs are not considered.

Activity: When is an inconvenience acceptable?

What about the five-year-old that is picking the neighbor's flowers? At what age is it okay to damage the property of another person? That's right; the flowers belong to someone else and, therefore, are the property of the neighbor, not the child. If, in the reader's value system, it is never okay to damage the property of another person, then it is not okay to allow the five-year-old to pick off the flowers, even if the child has a diagnosis of ASD. The fact that the flowers are along the sidewalk where the child is able to reach does not matter. The flowers do not belong to the child or the neighborhood. In the North American culture, the flowers are the neighbor's property and, therefore, it is never okay for the child to pick the flowers unless the neighbor tells the child to go ahead and pick the flowers. The decision to pick or not to pick the flowers belongs with the owner of the flowers, not the child or the child's parent.

Finally, the authors must help the reader understand that a diagnostic label such as ASD does not change the limits. It is no more acceptable for a child diagnosed with autism to pick the flowers in a neighbor's yard than it is for the neighbor's six-year-old without a DSM or IDEA diagnostic label. Yes, for the child with autism, the adults will need to draw out why and how and when the behavior is okay and not okay; and, therefore, it is more difficult for the adults to set limits for the child with autism than it is to use oral language to quickly explain to the six-year-old why picking the neighbor's flowers is not okay. But the child with autism deserves the right to learn to be social and needs more consistency with social limits that makes setting the limits even more important for this child.

Activity: When is it okay to hurt another person? When is it okay to destroy another person's property? When is it okay to destroy another person's property?

It is important to understand that the examples are presented for several different cognitive levels. *Table 3.4* provides the different levels and their interpretations. Remember that preoperational thinking is typically associated with three to seven-year-old behavior; concrete interpretation is associated with seven to 11-year-old behavior, and formal interpretations require the language and thinking of someone at a formal or 11+ age level.

Table 3.4. *Behavior is interpreted differently according to age.*

EXAMPLE OF BEHAVIOR	SOCIAL INTERPRETATION	COGNITIVE STAGE
Nine-month-old baby pulls Daddy's beard	1. Isn't the baby cute? 2. The baby might be hurting his dad 3. Never okay to hurt someone else	1. Preoperational interpretation 2. Concrete-rule (don't hurt) interpretation 3. Formal – others' perspective interpretation
A 2-year-old walks on a restaurant's table	1. Sally is so adorable 2. Sally might knock over the items on the table 3. Others are inconvenienced by Sally's behavior	1. Preoperational – I think she is cute 2. Concrete rule 3. Formal – not okay to inconvenient others – their perspective
A 5-year-old is picking neighbor's flower blossoms	1. He is only 5 2. I'd better tell him no before the neighbor sees him 3. It is not okay to damage someone else's property	1. Preoperational; he is the only one in the picture 2. Concrete – rule about the neighbor and "getting caught" doing something wrong 3. Formal – child needs to understand that the flowers belong to the neighbor and what the neighbor would think and feel if he picks them

Activity: What are the developmental levels that correspond to interpretation of behavior?

Corresponding Developmental Levels of Behavior. All behavior is okay. All behavior is learned. And all behavior is interpreted as acceptable or not. The conditions under which a behavior is acceptable or not acceptable are highly dependent on the meaning or value that others place on the behavior. In other words, the acceptability of a behavior is greatly dependent on others' levels of development. Others interpret behaviors according to their own levels of thinking.

A family that has difficulty setting limits is a family that will have difficulty assigning appropriate or pro-social meaning to a child's behavior. For example, if the family laughs at behavior that is interpreted as okay for a young child and then tells the child that the same behavior is not okay later when she is older, the child will have difficulty understanding when the behavior is okay or not okay. If the child has trouble understanding when a behavior is okay, she will not develop beyond the "me-centered" level of preoperational thinking. The language for such a level of thinking is all about the child: "Me;" "Mine;" "I didn't do anything wrong;" "It is someone else's fault," and so forth. Social development is limited to that "me level of thinking" if a child cannot determine the conditions under which a behavior is acceptable or not acceptable according to others. If a child stays at the preoperational level of thinking and language function, the child will not learn higher-order social development that allows for the understanding of formal concepts such as respect, consideration, kindness, and responsibility.

To help children develop the language and thinking that provides for learning to behave at a level higher than the preoperational level of the child seeing himself in his own picture, it is important for educators and parents to determine what their values are with regard to behaviors being okay or not.

Activity: At what thinking level are children or adults able to behave according to the language set by rules of society?

Like parents, educators sometimes have difficulty deciding whether a behavior is acceptable or not. Schools often are clear on their rules, but the interpretation is left to the educators. For example, in one school, the children are not allowed to eat or drink during class, but the teachers bring their water bottles, coffee cups, and so forth. During recess, Shontay is scolded for leaving the playground to get a drink from the water fountain while the playground duty teacher who stands and talks with other adults is sipping from a water bottle. This type of mixed message about behavior is not just confusing but is a matter of social trust. Can adults be trusted? If they say one thing and do something else, are they trustworthy?

Children who come from homes where it is explained that adults may engage in behavior that children are not allowed to engage in will sort through the concepts if they have good language and intact learning systems. For example, a child with good language might say, "This teacher is not consistent, but I must still do what the teacher says to do. The teacher is the adult." Children who do not have the same developmental level of language just see that the teacher cannot be trusted. Children who grow up with a lack of trust will have difficulty initiating and maintaining healthy (trusting) relationships for pro-social development resulting in social competence.

Activity: Why is it important to be consistent in assigning meaning while also considering the child's developmental language level?

"Disturbed" vs. "Disturbing Behavior"

As part of being consistent in assigning and interpreting behavior, adults must also decide if a behavior is merely irritating or if it constitutes a problem. For example, one classroom of fifth graders is working on social studies packets. Students are quietly talking to other students at the same table about the packet work. The teacher is monitoring the students' actions by walking around, talking to students or answering their questions. Jesemy is sitting on his feet in his chair. He is not completing much of the packet work. The teacher points out to him that he needs to get his work completed. As the teacher walks away, Jesemy asks the boy next to him about the words on a work page in the packet. The other boy tells Jesemy that he is finished with that page and that the teacher told Jesemy to do his work.

Right behind this table is another table with five students who are talking about their packet ideas. These five students are far ahead of any other table group in the room. The teacher briefly stops and provides some positive feedback for their efforts. Meanwhile, Jesemy decides to take the matter into his own hands. He gets up and walks over to another boy at a different table to ask him about the vocabulary sheet. The boy pulls out the sheet to give it to Jesemy just as the teacher sees Jesemy out of his seat.

Jesemy is given a warning on the board (check mark next to his name). The teacher says nothing but his name, "Jesemy!" Jesemy looks up and sees the check being marked next to his name but proceeds to take the other boy's sheet back to his table and begins to copy.

Another student at Jesemy's table returns from a pullout support and asks Jesemy about what they are supposed to be doing. Jesemy points to the board, the overhead example, and tells him that he has to do the words. This other boy pulls out his word sheet and also starts to copy, but he is in Jesemy's way, so Jesemy tells him to "move over." Jesemy's voice carries to the teacher's ears so the teacher walks to the board, says Jesemy's name, and gives him a second mark. Then the teacher announces that it is time for lunch and that the students have five minutes to pick up their materials and get ready for lunch.

Jesemy is trying to copy the paper, but the boy who lent his paper comes over and takes it back. Jesemy tries to hang onto the paper and copy but the other boy pulls the paper away, prompting Jesemy to say, "You aren't my friend." The teacher again hears Jesemy's voice, and he now receives check mark number three in less than 20 minutes. This third mark means that he will not have a lunch recess. Jesemy is upset. His face is red. He is saying mean things as he lines up for lunch.

Like all of the scenarios and case studies in this book, the example with Jesemy actually happened. One of the authors was observing in the classroom. She walked over to Jesemy and explained to him: "Jesemy, when you open your mouth, your words fall out. When your words fall out, they fill other students' and the teacher's space. When their space is filled, their pictures go away. When their pictures go away, they cannot do their work or get ready for lunch. So, for them to get ready for work, you must keep your mouth closed so the words do not fall out of your mouth and fill their space." Jesemy looked at the author's mouth and smiled. After lunch he came up to the author and said, "I didn't get in trouble at lunch." The teacher reported that it was the first time that Jesemy had not gotten in trouble at lunch for a long time.

Three important issues surround Jesemy's case: 1) Jesemy does not see himself doing the offending behavior and, therefore, he needs more visual words to be able to see what others hear; 2) Jesemy does not have the developmental language level to understand how to do his packet, so he must rely on others which sets him up for dependent interactions with others. Fifth graders want reciprocal interactions; therefore, they are not very supportive of Jesemy; 3) Because Jesemy has been in trouble a lot, the teacher no longer sees him in the way as she sees the other students. That is, other students engaged in the exact same behavior of helping each other, talking with each other, moving around the tables to work with each other did not receive reprimands. But only Jesemy received reprimands. Furthermore, it was discovered later that day that only Jesemy had a behavior plan that stated that he will do his own work. The plan did not consider Jesemy's level of language or his learning system (visual thinker). The behavior plan wanted to control Jesemy's behavior without considering why he behaves the way he does.

To the teacher, Jesemy's behavior was *disturbing*. The fact that Jesemy had been demonstrating disturbing behaviors more than any other student caused the teacher to seek help from a behavior consultant. The consultant had set up a token economy with a contract. Each time the teacher saw a behavior that Jesemy was not to do as stipulated in the contract, she gave him a check mark on the board. After three checks, he lost the next free time: recess, library, computer time, and so on. The behavior contract did not provide Jesemy with the tools to change his thinking so he had a choice about how to behave. Instead, the contract was about controlling the behavior as if Jesemy had the thinking and language to not be "irritating" or annoying. In other words, the contract as written expected Jesemy to be able to set his own limits, follow the limits set by rewards, and understand the thinking of the adults who set the behavior limits with the contract. The teacher said that the she did not think the contract with the token economy was working, so she referred Jesemy for a behavior evaluation to determine if he has a behavior disorder. At this point, since a different input from the author changed Jesemy's behavior, he does not have a behavior disorder, only disturbing behavior because he is trying to learn how to do his work. Unfortunately, he has a different learning system; and, for Jesemy to learn social limits of behavior, he needs the input to be in a different than sound (oral language) form.

Activity: When is a behavior considered disturbing?

Behavior Disorders

Behavior disordered (BD) is a term that most practitioners prefer over *emotionally behaviorally disturbed* (EBD). EBD is a term that is used in the Individuals with Disabilities Education Act (IDEA), a law ensuring services to children with disabilities throughout the US (US Department of Education, 2004). Emotionally disturbed refers to the way a child thinks about feelings and responses to feelings.

But, practitioners prefer the term behaviorally disturbed because practitioners deal with what they see, the behavior, not the emotional state of the child (for an explanation of the history of these definitions related to IDEA and the Diagnostic Statistics Manual (DSM) used by psychotherapists and medical personnel see Webber & Plotts, 2008.

For Jesemy, introduced earlier, to be considered as having a behavior disorder his behavior would have to be viewed as a problem in multiple settings by multiple people, which it was. Once the educators identified his behavior as a problem, then it was a problem. If the educators had seen Jesemy as needing academic help because he has a different way to think or learn, his behaviors would not have been interpreted as a problem. Jesemy was engaged in behaviors other students also exhibited, but the teacher had decided that this was a matter of degree and frequency and therefore no longer disturbing but disordered. But, in reality, he did not have a problem with behavior but a problem learning to behave.

Activity: What is a behavior disorder?

It is not uncommon to view students like Jesemy as having a behavior problem in one classroom but not in another. For example, Jesemy might not show a problem in a classroom that provides meaning for his behavior in a way that helps him learn to think. Students like Jesemy exhibit behaviors that some adults find *disturbing* because they cannot reach these students' way of thinking with sound words. If the adults see the behavior across multiple settings and across time, these disturbing behaviors come to be considered disordered.

One fifth-grade teacher set her class up to assign visual-motor meaning to academics, which resulted in her students being able to learn without her having to interpret behaviors as problems. One Friday, she left for a conference, and the substitute teacher immediately began to teach with the sound of her voice. Students had trouble understanding the tasks. One particular student began to ask lots of questions, talk to other students, and eventually quit working. When the substitute teacher asked him about his work, he gave a flip answer and was sent to the principal's office. When the principal asked him why he was sent to the office, the student called the substitute names and cursed. The principal and the student wrote out what he was to do: apologize to the substitute after lunch and go eat his lunch.

The student went to lunch, and once again he was flippant to a teacher and began to yell and name call. By the end of the day, the child had been put into a classroom for children with behavior disorders pending the approval of the classroom teacher. The student's parents had been called and they agreed to the placement. After all, the parents are not at school. How are they supposed to help the student from work and home? When the teacher returned on Monday, she challenged the placement and the student was put back into her classroom where he had no behavior problems.

Activity: What is the difference between behavior that is disturbing and behavior that is disturbed or disordered?

Summary

All behavior communicates. And, for behavior to communicate, behavior must be interpreted. Whether a behavior is acceptable or not is dependent on the interpretation and values of those who interpret the meaning of the behavior as well as set the limits. Since all behaviors are okay, whether a behavior is acceptable or not depends on the limits or conditions. A learner is always able to display disturbing behaviors, behaviors that others interpret as not acceptable. But whether or not these disturbing behaviors are diagnosed as disordered or disturbed, the learner must exhibit the unacceptable behaviors across time, settings, and to a severity of frequency so that a team of individuals sees the behaviors as not being typical. It should be noted that whether or not a person is able to assign meaning the way a child learns to think may result in differences in behavior and therefore may also result in whether or not a child's behavior is considered disturbed. *Chapter Four* will address how people learn to behave.

Important Concepts in *Chapter Four*

Readers should be able to explain each of these behavior principles upon completion of this chapter:

1. Everyone learns to behave.

2. All behavior is interpreted.

3. Different people may have different meanings for the same behavior.

4. Personal beliefs as well as cultural expectations help determine the meaning of behavior.

5. Learning occurs at several neurobiological levels resulting in developmental levels of behavior.

6. Learning of patterns, psychomotor skills, and copying or imitating a model is a low level of development.

7. Learning of concepts for thinking, viewing, and literacy forms such as speaking, reading, and writing requires a higher level of development.

8. Thinking about ideas that cannot be seen or touched, such as "to cooperate" or "to be kind," requires language.

CHAPTER FOUR
Learning to Think Helps Define Behavior

Seeing what I do is learning,
Thinking about what to do is learning to behave.
Seeing is thinking.
Thinking is a learning choice!

One of the authors has, on her office wall, a drawing from a first grader. The drawing shows some people in a classroom. Each person has a thought bubble. The child has written "Everyone thinks" as a caption. To demonstrate any behavior, a person must learn to think. Behavior is a product of the neurobiological learning system. So, behavior communicates the messages of society as well as how a child is learning. For example, a child pulls back his hand when he touches something hot. Later the child looks at the stove and says, "Hot" but does not touch. The child's behavior reflects the child's learning. The child first learned to reach out his hand and to touch. Then the hand automatically retracted. Someone assigned meaning to that response as "The stove is hot." Later the child adds more thinking to the behavior and says, "Hot!" The child is learning the behavior, the assigned meaning, and the language for the behavior. Since all children learn to act, all actions or behavior is okay and all behavior communicates based on the meaning assigned. The meaning assigned to behavior is determined by what is culturally appropriate, what families communicate is valuable, and how children learn.

This chapter will discuss differences in levels of thinking and learning. The relationship between learning to behave and how people believe behavior is learned will be refined. Examples of how behavior communicates what a person is learning will also be presented, along with examples of how thinking to behave utilizes language and cognition.

Learning and Behavior
Children learn to think, not only about others for social development; but also for learning to be literate. Therefore, children's behavior matches with what they know about the academic tasks given in a classroom. For example, many children exhibit unacceptable behaviors in classrooms because they are being asked to do an activity that does not match the way they learn or learn to think. Remember that learning to think is a process that involves forming concepts from patterns. But, many educators view learning as giving a response similar or the same as a modelled input. The teacher models the behavior such as writing a sentence. Then the child is asked to write four sentences. The child writes an idea. Then the teacher tells the child to write "some more." The teacher explains that she wants the child to write four sentences. Since the child does not know what "four sentences" means, her behavior matches what the child knows: The child interprets the teacher's words as "write." The child writes an idea and that is all the child understands. The teacher sees the child write but does not understand why

the child does not write more than one idea. According to the teacher, the child "knows" what the number "four" is and the teacher knows the child can "write a sentence," so why does the child not write four sentences? The teacher expects that the child can put together two parts, writing sentences and four into writing four sentences.

The child really does not know what a "sentence" is. The child sees the print and makes a picture in the child's head. The child is mentally seeing an idea, not a sentence. So, the child is able to write the idea. The child thinks that a sentence is an idea. On one hand, the child is acquiring the meaning of knowledge gradually through her neurobiological learning system, but the teacher expects the child's learning to occur as chunks of additive meaning. In the teacher's additive way of thinking, the teacher expects the child to know the "meaning" of "four" and the meaning of a sentence to be added together; and, therefore, the child should write four sentences.

The teacher interprets the child's behavior based on a *reductionist* approach: Take a task that an adult has acquired (the ability to write multiple sentences into a paragraph) and break the task down into smaller pieces (sentences to words to letters with sounds). Then, the teacher assumes that if she teaches these smaller pieces or parts in an additive approach, the parts will equal the whole. In other words, the breaking of the task into smaller pieces assumes that when the smaller pieces are added together, the pieces will make a whole.

This type of *task analysis* makes sense for skills or patterns such as helping a child print the letters of a word by holding the child's hand. The child prints the word with the adult or the child is able to copy the adult's printed word. Or a task analysis might break the adult word into letters and sounds and the teacher then teaches letters and sounds for the child to "learn" to spell the word by adding the letters and sounds together. The purpose of a task analysis is to determine which parts need to be taught to create a whole.

Activity: What is a task analysis? Perform a task analysis on learning to jump rope.

The assumption of the reductionist model is that the learner is able to: 1) imitate the model's behavior, such as holding the pencil with the adult or imitate the production of the sounds and letters; and 2) recall or retrieve the imitated model as part of a sequence of steps to create a whole. For example, it is assumed that a child who learns the sounds and letters of the alphabet is able to imitate and recall the sounds and letters as part of a whole task, spelling. This type of education assumes that the imitation of patterns is the basis of learning. But many children either don't learn sounds and letters or, in the case of children with ASD, learn the sounds and letters but are not able to integrate them into a whole process such as speaking or writing (this includes spelling).

Even though a task analysis is a good way to identify the adult's perspective of what constitutes a task or a behavior, a task analysis may assume the adult's learned belief system. For example, an adult is capable of using a full adult language grammar and, therefore, is able to think about spoken, written, or printed ideas as "words." But children do not acquire words. Children acquire the sensory input as patterns then the patterns overlap to form concepts (See *Chapters One-Three*). The result is that the adult tries to teach a child the unit of a word when, in fact, the child is thinking in ideas (concepts) at a child's level of thinking. In other words, the child's ideas may be incomplete pictures of what the child knows in a particular situation.

This process of matching what the adult assumes and how a child learns is further complicated by children who do not have the same process of learning as an adult. The adult not only teaches words like "respect" as words with additive parts of meaning; but, the teacher does so with the sound of her spoken voice or the sound of saying the words on a page (oral fluency of print). Those with different ways of creating mental ideas than the teacher's use of sound, such as individuals with ASD and related disorders, face the additional barrier of not being able to process the sound-based teaching. As a result, when the child's learning system does not automatically use the adult's input to create mental concepts in the way the adult teaches the child, the child may struggle to learn expected tasks, activities, or behavior. The child is not learning to think the way the adult expects or the way the adult assigns meaning.

Activity: How does the reductionist model of task analysis assume the way a person learns?

The relationship between the adult expecting a child to perform a certain behavior and how well the child is able to learn to behave depends on what the adult expects as well as the learner's neurobiological way of acquiring the concepts or ideas. For example, the adult expects that a child who learns the alphabet and the names of the letters will spell words correctly with practice. However, being able to imitate sounds and letters in isolation or to produce patterns such as the names and sounds of letters does not mean that the child's neurobiological learning system allows the sounds and the meaning of the word names to become mental concepts. Or take the example of a child who has learned how to say a rule back to the adult: "John, what is the rule about picking your nose?" John says, "I must use a tissue for my nose." John is able to give the rule but his behavior, picking his nose, continues which shows that John does not understand how his behavior matches with the spoken rule.

Learning to behave is the process of learning social concepts about what is acceptable or not acceptable. Concept learning is about thinking and viewing. Being able to learn to think and view with consideration for others requires the use of language. For example, being able to retrieve meaning from a page of print is different than saying the sounds of the names of the words on the page. Being able to follow the behavior expected from rules is different than just saying the rules. And, understanding when there are exceptions to rules or limits requires even more thinking and language.

Activity: Learning to think to behave requires concepts. How do concepts differ from imitating?

Learning to think in order to behave at higher levels requires that the neurobiological system is able to process through the four levels: 1) Sensory input forms perceptual patterns. The child's senses are checked to be sure the receptors are intact. 2) The sensory input forms patterns. At this pattern-recognition level, if a child is able to hear the patterns of an adult's voice, she is able to imitate the patterns such as being able to imitate a rule. If a child is able to recognize what she sees someone else do, then the child is typically able to imitate what she sees others do. Only these first two levels of learning are required for imitating. Children can be taught to imitate a lot of initial types of behavior…such as sitting down. But what is the child supposed to think about if she sits? And, as many of us have observed, that child who is able to imitate sits down, gets the reward, and jumps back up.

Activity: *What parts of the learning system are needed for a child to learn to imitate?*

In a human learning system, there is more than the imitation of sensed patterns. Typically, the learning system recognizes the patterns and so the patterns begin to integrate into overlapped units called ideas or concepts. The child begins to think about what the child hears, sees, smells, tastes, and touches. Concepts are thoughts or ideas at the third level of neuro-semantic learning.

To share the concepts with others, a learner must be able to acquire language patterns that will name the thoughts or concepts. This use of language is the fourth level of learning to think and behave. As a child acquires more language, the child's learning to think is also increasing. When a child has developed the language of a seven or eight year-old, he or she has an adult set of patterns or grammar. The learner can now use the adult grammar as a tool to give the learner more meaning of basic concepts. In other words, with the language of an adult grammar, language becomes a tool for learning more about how to think. A child learns to think and learns to think with language.

Activity: *What are the third and fourth levels of learning to think, behave, and use language?*

With more thinking, the child is able to make decisions, solve problems, and so forth. Behavior becomes more sophisticated as language and thinking increase. Learning to behave is a process of learning to think about the social concepts of behavior. Learning to think involves more than copied or imitated or matched patterns. Learning to think requires adding meaning for additional cognitive levels of thinking and assigning language to what those thoughts mean.

Activity: *How is learning to think different than imitating?*

The neurobiological system learns the meaning of a child's world through the reception of complex neurosemantic sensory input that forms patterns that create circuits of concepts for thinking and further learning through language (Arwood, 2011). This acquisition is a complex neurosemantic process that develops the child's thinking and higher order learning. So, learning to behave is about how to acquire the meaning of social concepts or how to think to behave with language. Language assigns meaning to behavior and to the learner's thinking.

The Meaning of Behavior.

As described in *Chapters One-Three*, the meaning of behavior is the result of the interpretation of what a child does through the lens of people's beliefs or philosophies. For example, a child with ASD is asked to sit at a table and point to pictures of vocabulary. As soon as the vocabulary cards come out of the educator's bag, the child quickly stands and moves toward the door. One adult, who is watching, sees a child who is "bolting." The adult judges the meaning of the behavior as "Roxanne does not want to do her vocabulary today. She is feeling a bit on edge because there are too many things going on in the classroom." The adult puts away the vocabulary cards and Roxanne begins to rock back and forth while flipping her fingers in front of her face.

Another adult sees Roxanne engage in the same behavior and says, "Roxanne is falling through space." She is literally moving upright through horizontal frames (see *Figure 4.1*). Roxanne needs more information about the behavior she is asked to do."

Figure 4.1. Roxanne falls through space.

The second adult immediately pulls out a piece of paper and draws Roxanne sitting at a table, thinking about her sitting; and Roxanne is also thinking about the educator sitting with her (*Figure 4.2*). Roxanne is learning to think about others. Roxanne is being put on the paper as an agent who can think, who can sit, and who can point to the pictures.

Figure 4.2. Roxanne thinks about the educator sitting with her.

The second adult draws Roxanne sitting with the other person in the picture so Roxanne can begin to see herself in relationship to others, see how her behavior affects others, and see what Roxanne is expected to look like. The educator writes the words below the behavior frames so that Roxanne is able to see what she looks like and see the visual-motor patterns of language that names the behavior. Roxanne is beginning to see what she looks like. Since Roxanne has little oral language, the second adult knows that using the sound of the adult's voice to help Roxanne learn to behave will not work. The drawing, writing, and talking about what can be seen helps provide Roxanne with the meaning of behavior.

For each of these adults, the meaning of Roxanne's behavior rests with the adult's knowledge about the acquisition of meaning (neurobiological learning) as well as with each adult's own philosophy about learning to behave. *Table 4.1* provides an analysis of the outcomes of the two adults' interpretations:

Table 4.1. Analysis of the Meaning of Behavior for Two Examples Using the Same Behavior

ADULT ONE	ADULT TWO
Roxanne is "bolting." She learned this behavior through modeling, imitation, or copying.	Roxanne is "falling through space." This behavior represents Roxanne's social, cognitive, and motor developmental levels.
Assumes that Roxanne has enough language to be intentional; that is, she knows what she wants and bolts to get away. But Roxanne has little language.	Observation interpretation is based on seeing Roxanne move on her toes, leaning forward, as part of being an extension of the environment. She is functioning at the sensori-motor level of development, which has little language to be able to think with intention.

Table 4.1. Continued

ADULT ONE	ADULT TWO
Reason for the bolting is that Roxanne does not want to do the vocabulary cards. This conclusion assumes that Roxanne has enough language to know that she does not want to do the cards. She also has enough cognition to understand why she doesn't want to do the vocabulary cards.	The adult assumes that if a child produces an undesired behavior, the child does not have enough learning to behave in an expected way.
The adult explains this behavior as too much going on in the room (other students doing their activities and so forth). This is "mind reading." The adult has no idea why Roxanne does or does not begin to do the vocabulary cards.	In order to bring Roxanne to a higher than sensori-motor level of understanding, the adult begins to draw more information for Roxanne so she can begin to see herself as an agent (early cognitive development). This adult wants to increase Roxanne's cognition so Roxanne will someday be able to explain her reasons for doing or not doing something.
The adult assumes that Roxanne's behavior occurs for the same reasons that the adult might engage in that type of behavior–reductionist model. The reductionist model does not take into account the way that a child learns through the neurobiological system. The adult is talking about the adult's motivations, not Roxanne's thinking or language levels.	The adult knows that children learn to conceptualize themselves as agents who are able to do something. Therefore, the adult draws the child on a piece of paper so the child begins to learn the cognitive piece of being an agent. This means that this adult realizes that learning to think for children with ASD requires the ability to see the shape of ideas (pictures and writing together) so the adult uses a visual-motor form if input.
Roxanne is left at the same cognitive or thinking level with which she began the task –sensori-motor rocking and flapping. In this way, she is using her fingers and body as ways to stimulate her body at a low level of pattern practicing. She is not learning to behave differently.	The adult realizes that if she wants Roxanne's behavior to change, she must help the child acquire more conceptual meaning about how to be an agent. Furthermore, the vocabulary cards are not at Roxanne's sensori-motor level of development so helping Roxanne see herself will help Roxanne begin to see the meaning of the task.
Unfortunately, Roxanne is practicing patterns with her body and hands that take the place of appropriate or pro-social patterns of behavior. Roxanne will grow bigger but without her thinking also growing. Over time, her behavior will be seen as aggressive and her large body will be out of control of the adults who work with Roxanne.	Roxanne is provided with input that allows her to begin to be an agent who is able to behave in the way that others expect. In this way, she begins to learn to think, and her behavior changes as she is learning.
Roxanne is learning that anti-social behavior provides her with a payoff. The payoff is that she is able to control her environment with this type of behavior.	Roxanne is learning how to behave pro-socially. She is developing social concepts that allow her to think about herself in relationship to others and their actions.

*Activity: **What do you choose to believe: Children's behaviors are learned through imitation or that children learn to behave by acquiring concepts?***

Thinking about Behavior

Children learn to think through the same learning system as they learn to be literate or to behave. The process of learning to think requires that the child is able to add meaning about basic concepts for acquiring more advanced concepts. Thinking increases in depth as the child learns more meaning. Therefore, behavior follows the developmental levels of cognition. For example, infants cry to get attention, to be fed, to be nurtured, to be loved, and so forth. Later the crying behavior becomes words, and the child asks for a hug or a snack or even throws her parent a kiss. The acquisition of learning to behave is a process that represents how well a child is learning. Learning occurs in the neurobiological system; therefore, a child learns to behave as well as the child's neurobiological system works and as well as others assign meaning in the way the child's learning system processes input. Likewise, a child learns which behavior works for the child's needs based on how others assign meaning (*Chapters One-Two*).

Learning to think "unfolds" a child's behavior as expected developmental forms: Crying becomes words, words become phrases, phrases become sentences, and so forth. The child's behavior reveals what the child learns. Physical forms of behavior also unfold: Crawling becomes walking, walking becomes running, and so forth. Behavior represents how well a person is learning what is accepted, what is meaningful, what works, and so forth.

Activity: Developmental behavior is the result of the learning system. What is the relationship between learning to behave and showing developmentally appropriate behavior?

The change from non-verbal behavior to the use of language also reflects the child's learning. The child's developmental products like talking or walking are the result of the child's ability to learn. So, a child who is not producing specific developmental behaviors is not learning how to behave as society expects. Learning to behave is a neurobiological function, or learning to think.

In other words, the behavior one sees is the result of what happens internally in the brain of the learner. This concept is important in understanding how to approach behavior: Is it more effective to treat Roxanne's behavior as something to be controlled with the assumption that she is able to understand what the behavior means? Or does Roxanne's behavior reflect what she understands, so if her behavior is to change, the adults must provide her with better thinking about her behavior?

The brain is responsible for thinking.

Thinking is not a behavior but the basis for choice.

Learning to think is learning to make a behavioral choice.

Choices increase as thinking increases.

Language assigns meaning to the choices.

Pro-social development is the result of healthy language-based choices.

Activity: How is thinking part of learning to behave?

Using an approach designed to deal with behavior separate from thinking ignores the basic fact that the brain is responsible for learning to behave. For example, most adults attending a lecture are able to sit in their seats because they are thinking about the lecture, not about the shirt tag on their neckline or the open door. But, if the adult sees the open door and has little if any language to continue to sit and think, the adult will run out the door. Language about the adult's thinking keeps the adult in his seat. Trying to address a child or adult running out of the room without consideration for what the child or adult is thinking does not accept the value that the brain is responsible for learning to think and thus the behavior of running out of the room.

Thinking begins to become conscious at the preoperational level (age 3-7) and, therefore, is the basis to most choices of simple behavior. For example, a child thinks about what the teacher's mouth movements mean so the child is focused on the teacher's information. If the child is able to turn the teacher's mouth movements into something that is meaningful, the child will not run out the door when the child looks at the door. For the child with preoperational thinking, thinking is greater than just doing. To sit and think requires more than just sitting. The child can sit and think. Learning to choose to stay seated is the result of learning to think and not just sit.

Activity: Is learning to think a process of learning to choose how to behave? Why or why not?

Learning to think is a function of the learning system. A child will learn as well as the learning system creates meaning for the child. Meaning can be created by overlapping input from the various sensory systems; eyes, ears, nose, mouth, and skin. These inputs create concepts in a neurotypical system. However, children diagnosed with ASD[5] learn best with the input of visual shapes. Shapes form from the overlap of seeing movement such as the lips moving to form the meaning of a word, the hand moving to sign an idea, the hand moving to write the shape of a word, and so forth. Therefore, children with ASD learn to behave as well as educators and parents provide them with the necessary, overlapping motor patterns or shapes to learn mental concepts or thinking that can then be refined through the use of language. The following case study highlights how thinking and behavior are related.

Case Study 1. Marguerita is a 15-year-old youngster from Guatemala, who is significantly impacted by autism. She and her family have been in the United States for 13 years and Marguerita has been in the public school system since early childhood. Spanish is the language of the home, but Spanish is not spoken in the educational placement in which Marguerita is currently enrolled. Marguerita is nonverbal and uses behaviors that include spitting, hitting, punching, and urinating as ways to communicate. Her family reports that she displays the same behaviors at home.

Her behaviors at school have caused her to be removed from her special education classroom into a separate space with a teacher who is responsible for Marguerita's programming along with two educational assistants who are trained in restraint procedures as well as behaviorism methods. Marguerita has very limited interactions with peers. Marguerita takes a long list of medications to reduce her aggression and increase her focus. The school staff has confided that Marguerita's family is inconsistent with the delivery of her medication and regularly changes the amount of her medication without her physicians' knowledge. This has proven to be very frustrating for school staff who believes that the changes in medication lead to Marguerita's behavior being very unpredictable.

Marguerita has learned many acoustic patterns for simple directives such as "sit down," "stand up," "put your backpack away," and "do your work." These are paired words or stimuli for an expected behavior or response; but, paired words or directives of what Marguerita is to do, *does not reflect Marguerita's ability to think about what the directives actually mean.* However, because Marguerita is able to recognize these learned patterns and respond with an expected behavior, the staff uses spoken English and some sign cues because they believe "Marguerita understands when [they] talk to her." Educators have used single objects on cards as symbolic pictures for visual schedules for many years, but Marguerita continues to need constant verbal cueing to "check her schedule" in order to move forward through her day. Marguerita loves to chew on tubing, loves to walk (staff reports that walking appears to calm Marguerita down when she is highly agitated), and loves music, especially Spanish music. The school uses these tasks as positive reinforcement when Marguerita is compliant and "does what she is told to do." Marguerita continues to physically grow; and she has developed little conceptual thinking.

After consulting with one of the authors, it was decided by the IEP (individualized education program) team to try some stick-figure line drawings of Marguerita in context performing her activities with some physical assistance in the form of hand-over-hand (HoH) writing and drawing to see if any changes in behavior would occur. The educators wrote and drew Marguerita within a context along with matching written print to show her what she was supposed to look like doing a task. To help Marguerita perform daily acts, the educators used hand-over-hand assistance. In a short period of time,

---

[5] It should be noted that there are other children with different diagnostic labels who also do not use sound for creating concepts; for example, those with ADD will act upon what they see.

it became evident that Marguerita was not only able to understand the stick-figure drawings; she would also attempt to make her body match the pictures. It is important to recognize that the easiest form of seeing an idea is a black-and-white line drawing (*Figure 4.3*) because the brain only sees two dimensions and because black on white provides the most neurological contrast.

Figure 4.3. *Marguerita learning her schedule in a line drawing.*

These drawings and hand-over-hand motor patterns provided Marguerita with the appropriate input for learning to behave. Her aggressive behaviors decreased and she began to be more independent with her developmentally appropriate visual schedule.[6] The fact that the parents were changing medications was not the reason for Marguerita not learning. The fact that they spoke Spanish at home was not the issue either. Marguerita had spent nine years in and around English speakers and had not picked up marketplace English. Furthermore, she also did not learn Spanish. She did not have a language system so what language was used for education was not the issue. Language interference was not the reason why she was not learning to behave.

Marguerita was not learning because the adults were not providing her with the information she needed to learn in the way that Marguerita learns. Furthermore, the adults were assuming an adult's reductionist approach to Marguerita's thinking, assuming that Marguerita could think like the adults and was "choosing" to behave inappropriately. Therefore, the adult's program focused on controlling her behavior rather than helping Marguerita learn to think at a higher level and, therefore, exhibit more socially appropriate behaviors.

Marguerita still resorts to old behavior patterns when new information is presented if the educators or parents have not prepared her through drawing and writing about what she will look like and think about. *Figure 4.4* shows how thinking relates to her learning to behave. Notice that there are

---

[6] Not all visuals are the same in developmental level or meaning. See Arwood, Kaulitz, and Brown (2009) for an explanation of how visuals create meaning and for an understanding of the developmental levels of visuals.

multiple thought bubbles for each frame. This shows Marguerita that she should have multiple thoughts or pictures so that she is able to learn how to behave based on her thinking.

Figure 4.4. Marguerita uses thinking to learn how to behave.

Marguerita is learning to think. Her thinking or conceptual development is helping her produce more appropriate social behavior. The staff are able to see that their assignment of meaning through visual-motor drawings and hand-over-hand pointing, doing activities of daily living through hand-over-hand drawing and writing helps Marguerita acquire the shape of the hands moving as concepts. Marguerita is learning to behave because she is learning to think.

Figure 4.5 shows Marguerita learning the shapes of others' hand movements as visual concepts. The educator is tracing around the shape of the idea in a picture so that Marguerita can see how the movement of the hand forms a shape like the shape of a person or agent.

Figure 4.5. Marguerita learns shapes of ideas.

Activity: How is Marguerita learning to think? How does learning to think help social behavior develop? How does learning to be pro-social develop from thinking?

Thinking to Learn Language

It is important to understand the relationship between thinking and language. A child learns the meaning of his environment and as a result develops concepts or ideas. Conceptual learning provides the child with ideas about what he knows, what others know, and what the child looks like in specific situations. When the adults draw the way the child looks, the child also learns how to look or behave to show what he knows.

In the previous example, Marguerita was learning to think and, therefore, was learning to behave through the acquisition of concepts about what she looks like when she does activities. For more meaning, Marguerita has to begin to show acquisition of language. Language represents thinking. And language is the tool that helps a person use his or her own thinking to increase understanding.

For example, a 2-year-old knows "table" as a pattern. Mom says, "Freddy, put your cup on the table." Freddy turns to see what Mom is looking at and then walks over to the table and puts his cup on the table. Freddy is learning to think about his world. Others, like Mom, provide Freddy with meaning about his actions. Freddy's learning system allows him to use those spoken patterns as *indicators* of Mom's expected behavior. Freddy has enough pattern recognition to allow him to think about his mom's words, his mom's eye movements focusing toward the table, and the object in his hand. Freddy is conceptually thinking about what he is able to do (agent and action) with the cup (object). Freddy is learning to think about what he sees, hears, and does. In short, he is learning to behave

Activity: How does thinking and doing affect learning?

As Freddy grows older, he continues to learn so that his concept development or thinking increases, and so does the complexity of his behavior. By the time he is five-years old, Mom can ask Freddy, "Where is your cup?" Freddy will either tell her where the cup is or he will look for the cup. Furthermore, Freddy will also be able to explain or tell a story about where he found the cup. When Freddy is 10 years old, he is able to talk about different types of cups and even categorize a cup as something that holds liquid. As Freddy learns more about the concept of cup from many different experiences, he learns that there is another type of cup, the kind of physical protection that he wears when he plays athletics. As Freddy's learning about the concept of cup increased, so did his thinking.

However, learning to think from experiences in the environment is only half of the equation. After seven to eight years of age, most neurotypical children like Freddy are also able to use their own language to help them think about complex or abstract (formal) concepts. In other words, before language is fully developed (7-8 years), children learn to think about what is in their immediate environment – what they see and do. But with language, a child over the age of seven is typically able to assign meaning to previous knowledge (concepts). For example, at eight years old, Freddy is able to tell a good story about his cup that he used for moving sand to make a castle at the beach. He is able to ask others to participate with him as he continues to build an "awesome castle." Building the castle requires that everyone working with Freddy are on the same page so Freddy thinks about the others in his picture and explains, "Let's make the castle about three feet tall and then we can watch the waves break it down. The tide is coming in so we have to hurry to get it built before the water gets up to the castle. I will dig a moat around the castle." From Freddy's lead, another child says, "I will build the tower," and another child says, "I will make taller walls."

The ability of these children to work together by thinking about each other's work as well as their own work is the result of the children having sufficient language to socially communicate with each other. Freddy is using cups to dig with, shovels to pile sand, and buckets to mold. In other words, he is using these objects in a variety of functions based on his thinking. And he is using his language to help him and others think about the outcome of the castle building. Freddy's ability to use his own language helps him learn more about the world of "cups." *Table 4.2* shows how language helps assign meaning to thinking.

Table 4.2. *Learning to Behave with an Increase of Language*

AGE	STAGE	LANGUAGE	BEHAVIOR
0-2	Sensori-motor – thinking is in response to patterns.	Pre-production – child responds to others' actions and words.	Child looks for adult cues, and needs are expressed through simple actions or motor responses such as crying when hungry and Mom hands the child a cup of milk
3-7	Preoperational – thinking is about self.	Preproduction to early language. Language is not complete, "me do it," "I no need dat." "My cat is big. She has two eyes and I love my cat." "I want the cup."	Child behaves as if he or she is the center of the universe. Others attend to child's needs. Child is dependent on others for assigning meaning.
7-11	Concrete – thinking is about others in relationship to self, rules, etc.	Full grammatical language that allows for reciprocal conversation: "I like to ride my bike in the coastal range." "Oh, have you tried any distance rides with others?" "Yes, my wife and I did the coastal 100-mile ride last weekend. How about you?" "No, we just ride in the neighborhood. Maybe we will do some short-distance rides …" Freddy's discussion of working to build a castle is also at this level.	Child follows rules because others are in the mental picture with the child; child realizes how his or her behavior affects others. Following rules is easy. Shared relationships around play, work, governance, and leadership.

Table 4.2. Continued

AGE	STAGE	LANGUAGE	BEHAVIOR
11+	Formal thinking is about the effects of one's actions on others and on society through principled and ethical thinking.	Language structures function to enable us to talk about ideas that we cannot see such as "being considerate" or being respectful." "Freddy is sharing his work with others with the same interests. Together they show respect for each other, each other's gifts to the project, and their beliefs about cooperative working and collaborative projects."	This person is able to take another person's perspective, capable of linking behavior with different emotions, complex behaviors, and outcomes or complex consequences

Table 4.3 shows the relationship of a person or agent with the cognitive level. The picture on the right depicts the way the child "sees" relationships to self and others based on the child's thinking.

Table 4.3. Cognition or Thinking

Sensori-Motor Level Agent is an extension of the environment.	
Preoperational Level Agent is about "me." The big "I."	
Concrete Level Agent is one who relates to others.	
Formal Level Agency is about taking another's perspective.	

Adapted from Arwood, E. (1991). *Semantic and pragmatic language disorders.* Portland, OR: Apricot, Inc. Used with permission.

Activity: How does thinking and cognition relate to learning to socially behave or socially think?

Learning to Think with Language

Children learn to think and their behavior represents how well they think. As each child's learning system creates meaning from the world through the sensory system, each child's thinking or cognition grows. And, for neurotypical learners, this learning results in language that represents their thinking. Likewise, behavior represents what the child's learning system has acquired. The child grows up, and so does the child's behavior. But many children, like those with ASD, do not acquire concepts or thinking in the way society expects. Learning to think occurs as a result of an interaction between those assigning meaning in a child's society with the child's parallel acquisition of language to name that thinking. Oral language uses sound to name the concepts. Children with ASD as well as most neurotypical learners in today's classrooms do not learn to think with sound-based processes. The result is that learning to translate the sound of ideas into behavior is difficult for many children. The following section describes how most people expect children to use the sound of language for learning to behave.

Acquiring the Language of Behavior. Most educators and parents expect children in English-speaking countries to learn to behave through the use of the adults' words telling children what to do or not to do. From the very first days of infancy, parents and educators talk to children about "taking a hand" to cross the street, "picking up" toys before snack, "being quiet" in the restaurant, and so forth. English-speaking countries expect children to use the sound of English for learning to behave. Furthermore, English is a sound-based language in that it uses the alphabet (sounds with letters) as the basis for language structure. And, English is a time-based language in that it changes verbs to show time (tenses), uses a lot of adverbs (time-based "how" words), and connects ideas with time words. Time is learned through the acoustic system (Arwood, 2011[7]) that means that children who can use sound for learning to think will be able to use time for organization. Children who don't use sound for thinking will have trouble with all of the time-based functions of English.

For neurotypical children who think in the sound of their own voices, this is an easy culture in which to learn to behave (about 15%). Many children are able to use the sound to connect to their mental pictures. Again, the culture works fairly well for these children as long as they are able to use their picture metacognition to translate the sounds of voices. But about 20-45% of the population, including those who are diagnosed with ASD, do not perceive the sound of their voices. They hear sound; but, sound does not form mental thoughts or thinking. In fact, many children with ASD are able to repeat exactly what they hear; but the sound of words do not necessarily turn into mental visual thoughts. This means that individuals with ASD typically do not use sound for learning the social concepts for acceptable behavior. So, other approaches to learning to behave must be used.

As previously mentioned, most individuals diagnosed with ASD think with the shape of the seen idea. So, learning to behave for a person with ASD occurs best when they can see the ideas. *Figures 4.2 and 4.3* showed ways to provide the visual thinking. To increase this thinking to more advanced social forms, language must be added.

Language provides the tool for increasing cognition to learn to make choices and to problem solve. Much time is spent on the behavior of children with ASD without equal emphasis on language, not just language structures but language that functions as a representation of thinking. As a result, some children with ASD, like Marguerita, grow larger, and their younger behaviors are perceived to be more aggressive. Doing without an emphasis on thinking and without a way to represent thinking through language limits how far a person will socially develop. For example, when Marguerita[8] was younger and her arm swung out to reach for others' arms, educators saw her behavior as meaning "she needs something." Now as an adolescent, when her arm swings out and touches someone's arm, she is seen as "hitting" because she is big and her arm touches harder. But the same methods to "control" her

---

[7] See this reference for explanations about English properties as well as for why the differences between English and other languages.
[8] This is the same case as earlier described in this chapter.

behavior have been used for 9 years in the school system: 1) Limit her unwanted behavior by reinforcing her wanted behavior; 2) limit what people say to her so as to increase her understanding; and 3) use the adult voice or sound input as a stimulus for visual or motor output such as pointing or sitting. Learning for all three of these methods is based on modeling and additive imitative steps. Let's analyze why these methods have not worked.

Primary emphasis on changing Marguerita's behavior into more acceptable social behavior has been to "Limit her unwanted behavior by reinforcing her wanted behavior." The problem is that Marguerita does see others' actions or behaviors in a way that allows her to imitate them. She is too big to physically direct her body into the wanted or targeted behaviors for reinforcing; and, she does not engage in a lot of wanted behaviors naturally to be reinforced. Furthermore, this type of method works well for "limited behaviors" such as hitting or pointing on cue of a stimulus, which Marguerita does. But after Marguerita sits or points, what is she supposed to do? THINK! Yes, she has to think to continue the behavior that is expected. Without an emphasis on how she learns concepts in the process of language acquisition, she does not learn to think so as to engage in behavior that is more pro-social or expected. So she sits on command and then jumps up, spits, yells, or engages in any other behavior to fill the space between the last stimulus and the next behavior.

2) Another method used with Marguerita has been to limit what people say to her so she learns to follow very short, specific verbal cues, such as "Be quiet!" "Sit down!" "Stop that!" Again, with limited input, Marguerita's learning is limited. *Limited input results in limited acquisition of patterns. The same patterns are used over and over; so, the patterns do not overlap and therefore will not create conceptual meaning.* Children learn to think as a result of the overlapping use of patterns that eventually form concepts or thoughts. With limited input given to Marguerita, there are not enough overlapping patterns to learn concepts. This results in Marguerita having to use her own behavior to activate her brain. Since she only has physical behavior for communicating, she also only has physical behavior for developing brain patterns. The result is more and more unwanted behaviors over time such as aggressive behaviors to fill the space of "nothing to think about" or more self-stimulation behavior to activate her brain.

3). Most behavior programming is done for Marguerita with the use of adult voices for cues or stimuli. Visuals are cues for responses. The input of sound does not allow Marguerita to learn concepts. If sound input would become conceptual, then she would have oral language because she lives in an auditory culture that uses an auditory language. Furthermore, children with ASD learn concepts through visual shapes. Neither the input nor the output is set up to match Marguerita's learning needs. Therefore, she also does not learn to think. So, her behavior is left at the sensori-motor level---hitting, kicking, spitting, and so on.

Activity: Why is learning language as important as children become older and have greater needs to communicate in conventional ways?

The aforementioned approaches to "controlling Marguerita's behavior" did not work. The philosophy used with her was based on behaviorism. Since all children learn to behave as a result of changes to the brain from assigned meaning to increase her thinking, a different approach was used to create meaning for Marguerita. The authors' effective approach is based on some simple principles grounded in neuroeducation; the translation of neuroscience to learning: 1) Provide Marguerita with the sensory input that matches the way she learns concepts (movement overlaps such as mouth movement overlapping with drawing and writing); 2) Increase language use by the adults since Marguerita has no language. This increase of language must be given in a visual way to match Marguerita's learning system; and 3) Make sure that the assignment of meaning with language is visual-motor in overlapping patterns such as drawing, writing, hand-over-hand, so that the input matches her thinking. This philosophy of increasing the use of language is opposite from the way that Marguerita was approached for nine school years. *The lower the person with ASD functions, the greater that person's need for more language, resulting in more meaning and more thinking for better behavior.*

The information in the following box is important to an understanding about how to help children with ASD learn to pro-socially behave.

Learning to See How to Behave

In an auditory, sound-based culture like the U.S., we always talk to children, giving them many acoustic patterns long before they talk. We assume that children are able to learn with these patterns. When most children connect what they see with the sound patterns or connect their mental visual thoughts with the sounds, they cognitively learn to talk and their behavior follows their thinking. They are also able to use this sound for writing and reading.

Children diagnosed with ASD cannot use sound for thinking and learning to act pro-socially. But, the human brain shows plasticity which means the brain is capable of using other sensory inputs than just sound. Furthermore, there is evidence in other cultures where people use thinking that is not sound based, such as with the acquisition of American Sign Language. Why not write and draw with children before they can read and write?

Drawing and writing for children with ASD from their very earliest years provides the same patterns that become conceptual for them that talking does for other children. It is not necessary to wait to teach sounds to teach a child to speak, read, or write. Reading and writing do not have to be accomplished with sounds and letters. Seeing print as patterns that go with pictures (concepts) provides visual-motor patterns that facilitate acquiring concepts necessary for language to behave. Seeing others write is like hearing others talk. For a child who thinks in the shape of movement, writing provides patterns for learning to speak, read, and write, just like speaking provides patterns for children learning to speak, read, and write who think in the sounds look.

WRITE! WRITE! WRITE TO THINK!

Activity: Why write and draw for children with ASD before they have oral language or the ability to read sounds and letters as alphabetic properties of English?

Summary

Everyone learns to think. Behavior represents the level of learning to think. In an English-speaking, auditory society the following learning is expected: 1) a neurotypical learning system that processes sound to allow the acquisition of typical language function from others' oral language; 2) the ability to form concepts from the sound of environmental sensory input; 3) an auditory environment that consistently assigns meaning and interprets behavior in the way that the adults of the dominant culture think; and 4) the use of limited oral language to explain the meaning of behavior to young children so children are not confused.

In order for children and adults diagnosed with ASD to learn to behave at the level expected for independence by the dominant U.S. society, the following must happen: 1) input about behavior must be in a visual-motor way for the learner to see him or her in a 2D picture or stick-figure cartoon that depicts how to look and think about others' actions; 2) all visuals must include written words to show what the mouth movements look like that assign meaning to the pictures; 3) all conceptual learning must include motor layers of meaning, such as writing followed by drawing (independent of age) and more writing, hand-over-hand finger spelling, writing, drawing, signing, and so forth so the learner with ASD can connect visual thoughts with visual patterns; and 4) the use of lots of rich visual language to name behavior in order to explain what social development means.

This summary shows how the dominant auditory culture does not always set up opportunities for children and adults with ASD to think with visual-motor concepts so as to learn to be pro-social thinkers. *Chapter Five* expands on how to use the knowledge about learning to behave to help a child develop pro-social behavior.

Important Concepts in *Chapter Five*

Readers should be able to explain each of these behavior principles upon completion of this chapter:

1. Pro-social development is learning to see others in one's own picture.

2. All behavior is acceptable, a form of communication, and interpreted by others. Therefore, learning to be pro-social is learning what others think about one's behavior.

3. Individuals with ASD learn to think in visual forms that are often made from the shape of movement of the hand, mouth, and eyes.

4. All interventions for individuals with ASD must consider the developmental level of the language so as to match thinking levels with literacy expectations for viewing, reading, writing, listening, speaking, and calculating.

5. Pro-social concepts represent how a learner thinks about self and others and what others think and do.

CHAPTER FIVE
Learning to Be Pro-Social

Others see me, but I don't see them.
My pictures are from me, inside out, not outside in.
I wonder what others see when they see me.
But I don't see me so I don't see them.

All children learn to behave (*Chapter Four*), but not all behavior contributes to pro-social relationships. *Pro-social* behavior supports the initiation and maintenance of healthy relationships. Learning to contribute to the wellbeing of others and their needs as well as take care of one's own needs through healthy relationships is difficult for everybody, but is especially difficult for children and adults diagnosed with ASD.

This chapter will discuss some of the factors involved in learning to be pro-social in the U.S. culture and present methods for helping those with ASD learn to be socially interdependent. Being social assumes appropriate behavior representative of learning to be social. Learning to behave represents social and cognitive development. Therefore, learning to be pro-social requires sufficient cognitive development to think with language about one's behavior in relationship to the effects or consequences of one's behavior on others.

To support pro-social development, the following learning principles (*Chapter Four*) are important to consider for individuals with ASD:

1. Provide the meaning of behavior in developmentally appropriate *visual-motor* forms.

2. Include written words to emphasize the shapes of ideas.

3. Include multiple *layers* of meaning through the shape of motor patterns.

4. *Overlap* motor movements to create changes in thinking or cognition.

The following section of this chapter will address each of the aforementioned principles of learning to be pro-social.

Visual-Motor Forms

For an individual diagnosed with ASD, all concepts about behavior must be presented in developmentally appropriate visual-motor forms. But not all visual-motor forms are effective. The visual-motor form must match the way the learner is able to create new concepts. In other words, the visual-motor forms must be presented in the type of patterns in which the person thinks. Thinking is conceptualizing! Visual-motor forms must match the way the learner thinks and must be at the learner's level of thinking.

Most people with ASD learn concepts by overlapping movements into meaningful shapes rather than by seeing the content or hearing the words. These shapes are like puzzle pieces where they interconnect to form the *context of events*. *Figure 5.1* is an example of thinking in shapes.

Figure 5.1. *Thinking in shapes.*

In order to be effective in helping individuals with ASD learn to be social and, therefore, behave in an acceptable pro-social manner, it is important to provide shapes of ideas about behavior. Shapes form from tracing the perimeter of an object. For example, moving one's hand along the edge of a table creates a mental understanding of the shape of the table. These shapes record in the visual cortex (Sadato, 1996). Thus, shapes create concepts in the visual thinking system. Others also report this ability to use shapes as a thinking process of learning in the brain (Arwood & Kaulitz, 2007; Arwood, 2011; Grandin & Panek, 2013).

Seeing a picture is also visual, but pictures may or may not create shapes. Pictures are what we can see within the space of the perimeter of the shape. Shapes are patterns, whereas pictures are the concepts or content of ideas. Content or concepts seen within a picture or photograph require thinking and language to name the thinking. Individuals with ASD do well with patterns but are not always able to quickly form concepts from patterns. As a result, they struggle with understanding what others think or sometimes how to develop language to represent thinking.

This is why many individuals with ASD do better with the print patterns of ideas than the meaning of pictures. The print patterns, when outlined or bubbled closely, show a shape. The meaning or content of the shape is the picture. In this way, the individual with ASD is able to read patterns that will form shapes when paired with contextual meaning of concepts. The shapes of print create meaningful concepts, whereas pictures are not patterns but the concept of someone else's thinking.

Consider a middle-school student, Randy. Randy frequently spoke about how others "annoyed" him or "teased" him and how it "made him angry." His teachers complained that Randy did not take "responsibility" for his actions. At the same time, Randy never ever saw an event from someone else's "perspective." Randy would name call a student because Randy might be "frustrated," but Randy's frustration might have little to do with the student Randy name called. For example, another student, Jack might say, "Randy, don't be so slow. Hurry up with the water at the fountain." Randy would then turn around and say to a bystander, Clark, "You are stupid." Clark would push Randy, and Randy would throw Clark down on the cement." Randy was a very large student compared to the other middle-school boys. When interviewed after the water fountain event, Randy said, "It's all Clark's fault. I take responsibility for my actions. I was minding my own business at the water fountain. Clark was mean." Randy did not act out on Jack, who was the one who rushed Randy. Instead, he acted out on Clark. The reason why Randy did not act out on Jack was that Randy did not see anyone else in his picture. Randy was functioning at a pre-operational level of thinking and doing. Randy just acted on whomever Randy saw.

Randy could talk on and on about the event, listing all of the school rules and how he never engaged in any behavior that had anything to do with a problem behavior such as the situation at the water fountain. Randy could use formal vocabulary like "accountability," "responsibility," and "trustworthy," but his actions showed he did not understand the meaning of these words.

Figure 5.2 (see next page) provides an example of a vocabulary sheet that Randy was asked to fill in each time he said a word that his actions or behavior did not show he understood. This sheet was completed over several weeks. He spoke all of these words, but he did not "know" their meanings well enough to change his behavior.

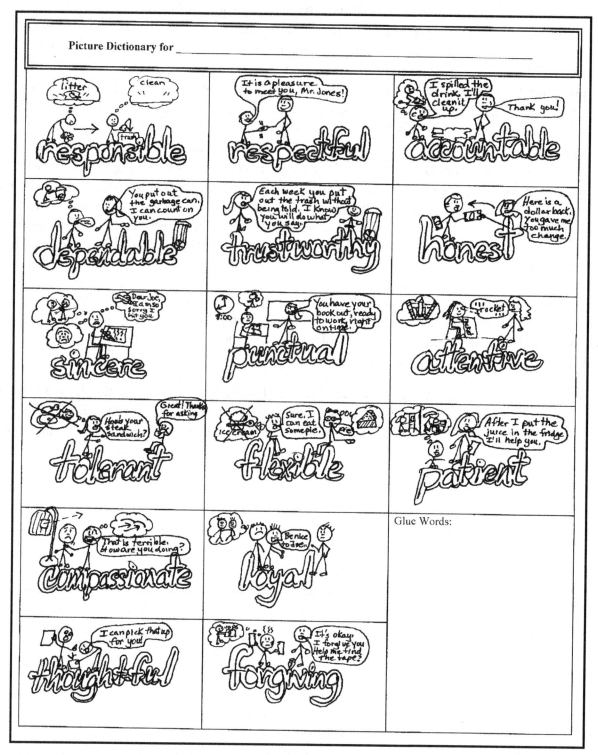

Figure 5.2. The concept "Responsibility" in a picture dictionary.

Randy could say the words. He learned the acoustic or sound patterns of the words and the rules about the words. But he could not connect the sound pattern of words with his mental pictures, so he did not really "know what behavior" went with which words. He could not see himself involved in activities in which he could see others. They were in a mental picture outside him while he was in his own picture. They were not together in one picture. Even in the picture dictionary, his drawings or meanings lacked people who are engaged in activities that would represent the conceptual understanding of how his behavior and their behavior interrelate.

Activity: At what developmental level is Randy if he is in his own picture?

Randy was in his own picture. His social development was preoperational at best. But he had learned the words and patterns of the rules so he could talk about what he saw others do. He could see how others were in his space, but he could not see how he was in their space. Because the adults heard Randy tell all of the rules about how he was responsible, and so on, they thought he understood these words and rules. Educators would often say, "He knows the rules. He just wants attention." Educators also blamed Randy's family for not being "strict enough;" but the educators were not able to make Randy behave at school, so how could the family be held responsible for the educators' actions? Because the educators believed that Randy understood his actions, they thought his behavior reflected a choice to not comply. The adults tried all sorts of activities and methods to get Randy to comply. They used token economies, motivational activities, bribes, punishment, but to no avail. Randy just keep growing larger, using more words, and his behavior becoming more unacceptable.

For compliance, Randy and the adults in his environment wrote many contracts using a variety of approaches. But Randy's behavior never changed. Sometimes he showed an immediate change, but his behavior always reverted back to him being in his own picture. The contracts did not improve his thinking, so contracts did not improve Randy's social behavior. Various support personnel wrote numerous social types of stories with him, but Randy did not understand how to make his behavior match the words in the stories. Over time his behavior remained anti-social.

As Randy became older, he appeared more aggressive and his behavior was seen as irritating or disturbing to most of the other students and adults. So, what is missing? He has the words, the rules, and the rewards/punishers as incentives, but this behavior was often inappropriate, sometimes aggressive, argumentative, or "non-compliant."

Randy needs *to see the behavior*, not hear the rules. He needs to see the concepts of the behavior, not the models by the adults. For Randy to be able to think about what he sees, and for Randy to see how his behavior affects others, he needs to be able to draw what he knows as well as what others see when they think about his behavior. *Helping Randy to see what behavior means requires adults to draw behavior as ideas so that Randy can record the meaning of behavior as shapes.* Further, these shapes or visual-motor meanings must be presented at an appropriate developmental level for Randy to understand the meanings.

Activity: What is the basic rule for presenting material about behavior to individuals with ASD?

The use of visual-motor concepts in the form of hand shapes for writing and drawing provided Randy with appropriate meaning to change his behavior. What eventually made the difference was the way the visual-motor concepts connected with his language. In order for concepts to be recalled, they must be learned with language. Any lower level of learning, such as rote memorization, imitating a model, copying words on a contract, saying meaningless words as rules that were imitated from others, will not create conceptual changes that allow for changes in behavior. This is why contracts and stories using others' language did not work for Randy. For Randy to use words and sentences that have meaning, he must be able to learn the shapes of those words and sentences, as he understands the meaning. He must be able to draw and write using his thinking to create his language about the situation.

Activity: How does language fit into the visual-motor piece of learning concepts?

The purpose of asking Randy to write the words he spoke along with drawing pictures of the meaning of the words was to create language. Language provides for long-term retention, or semantic memory. The patterns are the print or written words added to the drawings or the concepts. When patterns and concepts are linked together, the name or language of the concept is put into semantic memory. Language allows for long-term retrieval and understanding of concepts. Language in a visual-motor form consists of the visual-motor patterns or writing combined with the meaning of those patterns or the drawn concepts. Shape patterns or written forms connect to the pictures of the concepts (pictographs), which form language. To be certain that words were turned into shapes, *bubbling* the printed concept or word was then paired with a picture to help create a visual-motor shape for meaning.

Randy began to see the pattern (written word) attached to the meaning (drawing) of each concept. Soon his behavior began to change because he was learning to see or think with the meaning of shapes about social concepts. *When patterns and concepts are integrated, they become language-based or semantic for long term retrieval and understanding.* Because Randy is a visual-motor thinker, the patterns must be visual-motor (seeing movements of the hand drawing and writing) for him to learn the meaning of the concepts.

Activity: What does integration of patterns and concepts form?

All people acquire concepts as part of a semantic field or in relationship to each other. In other words, the meanings of the word "responsibility" and "respect" relate to each other. Semantic fields are like families. They relate to each other in some meaningful way. The arrows on Randy's picture (*Figure 5.2*) dictionary chart help organize how the different concepts meaningfully relate to each other. Concepts are learned, not taught, so, like many other students, Randy has to learn how different concepts relate to acquire the meaningful connections. For example, Randy considers himself "a responsible person," but he always blames others at school and at home. This means that he only sees himself in the pictures, not others. Randy lacks the meaning of how his behavior looks when he is responsible for his actions to and with others. Developmentally, he is thinking about himself at the preoperational level of social learning (see *Chapter Four* for a definition of levels).

At the preoperational level, Randy is dependent on others because he cannot see how he fits into society, into others' actions or events involving others, into classrooms with other students and adults, and so forth (Arwood, 2011; Winner, 2002, 2007). To behave at a level that matches societal expectations, Randy must learn to see others in his pictures. This conceptual level of seeing others is concrete and rule-governed. Without a concrete, rule-governed level of thinking, Randy's social behavior will not match society's expectations. Eventually, Randy will not be able to live alone without the language necessary to make choices or problem solve about how to behave in relationship to other people's needs .

Figure 5.3 shows a picture of Randy on the playground thinking about others' thinking. This picture also shows Randy behaving in a way that allows his actions to be a part of others' thinking.

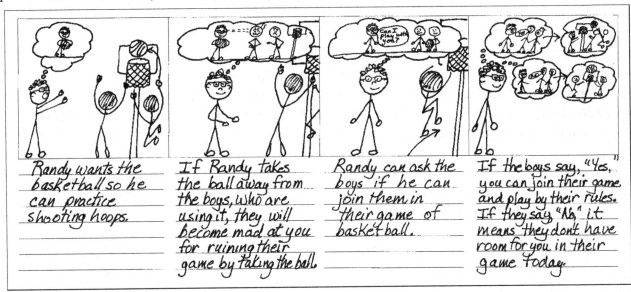

Figure 5.3. *Randy thinks about others in his pictures.*

Activity: At which developmental level must thinking be in order for behavior to fit in with society's expectations?

Shapes

Shapes occur from seeing the edges. Edges occur when a hand touches the outside of another hand. The eyes see the edges of objects, which is why we see the surface of a table or desk or person. The eyes do not see through the table or the bottom side of the table. The eyes cannot see through a human. The brain sees the surface points of light that reflect off people or objects, not the inside or backside. The language of thinking in shapes (Arwood, 2011) allows the learner to see the edges as a concept. Learners see the outside edges of a table, desk, Aunt Ruth, and so forth.

Thinking in shapes is not specific to individuals with ASD. It also works for many others. Children or adults who use movement for meaning such as those with ADHD (attention deficit hyperactivity disorder) or FAS (fetal alcohol syndrome) also use shapes of ideas for thinking. Anyone who uses movement for thinking does not think in the sound of others' voices and does not learn social development from watching what others do. This means that the social norms of what parents and educators expect must be turned into actions that can be seen through the shapes of movement. And these shapes of movement must be given the language patterns through print so that the learner begins to acquire the meaning of the shapes. Recent reports support the development of these shapes in the mind of those with autism (e.g., Grandin & Panek 2013).

Activity: How does a learner think in shapes?

People frequently ask, "What types of movements create shapes? Does walking on the track create shapes of thinking? Does sitting on a ball create shapes for thinking?" The answers to these questions relate to the concept of "thinking." Any movement that uses gross-motor muscles does not connect those muscle groups to the thinking part of the brain. For example, an educator gives a child some time on the track to "think" through the child's actions. The child is diagnosed with ASD and uses shapes for thinking. Gross-motor activities such as walking on the track do not create the shapes of thinking. But walking does change the child's movements, so as the child walks, such movement changes his thoughts. The child no longer is thinking about what happened that resulted in him being out on the track. Instead, the child is thinking about the walk around the track.

Activity: What types of movements create the shapes of an idea?

To learn with shapes a person must be able to think in shapes. For example, a child with ASD is in a general education classroom with a paraprofessional. The class is working on a task that has little meaning for this student, so he begins to talk loudly and make inappropriate vocalizations that "distract the other students." The paraprofessional is told to take the student with ASD outside to walk the track. The student is now walking on the track. He is no longer thinking about what happened in the classroom. He is now thinking about what he sees as he walks. When he returns to the classroom calmed down, the adults assume that he has used the time on the track to think about his inappropriate behavior.

First of all, he does not know his behavior was inappropriate. He was trying to make the classroom meaningful. Second, he returned calmed down because his movements changed his thinking. Unfortunately, such activity does not help the child learn about why he left the room, why he walked the track, what others think about him when he is using a loud voice or making sounds that distract others – he thinks with shapes and does not hear the sounds he makes that reach others. And, he does not think about others in his thoughts, because he has not learned enough shapes or concepts about what others think.

Figure 5.4 shows the student making noises and what the other class members look like when their thinking goes away as a result of his voice. Then in the second box we see the student thinking about what the students look like and what he needs to look like to change their faces and their thoughts.

The teacher's mouth is moving. That means the teacher is talking to you and everyone else in this room. It is your job and the job of every student, to watch the teacher's mouth move and make pictures in your head of what you see teacher say.

When teacher is talking and you open your mouth, you let noise fall out of your mouth and you cover up the thoughts of the people in this room. Your noise pops their thought bubbles and they cannot think.

When your mouth noise pops people's thought bubbles, they turn around and look at you to see why so much noise is falling out of your mouth.

Figure 5.4. *Seeing that others are talking.*

Notice that in *Figure 5.4*, the boy must learn the following concepts: 1) there are others in his space; 2) moving his mouth results in words that come out of his mouth and fill others' spaces; 3) moving his mouth might make others' pictures or thoughts go away because something comes out of his mouth when he moves; 4) others do not see him in their picture at lunch or recess or in the classroom if he makes their mental pictures go away so they cannot do their work.

For this student to become social so that his behavior is appropriate and so he can be pro-social or fit into the other students' thinking, he must be able to learn the concepts in the form of shapes – the shape of the hand moving to draw the pictures so he can see the people, see their thoughts, see his thoughts, see himself in their picture, and so forth.

To be able to see the shapes of the drawing movements, the child must be able to see the shape of the words that he cannot hear. So, anything with sound such as talking to him about his behavior, his feelings, his needs, and so forth will not create the mental shapes of his thinking. Writing the shapes of the words will help him see the ideas.

Figure 5.5 shows the writing. This student does not read and write so all of this work was completed in a hand-on-his-hand (H/H) manner so that he could learn the shape of the patterns of writing a form (word to the reader) that explains the meaning of the drawn concepts.

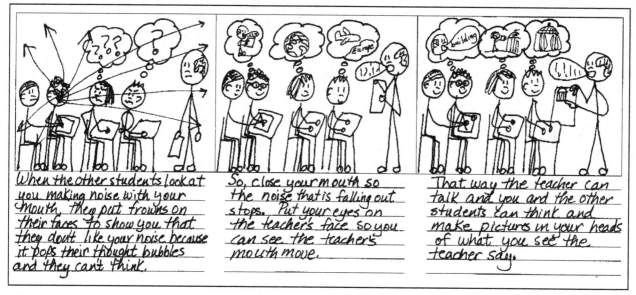

Figure 5.5. *Seeing others think.*

Activity: How does learning with movement help form mental shapes?

The student in *Figures 5.4 and 5.5* learns to think and be social through the fine-motor movements of the mouth and hands forming shapes of concepts, not the gross-motor movements of the large muscles for walking, sitting, and so forth. Exercise helps provide the brain with oxygen. Walking on the track allows the child to move so that his thinking is activated, but this type of movement does not provide the shapes of ideas. Sitting on a ball helps a child develop trunk support which helps stabilize the child's trunk while providing continuous feedback or *proprioceptive* feedback to the child's body about where the child is in space. Therefore, sitting on the ball helps the child to focus on sitting, but the feedback system connected to the muscles does not provide changes in thinking at the cortical level of the brain. In other words, the muscles do not help develop the thinking found in the brain.

Neither walking nor sitting provides the child with knowledge about how to be social. Concepts in the form of shapes from the fine-motor movements of the hand, eye, or mouth develop the child's thinking. These shapes represent the meaning of concepts that are named by language that may be spoken or written.

Activity: How do movements that create symbol shapes or thinking differ from gross-motor movements?

Layers

The learning system is set up in layers of complexity starting with the *sensory receptors*: eyes, ears, mouth, nose, and skin. The second layer is at the cellular level of neurons sending messages as groups or *patterns* on to areas of the brain. Multiple areas of the brain interconnect forming the third layer of circuits. These circuits create *concepts* or thinking when the patterns are recognized. When a learner is able to put shared patterns together to represent this thinking, he uses the fourth level or *language* to continue the learning. These layers create more and more complex forms of learning and behaving.

The first two levels of learning do not allow for thinking but for doing. The sensory input overlaps to form patterns. Behavior through imitation is in the form of patterns, the second layer of learning. Therefore, imitation or models of behavior to be copied are very low levels of learning and do not really provide for higher levels of learning or thinking.

Behavior from imitation will result in little, if any, thinking about one's actions. Examples of imitation include copying another person's behavior: An adult crosses her legs and the child also crosses his legs. The adult says something and the child says the same thing either immediately or at another time. Someone sings the national anthem and the child sings it exactly the way the professional sings it. The educator reads the words on a page and the child is able to read back exactly what the educator read. The child writes the teacher's words on a contract: "I will not hit other students. If I hit other students, then I will spend time in the detention room." This imitation of another's rule means that the student has little meaning for what the words represent in terms of behavior.

Often, patterns of behavior are found not just in behavior or social programs but also in academics. Copying and matching the correct answers on worksheets or tests require imitating the correct patterns. Saying the correct sounds to the words is a rote memorization of patterns as is taking a spelling test. Patterns are patterns! The brain loves patterns, and individuals with ASD do very well with patterns. But learning to be pro-social so as to behave in societally expected ways requires thinking. Thinking is more than copying, matching, and imitating patterns. Thinking is conceptual. People acquire concepts through this layering process in the neurosemantic language learning system (Arwood, 2011). The result is that concepts are always acquiring more meaning. Concepts layer! Concepts are ideas! Concepts make up thinking!

Activity: Why are patterns learned through imitation?

Learning to think requires layers of conceptual meaning. Conceptual learning occurs at a higher level than the first levels of input and imitated responses. Since individuals diagnosed with ASD learn new concepts through visual-motor access, they need layers of thinking about being pro-social in visual-motor ways. So, for a person with a motor access to be able to visually think, concepts must contain layers of visual-motor input.

Case Study● Aaron is an 11-year-old diagnosed with autism. He is nonverbal, aggressive, and does not have a conventional form of reading, writing, or speaking. He is ambulatory and dresses himself. Upon observation, the author notices that Aaron is able to pick up a magazine in the waiting room of the evaluation clinic and thumb through the pages in the way that most people read a book. While waiting, he climbs up on a chair, then a table, and changes the television to a different channel and then watches the program. Aaron's record shows eight years of speech therapy to develop speech movements, blowing, lip movements for sounds like /p?/ and /b?/. He has also had eight years of school with discrete trials for behavior to change his level of compliance. He has learned to imitate others' behavior. He sits when they sit. He points when he is to point, given a stimulus that he recognizes.

After some time in the waiting room, a student educator took Aaron to a room to begin to work with him. Aaron did not recognize the stimuli, the rewards, the room, or the adult. Without language, Aaron has no meaning for the changes, so he pushed the materials off the table, made faces in the two-way mirror, and eventually stood up on the table holding his shirt up while continuing to make faces in the mirror. The student educator talked, pointed, showed Aaron what to do, and explained the rewards of checks and smiling faces, but to no avail. When the student educator pulled out the candy, Aaron grabbed it and threw it across the room. He then began to jump while still standing on the table. The student educator tried to physically redirect him down from the table, but Aaron kicked at the educator's face.

The author, the student's supervisor, was sitting on the other side of the observation room. Seeing that Aaron could be dangerous and could hurt himself, the supervisor immediately went into the room and began to draw a picture of Aaron sitting in his chair while talking about what they would do when he sat. Aaron bent over to see the author's hand move. He then climbed off the table and sat down in his chair. The author used rudimentary American Sign Language to sign about the drawing and what they were to do, and Aaron slapped at her moving hands. So she wrote the words, "Aaron is sitting in his chair so his eyes are able to see the pictures." She drew him sitting and looking at the pictures and thinking (thought bubble) about what he saw. *Figure 5.6* shows Aaron sitting, looking at the pictures, and thinking about sitting and looking at the pictures.

***Figure 5.6.** Aaron sits and thinks.*

Aaron grabbed the picture and attempted to vocalize. The educator wrote the words that went with the picture. The picture was about a boy throwing a football. So the educator wrote, "Aaron is sitting so he is able to see the picture. Aaron looks at the picture and thinks about what he sees. Aaron thinks about the boy playing football. Aaron uses his hands to show the words he sees." The educator took Aaron's hands and used her own hand and to form the shape of the signs in Aaron's hands: "boy throw football." She then drew another picture of Aaron seeing the words and thinking about the movement of the hand signs. *Figure 5.7* shows Aaron thinking about what he sees and making the signs for the ideas that he sees.

Figure 5.7. Aaron thinks and signs.

Over the next three months, Aaron would look at pictures that the educator gave him and the educator would give the manual sign paired with the written word(s). Then the educator would shuffle the pictures and show Aaron the print. No matter what order the pictures were in, Aaron could sign the meaning of the picture after one paired meaning (hand movement, written word, and picture). Aaron's ability to acquire visual-motor layers of meaning was phenomenal. Aaron gradually began to use his knowledge (print and signs with pictures) to write about his needs and wants. *By the way, the day that the visual-motor layers began, all of the inappropriate behavior stopped.* Furthermore, his behavior changed in other environments. He could think! He could think because the author provided him with enough visual-motor layers to create concepts for him. These layers included drawing him into his picture, writing about what he sees in the picture, hand-over-hand signing the meaning of what he sees in the picture, drawing and writing what Aaron does to the pictures and, using the pictures in a variety of ways to create meaning for more visual-motor, shape-based thinking. These types of layers were necessary for Aaron to acquire conceptualization about how to behave or be pro-social.

Activity: What are layers in learning to be social?

Overlap

The person diagnosed with ASD learns best with visual-motor concepts. As we have seen, these concepts continue to develop in meaning with more layers (also see Arwood & Kaulitz, 2007;

Arwood, Kaulitz, & Brown, 2009). However, the layers of thinking also must overlap to create connections for higher order thinking and functioning. To be independent, a person with ASD must be able to think about others and what others' think. This ability to think about others begins to emerge around seven years of age.

Case Study. Troy is an eight-year-old child with ASD who is nonverbal and uses behaviors that include pinching, biting, yelling, and laughing to communicate his wants and needs. He is enrolled in a developmental special education program with other students with developmental delays. The teacher and the assistants lead Troy through his day with verbal and visual cues in the form of symbolic line drawings.[9] After seven months of discrete trial training with these drawings, Troy still does not recognize the symbolic drawings independently without cues. He is not receiving the visual-motor information in a way that connects his learning system to what he sees in the pictures and to what he sees others do. Furthermore, there are not enough layers to form concepts because Troy is only responding to the cues by imitating of patterns. Also, his responses do not overlap the visual-motor patterns with visual concepts so that he learns the language; that is, which words go with which pictures, what the pictures mean to him, what he can do with the pictures to alter his environment (agency), and how he fits in with other people. In other words, he is not learning to think about behavior so as to become pro-social. Finally, the line drawings do not put Troy in his picture to help him see how his behavior affects others or how he thinks about others in his picture. He is not learning to behave by acquiring social concepts.

Activity: What is the difference between learning to behave in response to others' cues and learning to think about being social?

Adults in Troy's environment attempt to reinforce Troy with the sound of words such as telling Troy that he is a "good boy." These words are sounds without specific meaning. In other words, what is a good boy? When is he a good boy? Is he good or is it his behavior that is good? Such words do not create mental pictures for Troy, nor do they help him learn what he is supposed to look like or think about. The adults also try to use rewards such as time on the computer for when he does a "good job" or presents 8 out of 10 correct responses to cards. But Troy does not know how these rewards connect to his behavior.

Likewise, when the adults do not like Troy's behavior, they say words such as "no" firmly and loudly. If the adults judge Troy's behavior as not fitting into a setting, then the adults isolate him from his peers based on the assumption that Troy wants to be with his peers and that he understands why he is not with the peers. However, since he is not verbal, he does not have the language to be able to mentally understand how others fit into his mental pictures. Furthermore, he does not have the meaning for spoken words, as he learns concepts with visual-motor patterns, not sound. To learn to think about others so that Troy changes his behavior to fit into the classroom setting, Troy needs more overlap of visual-motor meaning to create more depth of understanding.

---

[9] Symbolic line drawings are line drawings that depict a set of ideas. For example, a toilet might represent the process of learning to go to the bathroom.

Overlapping patterns form concepts only when the patterns match the way the learner thinks. And as the concepts overlap with each other, new depth in the meaning of the concepts as well as interconnectedness among meanings occurs. For example, a child sits so he can do a variety of tasks such as eat, look at pictures, write, draw, and so forth. When the child sits to do these types of tasks, the child's brain is acquiring meaning about each of the acts as well as meaning from those around the child. As the adults in the child's environment add layers of meaning about these acts through drawings, writings, manual signing, and so forth; the child is also learning about how the child is a social agent. The child is learning how others fit into these acts. The adult adds more visual-motor representations about how others think as the child engages in these acts and so the child is learning to be more social, to fit into others' pictures.

Overlapping concepts helps the child move from being in his own picture to being in the pictures of others. Overlapping these visual-motor concepts also helps the person diagnosed with ASD learn how to be pro-social, how to fit with others. So, patterns become concepts and concepts overlap to create layers of meaning to increase the complexity of meaning in the concepts.

Activity: What does overlapping concepts do to help learn to be pro-social in learning to behave?

When a child learns to behave, she learns to be pro-social through cognitive acquisition of concepts for language function or purpose. Providing individuals diagnosed with ASD with visual-motor input that forms shapes through layers of meanings overlapped with multiple uses has a powerful effect. If the type of input matches their learning systems, their thinking provides the meaning for their pro-social behavior or their doing.

The meaning others assign is a form of input. Therefore, how others assign meaning is important. What adults value as meaningful, determines what meaning the child learns. For example, according to the adults, one of Troy's especially annoying behaviors is his laughing. He tends to laugh in response to demands being placed on him. The adults have made an assumption that the laughter means that Troy thinks the situation is funny and that he is laughing on purpose to avoid the task he is being asked to do. With the help of this author and an occupational therapist with expertise in language, the staff has been exploring the idea that although it appears that the laughter is often a response to anxiety/sensory[10] issues, it is more likely a symptom of a child with a motor (shapes from movements) access to his visual language system who is struggling to find meaning in his world. As a result, they have stopped assuming that the laughter is because Troy thinks what is happening is funny and have introduced stick figure line drawings as well as hand-over-hand writing to assign additional meaning to the tasks that Troy is being asked to do. The drawings show Troy what his body needs to look like in relation to other bodies in the room when he is performing a task. Visual information in the form of stick figure drawings appears to greatly reduce his anxiety/sensory issues because these types of input provide Troy with meaning in the way he learns concepts. In other words, he is learning to think. The laughter has stopped. The Hand-Over-Hand (HoH) writing has created enough overlap of

---

[10] Anxiety is the product of stress. Stressors include unknown sensory inputs, uncomfortable physical situations, physical problems such as a new diet, non-meaningful input such as external noise, and so forth. Meaning that is attached to these stressors tends to decrease the resulting anxiety.

concepts to allow Troy to be able to write his name on his papers and school projects and to begin writing and drawing ideas on his own. Troy is learning to think as a social being, an agent who is capable of writing, doing his projects, and so forth.

Activity: What does overlapping concepts do to increase meaning?

Learning Pro-Social Meaning

People don't view behavior in the same way or even think that behavior means the same thing. For example, sometimes parents and educators see very different behavior in children at school than at home. Sometimes the same educators or parents see different behavior in the same setting. Part of the reason for these differences is that different people have different ideas about which behavior is okay or not okay. In other words, differences in philosophical beliefs about how to deal with behavior reflect differences in thinking, which results in assigning different meanings to the same behavior, to different behaviors, or to setting different limits. Therefore, different environments or settings provide different opportunities for learning and for acquiring different meanings.

These differences are easily resolved for most people through the acquisition of additional concepts represented as more complex language across developmental ages. But sometimes these differences in meaning for different situations and for different people are difficult to understand. Sometimes children struggle in learning how to behave in a pro-social way.

Activity: Why do differences in meaning result in confusion in learning to be pro-social?

Case Study. Jackson is a 13-year-old male who is often in "trouble" for not understanding rules or for noncompliance. Furthermore, he argues about the meaning of concepts, about whether or not others are "fair" in their interpretation of meaning. Students and faculty see Jackson as "belligerent," "difficult to be around," and "unlikeable." Jackson greets people and appears to initiate social interactions but his behavior gets in the way of him becoming "pro-social." He is not learning how to "get along" or maintain healthy relationships with others. He tends to follow those who bully others and even shows some tendency to "fit in" with those who aggressively attack others. Over time, Jackson has been showing more anger and lack of thinking or concern about others. Instead of learning to be pro-social by learning the concepts about himself in relationship to others, he is learning to be more anti-social.

His speech-language (SLP) therapist, Loretta Walsh, has begun to draw and write out the meaning of what others see and what others mean when Jackson behaves a certain way. *Figure 5.8* shows a situation in which a teacher questioned Jackson about jumping down the stairs. Here are the meanings: Jackson jumps and Jackson "goes" down the stairs, so when these meanings are put together, then Jackson jumps down the stairs. From Jackson's perspective he is doing what he is supposed to be doing. From the teacher's perspective, Jackson is not walking down the stairs but jumping. When the SLP sat down and began to draw, Jackson took over the task. The SLP had written a question to Jackson that the teacher had asked, "Is that a safe way to go down the stairs?" This question is not very specific and is "colloquial" in nature, making the teacher's intention a mixed message. Is the teacher being funny or sarcastic? Or does the teacher want some specific information from Jackson that would suggest that he has to change his action?

Figure 5.8. *Jackson does what he thinks.*

Because of previous work with the SLP, Jackson realized that there has to be thoughts to go with the spoken language, so he drew, and then he began to think about the other people and what they were thinking. By thinking about others, Jackson began to put other people into his own picture, which means he also began to function at more of a concrete level of thinking. He could then think about the rules and what the rules mean in relationship to others (Winner, 2007). By the end of the drawing and writing, Jackson calmly could explain what the consequences of his jumping behavior meant and what he needed to do to change his behavior to be safe around others. He also began to realize that his behavior had not only a physical impact on others but also a thinking impact. To learn to be pro-social, Jackson needs to learn about others and how his behavior affects others' thinking and their behaviors.

By drawing out what Jackson was doing and what he was thinking, Jackson never again jumped down the stairs. By overlapping multiple examples of how to think about others and have others think about Jackson, Jackson will begin to learn that he is in a relationship with others. If others think about him in a pro-social way, he must think about them to develop healthy relationships. A healthy relationship is one where Jackson thinks about others and his friends think about him. They support, nurture, and protect each other. Jackson is beginning to change his behavior so that he is thinking more like a pro-social being, an agent who is able to initiate and maintain healthy relationships with others.

---

*Activity: **What does Jackson begin to learn so that his behavior is more pro-social?***

In order for children to be able to learn to be pro-social, it is important that adults view the children's behavior as separate from the children's thinking. A child's thinking is part of "who" the child is, not what the child does. Therefore, it is important that the adult not judge or interpret the behavior based on what the adult thinks. *Chapter Six* will provide more examples of how meaning layered, overlapped, and provided in visual-motor ways helps individuals with ASD learn to act as agents in their pro-social relationships.

Summary

To learn to behave in pro-social ways, a person must be able to think about how his or her behaviors affect others. To think about others means that we must be able to see others in our picture, but many individuals diagnosed with ASD without language cannot see themselves in their mental pictures. Educators and parents must first draw these learners into pictures and then, add written meaning so that the learners are able to see themselves and their behavior in relationship to others who are also in the pictures. By being able to see themselves, their behavior, and their behavior effects on others with the written meaning (language), individuals with motor access to visual thinking, including those with ASD, can learn to think about behavior. Thinking about behavior allows learners to initiate and maintain healthy social relationships or become pro-social.

Section II
Practical Tools for Learning Pro-Social Behavior

This section of the book will discuss the purpose and rationale for a variety of methods to increase pro-social behavior while preventing unwanted behavior. Prevention measures include increasing the child's ability to successfully think in society (agency) (*Chapter Six*), to have the knowledge or power to make choices (*Chapter Seven*), to be able to use effective language (*Chapter Eight*), and to behave at a pro-socially appropriate developmental age (*Chapter Nine*). Language represents thinking, so methods that increase knowledge about behavior and thinking stem from current and future neuroscience (*Chapter Ten*). Methods to interpret the meaning of behavior use the language of emotion (*Chapter Eleven*), but emotions are not the same as feelings. Understanding how language, thinking, and feelings interconnect helps prevent anti-social behavior such as bullying (*Chapter Twelve*). Finally, how to create a pro-social model of prevention and intervention will be summarized (*Chapter Thirteen*). This section of the book will also highlight case studies that show the principles of prevention for better pro-social development.

In *Chapter Six*, the reader will learn how important the development of the concept of agency is for improving social development. As pro-social development increases, so does appropriate behavior. This chapter will also provide suggestions for how to increase the development of agency. Being an agent means that the learner is empowered. *Chapter Seven* provides the reader with a better understanding of the difference between power and control; that is, power increases pro-social development whereas controlling another person's behavior tends to create anti-social development. Suggestions for how to increase pro-social development will be provided.

Many programs attempt to deal with behavior after it occurs. The emphasis in this book continues to be on how to prevent unwanted behavior by increasing appropriate pro-social development. Probably, the most effective way to prevent unwanted behavior is to provide the learner with pro-socially appropriate ways to communicate. Such communication requires adequate language. In *Chapter Eight*, the reader will be introduced to ways to set up events that provide improved language development, therefore increasing thinking and learning for pro-social development. In order to provide appropriate materials for language development, the child's social, cognitive, and language developmental levels must be considered. *Chapter Nine* provides the reader with the opportunity to adjust the developmental level of materials, language, and behavior intervention methods to better meet the learner's developmental needs. The rationale for using the learner's way of thinking as a basis for how to prevent unwanted behavior through increased language comes from understanding neuroscience about the brain. So *Chapter Ten* will provide some pertinent information about neuroscience – a translation of neuroscience into learning to behave.

Often, adults want to understand the motivation behind certain behavior; so, adults will interpret behavior based on the adults' emotional states if they were to behave in a particular way. But emotions are adult-based. Adults possess a lot of meaning and therefore a lot of language about their feelings. Children learn through their senses about feelings (not emotions). Emotions are language-based. With sufficient meaning added by adults, children learn the language labels that represent those feelings over many years of assigned meaning. Language labels for feelings are called "emotions" by adults. *Chapter Eleven* provides the reader with an understanding of feelings versus emotions along with information about intervention and prevention of behavior.

Even though pro-social development is the goal for all children, not all assigned meaning is pro-social in nature. For example, bullying is anti-social in nature, which means that the bully and/or the victim are engaged in an anti-social form of communication. *Chapter Twelve* will suggests several methods for preventing bullying, for assigning meaning to bullying, and for intervening. The last chapter is designed to help explain how all of the content in this book is aimed at going beyond controlling behavior to increasing thinking through language methods that connect pro-social behavior to thinking. The goal is to provide the reader with strategies to initiate and maintain healthy relationships so as to develop pro-social development for all learners. Learning to be socially competent is the ability to initiate and maintain positive (pro-social) healthy relationships.

Important Concepts in *Chapter Six*

Readers should be able to explain each of these behavior principles upon completion of this chapter:

1. Learning "to behave" is learning to be pro-social.

2. Learning to be social requires learning to become an agent.

3. An agent is a person who is capable of doing something.

4. Learning to be a competent agent occurs in a series of conceptual stages.

5. Conceptual stages occur through a scaffold of learning.

6. Social concepts scaffold either into pro-social behavior or anti-social behavior.

7. Pro-social development requires becoming an agent in relationship to thinking about other agents.

CHAPTER SIX
Developing Agency

I do it!
I see it!
I learn it!
I am who I am!

Learning "to behave" is often thought of as discipline; a way to control a child's or adult's behavior. But behavior represents a person's thinking about the person and about other people. This process of thinking about one's self and about others is social development. To be "social" means to make decisions and choices which positively affect others as well as one's self. This process of learning to be pro-social as a person, or agent, covers a continuum of behavior from behaviors that are not acceptable by society to those behaviors that help promote social competence. Social competence is the ability to initiate and maintain healthy relationships. Learning to be social is a process of becoming a social being. A social being or agent is a person who is empowered to perform pro-social behavior.

This chapter will introduce the reader to the continuum of social development and the relationship between social development and developing the learner as an agent. Adults help learners produce positive or pro-social behavior by assigning meaning through setting limits and by providing the necessary language so that thinkers learn to socially think as agents. Since the acquisition of pro-social development is based on the concept of how to become an agent in relationship to others, the authors will provide suggestions for how to develop the learner as an agent. As a learner becomes more socially competent, or more capable of being a pro-social agent, then the learner is able to see others' perspectives. When a learner's thinking about agency increases, then the learner's behavior changes to show the improved social development.

Continuum of Social Development

Learning to be an agent occurs according to a three-scale model. First there is the linear increase of social development across time. Children with neurotypical learning systems are expected to increase in their ability to think about others as they grow older. In other words, the ability to be an agent in positive, pro-social, relationships with others increases in most neurotypical children across developmental time. Second, social development parallels thinking or cognitive development and language function (Arwood, 2011; Arwood & Young, 2000; Arwood & Kaakinen, 2010). As children become older thinkers, their language increases and so does their pro-social thinking. And, across both time of development and parallel language function (cognition) is a continuum of social development that addresses what is rational behavior. On one end of the continuum about rational behavior, the development positively affects social development and at the other end social behavior is not acceptable to society. *Figure 6.1* shows this three-scale model of social development.

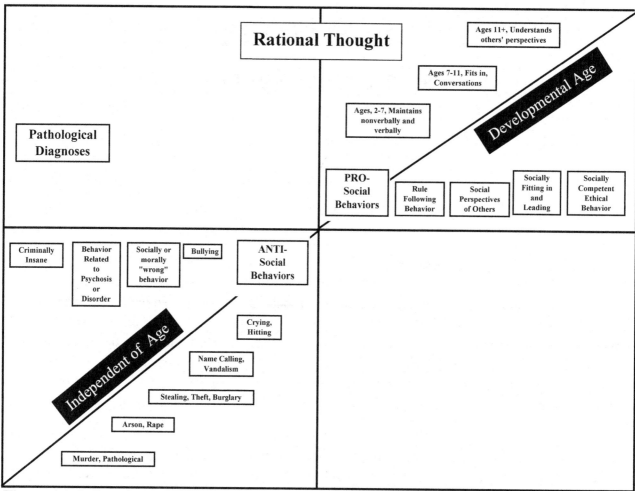

Figure 6.1. *Rational thought.*

Across the mid-page, horizontal line is a continuum related to behavior that leads to social competence, ethical behavior on the right and less social functioning to criminally insane on the left. This continuum represents social behavior that occurs as a person learns to become an agent. If a child or adult is unable to pro-socially develop as an agent, anti-social behaviors increase. This increase of anti-social behavior is independent of age, which means that these anti-social behaviors may occur at any age and do not need to occur at any specific age. To behave in either a pro-social or anti-social way a child's learner's thinking changes based on how the learner is able to process society's input.

Activity: What are the three dimensions of social development for rational thought?

Learning to Be Socially Rational. A newborn child is expected to be able to take in the sensory input of the parent and those around the child. The parent nurtures the baby by responding to the baby's physical needs, and the baby learns to interact with the parent. This interaction is a form of maintenance. The baby does something and then the adult does something. For example, the baby cries and the parent picks her up. The child stops crying. The baby is physically and cognitively learning the social meaning of the parent's actions. The baby is learning to socially maintain with the adult.

By about 18-24 months, the neurotypically developing child is able to say "my toy" and stomp her foot to show that she is an agent; she is letting others know that she is able to do something with her toy. The child is showing that she is becoming an agent who, like her parents, is able to assign meaning to her world. The child is learning to assign meaning in similar ways that the parents assign meaning to her world. The child not only stomps her foot but looks at the parents to signal that she is an agent who acts in relationship to those around her. How the parent assigns meaning to the child's behavior helps develop the child's meaning for her behavior. The child is learning to think about her actions the way others assign meaning to her and her actions. She is learning to be rational. Learning to be socially rational requires not only neurotypical agency but also a learning system that allows the child to receive and perceive others' assigned meanings in the way that society expects. Rational behavior represents thinking that is acceptable by society.

Activity: How does a child learn to be rational?

Children who are severely impacted by ASD and/or related social disorders are not always able to receive the input of the world around them and turn that input into concepts. Agency includes a large group of concepts about how to be social in relationship to others. Therefore, if children are not able to process the input into social concepts such as agency, then these children may show behavior that is not societally acceptable. This unacceptable behavior may begin as unwanted behavior but can become aggressive, even violent over time. The thinking behind this behavior is viewed as not being rational. For example, a 28 year-old-male diagnosed with an ASD, blamed his parents for not making the popcorn so he could not have popcorn, even though he knew how to make popcorn. This is not rational thinking from a societal viewpoint. This same adult would have physical meltdowns that included throwing objects, screaming, hitting, and so forth. Irrational behavior is anti-social and will increase in severity over time if intervention does not attempt to change the thinking to more pro-social ideas. By helping these individuals to develop the concepts of agency, these learners change many infant-like behaviors such as crying, hitting, biting, screaming, and so forth, into more agent-like behaviors such as looking, walking, talking, pointing, eating, and so on.

Methods aimed at increasing agency are designed to create a visual mental picture of how the learner is to think and behave based on language about one's self and others.

Methods for helping these individuals become agents include the following:

- Draw and name the child in his/her picture.

- Put the child through his day using drawn stick figure pictures that show the child who he is through what he does.

- Use hand-over-hand writing, pointing, and drawing so the child is able to create a mental movement of the shapes of words, objects, and people within context.

- Physically stay "velcroed" to the child so that the child cannot do unwanted behavior, with all behavior being desired behavior, the child is still being an agent.

- Put the child into activities of daily living such as eating as an agent, hand-over-hand making the child's food, pointing to what the child is to eating, cartooning the actions of the child with the event, and so forth.

- Put writing with pictures to show what the adults say, what the patterns of ideas look like that go with the concepts of the pictures. WRITE even when the child does not know letters or sounds. Written ideas provide visual-motor patterns. These patterns help develop thoughts just like using speech with a baby before a baby is able to talk. Visual patterns will provide visual ideas.

Figures 6.2a -6.2e show Haylee, a 14-year-old female, who is severely impacted by an ASD. Through the visual motor patterns of drawing and writing, Haylee is learning to see what she looks like as an agent, what she acts like, and what others expect of her. Haylee learned to think as an agent through the methods listed above.

Notice that everything she does is cartooned and written about. Intervention requires teaching Haylee how to be an agent in a visual-motor way of thinking. Haylee lives in an auditory world (typical U.S. society) but she thinks visually (Arwood & Kaulitz, 2007). The cartoons put Haylee into her picture and the writing helps her see what others say Haylee sees the actions in real time. The drawings are concepts, and the writing is a set of visual-motor patterns. When the concepts and visual-motor patterns are put together in context of an event, then Haylee is provided the language of how to become an agent. Language-based behavior is semantic or meaningful and will become part of long-term or semantic memory. Haylee will be able to act the way she is conceptually learning.

Figure 6.2.a. *Haylee prepares to make her lunch*

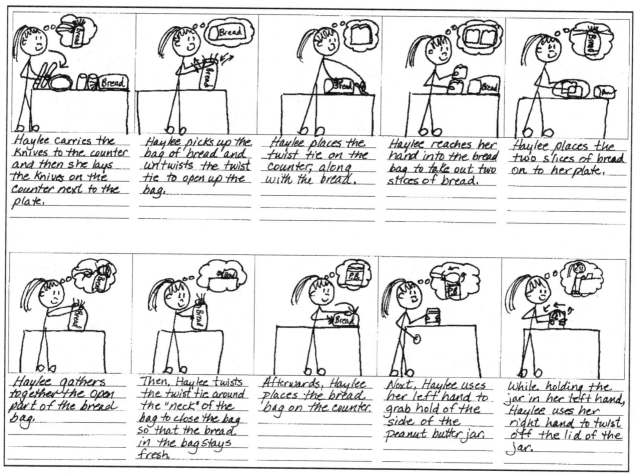

Figure 6.2b. *Haylee makes a sandwich.*

Figure 6.2c. *Haylee continues to make a sandwich.*

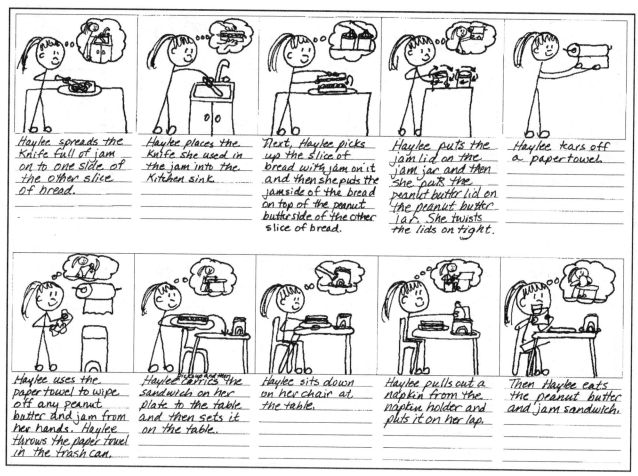

Figure 6.2d. *Haylee eats her sandwich.*

Figure 6.2e. Haylee cleans up after eating.

Notice that in *Figures 6.2a-6.2e*, there is simple agent-action-object overlap. Haylee needs to be able to learn the simplest of concepts about who she is and what she does. She thinks much like a young 12 to18 month-old child learning to become a person who is successful, also known as learning to be an agent. Too much background in the picture, such as adding other objects like cabinets or drawers actually, takes away from what Haylee is able to see and do. On the other hand, failure to provide Haylee with her whole body acting as an agent across an event (cartoon) would not give her enough information.

Activity: At what level is Haylee learning to be an agent?

At the beginning of intervention, Haylee acted like an instrument hitting, kicking – objectifying others – in her environment. As the drawings increased in multiple events across Haylee's day, the more she began to see how she was to act or behave. Because Haylee needed visual-motor patterns to learn to be an agent, a lot of hand-over-hand input was provided. The more events in Haylee's environment that were hand-over-hand signed, written, and drawn to afford Haylee the visuals she needed to make choices by pointing and by acting as an agent, the more social she became. For 11 years, attempts to teach her "to behave" through systems of reinforcement, rewards/punishments with objects and simplified pictures had been unsuccessful. But Haylee began to become an agent in only six weeks when the adults working with her assigned pro-social meaning to her through helping her be an agent.

Prior to this social and cognitive language-based intervention, Haylee's behavior was out of control and she had been recommended for an institution. Because of her growing size, intervention sometimes meant that two or three people were holding her hands, talking to her, drawing and writing for her at the same time. Haylee learned to become an agent when the educators created an environment where she could act like an agent, through hand-over-hand signing, pointing to pictures, making choices by pointing or choosing objects such as picking up her bowl to fill for her breakfast or responding to her pointing to what she wanted in her bowl. Once Haylee was treated like an agent, she became an agent! She learned through visual-motor patterns how to be an agent. In this way, Haylee is learning the concepts of agency; "who" she is and how to relate to others.

Activity: What are some ways to help develop agency for children who think with visual conceptualization like those with ASD?

Being an Agent in a Picture. Haylee learned to be an agent through seeing herself in pictures while completing tasks in a hand-over-hand (HoH) manner. In a HoH situation, other people or agents assign meaning by putting their hands on Haylee's hands to do the tasks. The pictures along with the HoH activities are then written and drawn. As a person able to perform expected tasks, she was an agent. But, the concepts of agency have conceptual levels; and, the conceptual level of agency for Haylee was as an agent within the world. The world still came to her and revolved around her needs. This level of agency is preoperational or egocentric in nature. But, she no longer functioned at a sensory level of hitting, biting, kicking, throwing, etc.

The next level of agency would allow Haylee to become an agent in relationship to others. At that point, she would be able to follow group rules. To follow group rules, she had to be able to see herself in relationship to others, because others set the rules. And, rules require that a person has the language to name the relationship between the person following the rule and others who may also follow or not follow the rule. Rules require that agency, or thinking about one's self, is at a concrete level. Concrete thinking means that the learner is able to see how the learner fits within a group according to the rules. Ideally, Haylee, like most citizens will someday fit into society and be able to follow society's rules.

Another case, Sean, a 6-year-old male diagnosed with autism also needs to learn about becoming an agent. Sean functioned at a higher level of agency than Haylee. Sean could point, sometimes echoing what he heard others say and he did not act as an instrument, hurting others like Haylee. But, Sean frequently cried and cried rather than perform educational tasks. His parents found it difficult to take Sean places because he might not fit into the expectations or rules of others. *Figure 6.3* shows a cartoon of Sean learning to be in the picture with one of the authors, Mabel Brown.

Figure 6.3. Sean learns to be in the picture with another person.

Sean is an agent who needs to learn how he fits in with others. This means that Sean must see himself as an agent interacting with others in the same activity. Once Sean could see his environment (home, school, and therapy) drawn out showing him as an agent in the same picture with other agents, then Sean would be able to act appropriately anywhere his parents would take him – to a baseball game, church, and so on.

Furthermore, when Brown worked with Sean at his level of understanding and with the visual-motor patterns of drawing and writing, his body posture was natural. Natural body posture indicates that the central nervous system (spinal cord and brain) is able to process the sensory input into meaningful overlapping patterns called concepts. Brown provided many layers of visual-motor patterns that formed mental shapes for Sean. Sean was able to use these shapes as concepts or ideas. In response to what he wrote with the movement of Brown's hand on his hand (HoH), Sean began to say what was written with the pictures so that his oral language began to develop. By developing oral language, Sean could use his oral language as a way to more efficiently communicate his needs. Behavior problems were eliminated. Sean was learning to relate to others and to fit in, typical of a 7 to 11-year-old. As long as the adults in Sean's environment provided him with visual-motor patterns of learning to think, Sean's behavior continued to show improvement. However he changed schools and could no longer work with Brown.

His new school placement believed that because Sean could speak, that he could use sound to think. So, they used oral language along with using token rewards to attempt to control Sean's behavior. Within two years, Sean's behavior had become aggressive to the point of being out of control. The educators at his placement did not meet Sean at his level of thinking and they did not provide the meaning of his environment through shapes to assign visual-motor meaning. Without meaning being presented in the way that Sean could learn, the environment was no longer meaningful to Sean. His behavior showed that he could no longer share the expectations of others. Remember that all behavior communicates and his new out-of-control behavior was communicating that his environment was not meaningful; whereas, the natural shared pro-social interaction with the adult, Mabel, showed that she was providing input in the way Sean learns to think.

It should be noted that when Sean is physically redirected at school without adequate visual language, he often has a crying meltdown. The physical redirection is moving him as an object. Instead of the adults at school trying to follow Sean's lead for how Sean learns to think, the adults are insisting that Sean learn the way they want to teach. Since the adults' teaching methods are not meaningful to Sean, Sean responds to the sensory input by crying, pushing, kicking, and biting. The adults in Sean's school do not allow Sean to be an agent, a person who is heard and therefore who is given what he needs to learn. Instead, they try to control his behavior through physically redirecting him like he is an object; and, they insist on using the sound of their voices even though this input does not form concepts for Sean. Sean, like most people, does not do well when he is treated like an object, something that is acted on. But when respected and treated as a person who is heard and whose needs are met, he begins to learn to be an agent and develop pro-socially. To be treated as an agent, he must be able to successfully act on his environment: read, write, talk, draw, sign, point, show others what he wants, and so forth. It should be noted that Sean needs a lot of layered movements to be able to think and behave in a way that shows he is an agent. His environment continues to struggle with providing enough of these shapes of movement to form concepts so he is able to act in pro-social ways.

Activity: What does it mean to be an agent and to fit into others' pictures?

Being an Agent Who Takes Others' Perspectives. Educators and parents often think of social development as learning to take others' perspectives, but that is only part of the pro-social continuum. Haylee needed to become an agent (sensori-motor thinking to preoperational thinking). Sean was learning how to relate to others as an agent so as to see himself as an agent in relationship to others in the classroom, his family, and so on (preoperational thinking to concrete thinking). Once Sean learned to be a part of others' pictures, he was ready to learn to see ideas from others' perspectives. Learning about rules means that Sean is also learning to think about what others are thinking.

Figure 6.4. *Sean learns to think about others' thinking.*

In *Figure 6.4*, Sean is sitting with his mom watching his sister dance on stage. Sean is hungry and he is thinking about eating. He wants to leave, so he begins to get up. But his mom gestures for him to sit. Sean begins to say he is hungry and is going to starve if he cannot leave now. Mom pulls out a piece of paper and draws thought bubbles and writes words for him so that he can see what is expected. Sean is now in the picture thinking about (a) what his sister is thinking about, (b) what his mother is thinking about, and (c) what his behavior must be to stay and watch his sister. Sean is learning to think in the way that others expect. As a result, his behavior changes and he sits down, looks at the page and matches the pictures his mother drew with what he is seeing. He is watching and waiting for the dancers to finish so that he and his mother can find his sister to help her with the costumes. After he helps his sister with her costumes, they will go to the car and ride home and he will be able to eat.

Activity: How is Sean learning to think about his actions in relationship to others'
actions?

Learning to think about his actions allows Sean to learn about being an agent in relationship to other agents and their actions. These actions or behaviors can be seen when drawn in cartoons. Understanding how Sean's actions or behavior affects others and how others' behaviors affect Sean helps him learn how to fit into what others expect. Learning to think about others is a prerequisite to learning to think from others' perspectives. Such thinking requires a lot of conceptualization as well as language. But, Sean must continue to use his way of learning to think. He learns with visual-motor patterns to form shapes of concepts. If his environment does not continue to provide this type of input, then Sean does not continue to learn to think. And, if Sean does not continue to be pro-social, then his social development will become anti-social, aggressive and possibly even violent.

Sean thinks in a visual-motor way. He uses the shapes created from movements to form overlapping patterns as visual mental concepts. In the dominant culture, many concepts about behavior are presented in words that cannot be seen, touched, or felt. Words are sound based. So, for Sean to understand the relationships between and among others, he must also learn the visual mental concepts of what others mean by words that he cannot see such as "considerate," "respectful," "generous," and "kind." These concepts require that Sean learn to be an agent in relationship to others' thoughts and behaviors that others think about. These thoughts require a lot of visual language about him in relationship to others, how he fits in with others. He needs to know what the thoughts and behavior look like to be considerate, respectful, generous, and kind to others. Once Sean is able to think at this level, he can become socially competent. Social competence is the ability to initiate and maintain healthy relationships, the greatest positive pro-social level of development (see *Figure 6.1*).

Activity: How much language does learning to think from others' perspectives requires?

As shown with the examples of Haylee and Sean, learning to be an agent is part of pro-social development. This pro-social part of the continuum in *Figure 6.1* represents the increasingly more complex process of learning to conceptualize as an agent. Pro-social development is a hierarchy that unfolds because others assign pro-social meaning. In other words, others initiate and maintain a healthy social relationship with the learner who, in turn, learns to be an agent using pro-social behavior. The learner must be able to process the adults' assigned meaning in order to develop pro-socially. In the cases of Haylee and Sean, this meaning has to be put in a visual-motor way so that they are able to learn to conceptualize themselves in relationship to others for learning to be an agent.

Activity: Why does taking others' perspectives represent a formal level of thinking?

Learning to Be Anti-Social. When a person learns to be an agent, the agent's thinking increases in complexity. Ultimately, the pro-social development unfolds, resulting in more complex thinking about others' expectations and their perspectives. The learner is able to fit in and, ultimately, initiate and maintain healthy relationships with others. The learner fits into pro-social development and is a rationale thinker. This increase in social agency occurs as a scaffold of the child trying a behavior and the adults assigning meaning that in turn changes the child's thinking. This back-and-forth thinking and doing occurs over time.

The same scaffolded learning that yields pro-social development can occur on the anti-social development or left side of the continuum in *Figure 6.1*. Unfortunately, the learner acquires more complex anti-social behavior the same way as a learner acquires pro-social development. The anti-social development is not attached to age, since society does not expect anti-social development.

However, the learning process works the same way. For example, when Haylee was in pre-school, she did not respond to the words of others and, therefore, did not learn to behave through the sound of voices like neurotypical children.

Adults began to try to teach Haylee to behave. First, by doing a functional behavior assessment (FBA), the educators examined Haylee's behaviors, her antecedent behaviors, and the consequences to her behavior. From this analysis, they targeted behaviors they wanted from Haylee and then began to teach her to behave. Adults used primary reinforcement consisting of pureed food paired with gestural signs (restricted forms of American Sign Language) and pictures of objects to try to *control*[11] her behavior, to reinforce simple behavior such as sitting so as to increase the likelihood of Haylee performing desired behaviors of compliance. Haylee would sit down in response to the pairing of the sign with a reward. At 14 years of age, she still tried to sign "eat" every time she sat down, no matter what she was going to do.

Why didn't she go beyond this early schedule of reinforcement? She did not learn to use signs or the pictures for choices and she did not learn to sit and do an expected task even though she had years of behavioral training or practice at performing specific behaviors in response to cues or reinforcers that acted as stimuli for the next response. In fact, over time, Haylee became more aggressive and her behavior became more anti-social. Instead of learning to behave as an agent, Haylee learned to be more anti-social. This was the result of her inability to understand her world with the sounds and sights given to her. The more aggressive she became, the more the adults tried to control her. By trying to control Haylee's behavior instead of assigning meaning to her behavior, the adults acted on Haylee as an object. Haylee was not an agent but an object.

Anti-social behavior is about controlling what others do. So, Haylee was learning how to act on others just like she was being acted on. Haylee learned to objectify others just as the adults objectified her. Haylee learned to be an instrument and use others as objects. By being an instrument that objectified others, she had not learned to be an agent. She could fill her space, hitting, kicking and biting. She was controlling her space. Emphasis on intervention for Haylee had been on controlling behavior, not on helping her learn to think at a higher level. She was learning to be anti-social.

Activity: How is learning to be anti-social a result of others treating a child in anti-social ways?

To be social, Haylee needed to become an agent, to see herself doing tasks and, eventually, to see herself in others pictures of what others expected. Becoming an agent means that Haylee and other children must learn to think as an agent. Instead of being "controlled," an agent learns how to think and use thinking to be an agent in relationship to others. Learning to be an agent necessitates that the adults in the learners' environments must also provide opportunities for learners to make choices based on thinking.

Learning to think increases the meaningful relationships (semantic relationships) among people or agents and actions. Language names or assigns meaning to thinking. Haylee did not learn language

[11] See *Chapter Seven* about the difference between power and control.

because she was not given a full grammar of language through the visual-motor way she learned concepts. Adults continued to talk to her with "mands" or simplified sound-based language patterns such as "sit," "stand," "walk," and so forth. Adults also continued to physically try to redirect Haylee to do tasks, pointing to the tasks, talking to her about the tasks, and modeling the tasks while talking (sound-based). In response, Haylee pushed the materials, fell through space (as if she were running away), hit, kicked, threw objects, pounded with her fist on the wall, and so forth. These sound words as commands did not provide Haylee with the type of thinking patterns she needed to be able to learn to be an agent or to name the activities with language. Because Haylee could not talk, read, write, or use any form of language to express her needs, she could not act as a pro-social agent. When adults modeled behaviors, the modeling did not work for Haylee since she did not have the language to process the modeled task; and, she did not have an auditory learning system to understand the words of what she saw the adults say and do. The only activity of daily living that Haylee had learned over the previous years of intervention was pro-socially eating. When the food appeared, she became an agent, eating the food. Therefore, her own eating actions created the opportunity for her to be an agent. In no other activity was she the agent.

Activity: Eating for Haylee allowed her to be an agent. Why was eating the only behavior that was appropriate for her at age 14?

Most children learn the social expectations of others by how they are treated. Treating a child as an agent means giving the child the meaning of the world so the child is able to function as a person capable of acting on his own world. Meaning is only acquired through the way the child is able to neurologically learn concepts. Haylee learned to think with a visual system. Limiting the amount of visual language for Haylee left her without conceptualization of being an agent. Agency is about being able to communicate with, for, and to others.

Haylee like Sean and some of the others described in this book experienced a lot of physical redirection that was not meaningful. Physically redirecting[12] an older child is a form of manipulation that does not develop pro-social behavior. The child in turn learns to push and manipulate others. Physical redirection and verbal manipulation go together. For example, a child with ASD who pushes another child until she falls down often sees the pushing as a result of something the other child did. The child with ASD only sees his hands, not his own face. The child with ASD sees his hands touch the other child, but the other child fell, which seems to be the other child's act, not the result of the behavior of the child with ASD. The child with ASD is not an agent until he is able to see himself in a mental picture or is able to see the shape of how others' behaviors change as a result of seeing how others' behaviors affect one another. This is one of many reasons why explanations about behavior must be visual concepts (drawing) and then written (language patterns) for the child to begin to learn to see behavior and the thinking that goes with the behavior. So, learning to be an agent is critically

---

[12] Physical redirection is used for toddlers. Typically, the adult puts her arms on the child's shoulders and helps the child's body begin the expected task, such as picking up toys. The adult acts as the agent for the child. Physical redirection for older children results in the adult moving the child's body like an object. This objectifies the child. However, when the adult uses an older child's hand in hand-over-hand activities, the hand is an instrument as long as the adult is looking at the hand and acting like an agent in relationship to the child being an agent, doing the activity.

important to pro-social behavior whereas being treated or treating others as objects develops anti-social thinking.

Activity: Why does learning to be pro-social require the ability to see oneself as an agent?

This inability to see oneself as an agent also means that name calling, teasing, tripping, scaring and other bullying tactics are seen as the result of someone else's behavior. For example,

"I tease her because she likes it." Or "I call her names because she is an idiot." This thinking may seem irrational and it is irrational. The left side of the social continuum (see *Figure 6.1*) represents irrational thinking. Irrational thought occurs for all sorts of perceptual and conceptual reasons, but there is always some payoff if the anti-social behavior continues. For example, the more some children are teased, the more they tease. Feeling objectified by the teaser results in fewer feelings of being an agent who is able to make a choice. So the more the child is teased, the more he teases others. The result is a lot of bullying at schools and in the work place. (*Chapter Twelve* expands on the anti-social behavior called bullying.) Similarly, the more rewards (punishers)[13] that educators and parents use to control children's behavior, the more the children identify with the objects. They are the objects of the rewards. They then become aggressive, objectifying others and, ultimately, their behavior can result in forms of violence. Treating children as objects comes from asking children to follow control demands, absent of the thinking an agent does. To become agents, children must be given opportunities to think and act as agents.

Activity: Explain the scaffold of anti-social behavior.

Social Acts: Pro-Social Behavior

As a child becomes an agent, the child's behavior or social acts reflect the child's thinking about social development. Social development requires thinking about one's own behavior as well as the behavior of others (Arwood & Young, 2000; Winner, 2002, 2007). Teaching social skills without attention to the development of the concepts of agency may result in more skills that reflect anti-social behavior than the development of pro-social behavior. Pro-social concepts, not skills, must be acquired to be able to think about how to act.

For example, a child learns how to introduce himself to strangers. He has practiced the skills and can perform them with mastery. He is walking down the school hallway and sees a teacher. He knows this is a teacher because he had the teacher for homeroom the year before. He looks at her and

---

[13] Rewards are objects (time, activity, food, money) that are paired with a targeted behavior. The child is to associate the reward or object with the behavior. The assumption is that the reward will increase desired behavior. But, the emphasis is on what the child does, not who the child is. Because the emphasis is on controlling behavior, not on helping the child learn to think, then rewards are about the child's what's, not the child's who. In this way, rewards may or may not be effective, depending on the child's thinking. Depending on how the child understands the pairing of the rewards with behavior determines if the paired object is a reward or punisher. In this way, all rewards are punishers and all punishers are rewards.

says, "Hello, my name is Arnie and I have new blue pants on." He has developed social skills. He is able to introduce himself. He has language. He is able to talk about his new blue pants. But he already knows the teacher and the teacher knows him, so he does not need to introduce himself. Furthermore, his pants are six months old. The pants are not new. Ultimately, a social introduction would be in the form of a greeting such as "Hello, how are you?"

Arnie has learned social skills, but he lacks pro-social development. The ability to initiate and maintain healthy relationships as an agent requires pro-social development of concepts, not the mastery of skills or imitated patterns. Most parents and educators want children who struggle with pro-social development to become socially competent; but teaching social skills without emphasizing social and cognitive thinking, as is often the case, will not help the child become socially competent. Pro-social development is the acquisition of meaning about being an agent, a person who is able to think about what he or she does. Thinking about being an agent involves conceptual development.

Here are some examples of rules to increase pro-social development:

- Rules must be drawn, written, signed, and perhaps provided using hand-over-hand methods to create a meaningful picture. *Figure 6.5* shows how a rule is drawn for a youth to learn what it means to be on time.

Figure 6.5. *Learning the rule about being on time.*

- *More language is better!* But the language must be presented in a pictorial form. In other words, simple demands such as "sit," or "Don't run" or "Put down your skirt" does not create any mental pictures. But, when language is given in a way that relates all the thinking of "who, what, where, when, why, and how "into a verbal pictured form, then the child can "mentally see" what the words mean and what is expected. For example, "Marsha, when you are in the classroom and you pick up the sides of your dress with your hands and raise your hands over your head, the dress goes over your head. You cannot see others when your dress is over your head, but others in the classroom are still able to see you. The girls and boys and the teacher cannot see your face, but the girls and boys and the teacher can see your underpants. They can also see your body. They do not want to see your underwear or your private body parts. When the boys and girls in the classroom see your underwear, they do not want to walk to lunch and sit with you. They think you might lift your skirt up when they are at lunch. So in order for the boys and girls to not see your underwear, Marsha, you need to keep your hands down. When your hands are down then your dress is down. And the boys, girls, and teacher in the classroom are not able to see your underpants or your body. They will be able to see your face. If the boys and girls and teacher in the classroom are able to see your face, then they can think about you. If they are thinking about you, then they might think you would want to sit with them in the cafeteria for lunch." This language is semantically relational. (More about language is found in *Chapter Eight*.)

- *Always put the child, youth, or adult learner into the picture so he is able to see him or herself as an agent* (for example, see *Figures 6.2a-6.2e*). Even the oral language in the example with Marsha showed how she was told about what she looked like. This is "putting her into her picture."

- *Create choice through "sabotaging" the environment and then help the learner act in socially acceptable ways.* For example, the child is on a field trip and the teacher tells the students that they will have a special treat, ice cream. As soon as they walk into the ice cream store, the teacher walks over to the student with ASD, Gabe, to help him work through the socially appropriate way to order ice cream. As they sit to eat the ice cream, Gabe jumps up to go find a napkin. When he returns to his seat, the teacher has moved Gabe's ice cream out of sight. The teacher then helps Gabe learn to problem solve about the missing ice cream by telling him who to ask and what to say to find his ice cream Such help keeps Gabe feeling like an agent, and when he is able to find his ice cream, he has learned to socially problem solve, part of pro-social development.

- *Create opportunities for learners to be agents.* In addition to choices, learning to do activities such as making beds hand-over-hand, putting on clothes with a visual chart of how to do the task, learning how to wash the dishes, play a musical instrument, make a choice on a board, and so on, are all ways to act like an agent in order to develop the concept of agency.

Pro-social behavior is the result of learning the concepts that correspond to being an agent. A child learns to behave because she learns to think. The child will behave in the way the child is thinking. If the child hits and kicks, then the child is thinking as a sensori-motor child (0-2 years of age) no matter how old she is. The child kicks and hits in response to sensory input that the person does not understand. To learn socially how to be an agent means to learn the meaning of the input so as to act like an agent.

- *Always write spoken words as complete sentences and always write to drawn pictures.* The movement of the hand while writing forms shapes, not words. The child watches the hand write and the child is learning written shapes. Children do not need letters and sounds to write shapes or to read shapes. Shapes are pictures. So write, write, and write – for all children with ASD, no matter how severely impacted or how high in functioning (Arwood, 2011; Arwood & Kaulitz, 2007; Arwood, Kaulitz, & Brown, 2009). In fact, most children who struggle with social communication disorders benefit from writing in shapes (not letters and sounds).

- *Always tell children and youth what you expect using as many oral pictures or drawn cartoons as possible.* Expectations must be clear and not hidden in words. "Look with your eyes, not your hands" is so much clearer than "don't touch!" Drawing creates the meaning of the concepts while writing creates the visual language patterns that go with the concepts. When the concepts and language are interconnected, then the long term or semantic memory is activated.

- *Follow through with expectations so an assigned meaning always follows the behavior.* The adult says, "Look with your eyes, not your hands." The child puts his hands down, and the parent says, "These pears look so good. I like to look at the pears with my eyes."

Activity: What are some ways to help develop agency in children so that they develop pro-social behavior?

The following case studies provide some pro-social applications of the aforementioned rules.

Case Study – Sheryl

Sheryl is a 9-year-old female enrolled in a general education public second grade. The general education classroom teacher has struggled the entire school year with Sheryl's behavior. Sheryl is diagnosed as having learning disabilities and was recently diagnosed with Asperger Syndrome. Sheryl receives special education and speech-language therapy. The special education teacher finds Sheryl's behavior to be "something you work with" and "funny." The general educator does not find the behavior funny and is "worn out" by having to deal with it. In her words, "Sheryl is difficult at best. She cannot work with the other students. Some of the other students are afraid of her." When asked if Sheryl ever hurt the other students, the teacher said, "No, the threat is all verbal, but the students don't know that."

The administrative personnel at Sheryl's school asked Mabel Brown, one of the authors, to assess Sheryl and make suggestions about how to help her. The assessment was supposed to be for academics and nothing in the paperwork indicated any behavior issues. The school's rationale for omitting the behavior issue was that they wanted to see what Brown would do with the behavior.

Assessment. Sheryl entered the room and sat down. Brown introduced herself and looked at Sheryl's face, treating her as an agent. Brown said they were going to do some talking, reading, writing, and drawing. Sheryl smiled when she was introduced. But, as soon as Brown told her what they would be doing, Sheryl looked forward, assumed a withdrawn posture, and began to use a whining voice to tell Brown that she was tired. Brown ignored the whine and focused on the task using visual oral language. "Sheryl, let's draw out what we will do today." Brown then began to draw a stick cartoon of Sheryl looking at the picture and beginning to work (*Figure 6.6*).

Sheryl puts her bottom on the chair, puts her eyes on the picture and thinks about the people she sees.

Figure 6.6. *Sheryl beginning to work.*

Sheryl continued to talk in a loud, whiny voice about what she could not do. Then she insisted she had to go to the bathroom. (Notice that the drawing is interrupted by Sheryl's request to use the bathroom.) Since Brown had never worked with Sheryl before and did not know when Sheryl had last been to the bathroom, she allowed her to go to the bathroom. Another teacher escorted Sheryl to and from the bathroom. In the process, Sheryl jumped up and began to fall through space (walking on tip toes) as if she were bolting. This behavior, falling through space, told Brown that Sheryl was functioning as an extension of the walls as if she were horizontal to the walls, moving through frame after frame. (More about developmental levels is found in *Chapter Eight*).

When Sheryl returned to the room to work with Brown, she once again began to whine. She was "tired" and did "not want to work." She began to make louder and more oppositional statements such as, "This is horrific. Like a horror movie show." "You hurt me. I am going to stab you." Sheryl even lifted up a pencil as if to stab Brown. Brown calmly reassigned meaning to her behavior. "I see you holding the pencil like a javelin. The pencil is not a javelin. To write with the pencil, you will need to put the pencil point onto the paper." Sheryl began to jump up, but Brown calmly wrapped her legs around the chair so that she had to sit down. Brown did not look at Sheryl or say anything to her about the behavior. Brown continued to draw about what they were doing and calmly talked using "visual picture language" or language that helps create visual images in Sheryl's head. "Sheryl, I see you sitting and looking at the paper. When you look at the paper, you make pictures in your head. When you make the pictures in your head, you can tell me what the pictures are or you can draw the pictures so we can write about the pictures." This type of visual picture language helps Sheryl develop visual ways of thinking about her behavior. The emphasis on what Sheryl can do (rather than the behavior) helps Sheryl function as a pro-social agent.

Sheryl's special education teacher, principal, second-grade teacher, and several others were watching the event unfold through a two-way mirror. The special education teacher became anxious and wanted to rescue Brown and Sheryl. One of the authors told the special educator not to intervene as Brown was handling Sheryl's behavior in a calm, respectful manner while orally, and with drawing, setting limits of what was okay and not okay. But the special educator went ahead and intervened. As soon as she walked into the intervention room, the special educator told Sheryl, "Calm down." But these words create no pictures, and Sheryl's behavior escalated into swinging her body to hit while she yelled with a fake cry. Brown immediately grabbed a piece of paper and began to write to Sheryl what she had to do (the tasks assigned) before she could leave. The principal saw the escalation and went into the room and escorted the special educator out. Brown and Sheryl resumed, and Sheryl produced, under protest, what she had to produce and then returned to her room.

Debriefing Comments. During the follow-up debriefing, the special educator said she never has behavior problems with Sheryl like she saw with Brown, but she also admitted that she wanted to see what Brown could do with Sheryl. The second-grade teacher was relieved to see that she was not the only adult who saw this type of behavior. Every time, this teacher expects Sheryl to do an activity, the type of behavior Sheryl exhibited with Brown would happen. With 24 other students in the classroom, the behavior is difficult to deal with as well as scary for the many of the other students. The second-grade teacher said it was easier to not ask Sheryl to do any of the expected tasks and to let Sheryl do what she chooses from within the class learning centers. Likewise, the special educator had learned to provide Sheryl with only the activities that Sheryl will do. So neither environment is expecting Sheryl to act like an agent in relationship to other agents.

Interpretation. If the adults in Sheryl's environment do not expect Sheryl to perform tasks, Sheryl remains the object of the world around her. In other words, the adults in Sheryl's world do not expect her to be an agent. This means that the adults and other students are the agents who act upon Sheryl, the object. Most of us would think that the relationship would be the other way around – Sheryl's behavior is abusive and she is acting on those in her environment, but that is not true. Sheryl is functioning in response to sensory input, so she responds to the sensory input with behavior that communicates what she does understand. She learns to behave in the way that she is treated. Her behavior, at its best, shows that she is the only person in her mental picture. When she whines and complains and people ignore her by telling her to "calm down," her behavior escalates. On the other hand, when she is given more information about what she can do, along with strategies to be able to do the task, then her behavior is socially acceptable.

In order for Sheryl's behavior to be age-appropriate, she must act like an agent and begin to see how her behavior affects others and vice versa. When the adults in Sheryl's world do not assign more meaning to Sheryl's behavior through visual-motor acts such as writing and drawing, Sheryl continues to grow bigger but her thinking remains at a lower level. The result is that (a) she does not become an agent in others' pictures and (b) she learns how to maintain the ability to keep others out of her pictures. No one else is allowed in her picture; nor does anyone expect Sheryl to learn how to be in his/her picture.

Because Sheryl is in her own picture, the adults and students around her continue to grow, learn, and be empowered as agents to make choices. But Sheryl's environment does not expect her to be an agent, so her growth is restricted to the sensori-motor level of cognition where she whines, cries, hits, stabs, and so on, and/or the preoperational level where she is the only one in her picture, doing what she chooses. The adults' expectations are restricting Sheryl's development socially and cognitively. Learning is a socio-cognitive process. Because Sheryl's thinking is restricted socially, Sheryl's cognitive development is also restricted with her agency development limited.

Finally, during the debriefing after the assessment, Brown asked the adults why they had not mentioned anything about Sheryl's behavior. They replied that they wanted to see what Brown would do with the behavior. These adults were interested in controlling unwanted behavior after the fact. This is definitely an adult agenda since most children want to be successful. To be successful at a task is pro-social. Being controlled by others is anti-social.

Had Brown known about Sheryl's behavior challenges, Brown would have set up the environment for Sheryl to be more successful much more quickly. But because the adults did not say anything about the behavior challenges, Brown expected a student who had some academic deficits, but who would relate more like a 7- to 11-year-old. Thus, Brown immediately looked at Sheryl and began to treat Sheryl as an agent (Brown) talking to Sheryl as an agent to an agent. This developmental level is socially age appropriate (agent to agent) at a concrete level of thinking. Such interaction by Brown placed a lot of pressure on Sheryl. Brown was expecting Sheryl to process what Brown said and did and then to relate to Brown, which made the situation more difficult for Sheryl. Had Brown known Sheryl's developmental level of agency was so low, she would immediately have drawn Sheryl on the paper sitting and looking at the paper, with Brown and Sheryl thinking about what they were to do. See *Figure 6. 7* for an example of what Brown would have drawn.

Figure 6.7. Sheryl thinks about doing.

Brown would have talked about the words written with the pictures so that Sheryl could see herself as part of the picture. In *Figure 6.8,* Sheryl is part of the picture and learns how she relates to Brown so that, as an agent, Sheryl is learning to do her job.

Figure 6.8. *Sheryl learns about her job as an agent.*

In this way, Brown would be helping Sheryl develop the concept of being an agent, a person who could see herself think, write, draw, and so forth. Furthermore, the adults told Sheryl that she was going to see "this nice lady and that they would play games." These words do not match the mental pictures of the situation Sheryl walked into. Brown told her that they would draw, write, read which is not playing games. So Sheryl was "set up" to struggle by being given words that did not match her pictures and by setting Brown up to expect Sheryl to act as an agent in response to Brown's behavior.

Figure 6.9 is a picture of what Brown drew to help Sheryl and Brown finish their task together so that Sheryl could leave acting as a successful agent. In other words, Brown had to be sure that Sheryl completed a task so that Sheryl would leave having acted like a pro-social agent. Ending the assessment with pro-social behavior is critical to developing a positive relationship.

Figure 6.9. *Brown and Sheryl draw and write together, as agents.*

Activity: Why does an agent have to be successful at completing expected tasks?

Recommendations. Based on the assessment, it was recommended that the special educator (a) set limits by drawing the entire day with thought bubbles about what happened, is happening, and is going to happen; (b) write complete ideas with all of the drawings and writings; (c) use writing to explain behavior and help Sheryl learn who she is as an agent; (d) develop agency by providing Sheryl with language strategies so that she is able to read, write, draw, and talk like the other students in the class.

To the general educator, it was recommended that she draw for all students and help Sheryl use her writing to interact with the classmates and the teacher and that all activities that emphasized sound be switched to visual-motor acts. For example, reading aloud, writing with sounding out of words, spelling activities, learning math facts through saying the multiplication tables, and so forth be replaced with cartoons, stories that create visual context, scanning the page silently for visual mental language, drawing out math concepts and then writing about the concepts, and so forth. Sheryl needs to be academic successful to be an agent. She learns with a visual-motor way of thinking accessed through movement that develops mental shapes. So in order for Sheryl to develop more thinking to behave, she needs the language presented by combining writing with drawing (Arwood, 2011; Arwood & Kaulitz, 2007; Arwood, Kaulitz & Brown, 2009).

Activity: Why does intervention to prevent Sheryl's behavior problems depend on helping her learn to be an agent in relationship to other agents' expectations?

Summary

Learning to be an agent is a pro-social, developmental, cognitive process. As cognition increases through the development of language, behavior becomes more socially acceptable. This process of learning to be an agent is dependent on how others assign meaning to one's actions. Learning to be pro-social as an agent is also dependent on how well the environmental input matches the way the learner is able to acquire concepts. That is, the learner acquires the concept of agency over time and is able to process others' assigned meaning as an agent. If others assign meaning that is not processed, the learner does not develop the social development of an agent who will become socially competent. Learning to be pro-social is a hierarchy or scaffold of adding meaning over time through layers of learning to be an agent.

Important Concepts in *Chapter Seven*

Readers should be able to explain each of these behavior principles upon completion of this chapter:

1. Power is the ability to be interdependent.

2. To choose to behave requires language.

3. Not all choices are real.

4. Options are real choices.

5. Learning to problem solve means learning to choose.

6. Control means to impose one's thinking on someone else's behavior.

7. Learning to be empowered requires some conflict in thinking in order to refine thinking.

8. Behavior is always a choice of thinking.

9. Thinking about behavior provides choices.

10. Each choice results in different behaviors.

CHAPTER SEVEN
Empowerment, Not Control

I am capable, let me!
Let me try.
Let me want to be free.
Let me be!

The previous chapter emphasized how developing agency improves pro-social behavior. Agency increases from being in one's own thoughts to thinking about others. When an individual is able to think about others in relationship to others' needs, the individual becomes empowered. *Empowerment* refers to the ability to think as a socially competent person who is capable of being interdependent. *Interdependence* refers to the ability to function independently while recognizing the needs of others and considering others' perspectives.

The ability of children to grow up into individuals who are capable of caring for themselves while also thinking about others' needs and considering others' perspectives is dependent on three areas of development: social development, language development, and cognitive development. This chapter will discuss how development in these domains results in empowerment. (*Chapter Eight* will discuss methods for improving pro-social development or empowerment through the increase of language for various developmental levels.)

Empowerment

Empowerment is the social outcome of a child who grows up able to initiate and maintain healthy relationships (social competence). In order for empowerment to occur, children must have the opportunity to be powerful agents. Powerful agents are able to make choices, be successful with expected tasks, and eventually learn that their behavior affects others, who are also agents. Methods that help develop agency (*Chapter Six*) offer a good start to becoming powerful agents. A powerful agent is able to live alone, take care of self as well as those who are dependent. For example, a person who is her own agent is able to provide for a family psychologically, financially, and emotionally.

Most parents and educators recognize that this type of interdependence does not develop overnight for anyone. But too often, the "work" towards such empowerment does not begin until the transition between youth and adulthood (Winner & Crooke, 2011). Unfortunately, in many cases, this is too late, leading to dependency. These authors suggest that the work towards empowerment should begin in early childhood and never stop. The development of empowerment consists of three basic elements: Making choices, solving problems, and refining thoughts.

Activity: What is empowerment?

Making Choices

The brain is set up to make choices, to recognize the existence or nonexistence of an input. Children do not need to "learn" to make choices, but they do need opportunities to use their brains for choice making. As stated many times in this book, in order for a child to learn, the child must be able to process the input. The sensory input to a child must be such that the child's brain is able to recognize it. For children with ASD, this means that the input must be a visual thinking form that creates the shapes of thought (Arwood, 2011; Arwood & Kaulitz, 2007; Arwood, Kaulitz, & Brown, 2009). For many individuals with ASD as well as other social communication disorders, the most meaningful input is in the form of movement of the mouth and/or hand to create shapes.[14]

Activity: What is the way that information must be given to children with ASD in order for them to acquire the ability to think?

As children learn to think as agents (*Chapter Six*), they are able to "think" about their behaviors, to make choices about their behaviors. For children with ASD, such thinking is not an automatic process. Adults must provide opportunities to think in visual ways that match the children's abilities to process information. For example, with neurotypical development, a parent might say, "John, sit down." John sits down because he is able to recognize that there will be consequences if he does not sit down. This means that John has the language development to think about how he relates to others. John's parent is consistent in her responses. If John does not sit, John's mom helps him sit. After all, he is only two-years-old and does not know all of the rules. Mom continues to talk with John, "Okay, let's finish eating our lunch so we will have time to play on the swings before we go to the store." John is able to hear about the three relationships: sitting down, eating lunch, and then playing on the swings. John eats a couple of bites, and now it is time for the swings. This "talking" exchange works for John. This type of input is typical of a "sound-based" or auditory culture (Arwood, 2011; Arwood & Kaulitz, 2007). However, such talking to "learn how to behave" does not work for children with ASD. Frankly, it does not work for most children in the U.S. culture as most thinkers today think with visual ideas such as mental pictures or graphics (Arwood, 1991; Arwood, 2011).

Activity: How do children typically learn to make choices about behaviors such as "to sit" or "not to sit?"

---

[14] Individuals with ADHD or FAS and syndromes such as Down syndrome also use the movement of shapes for the best meaning.

For children with ASD to learn *choices* such as to sit or not to sit, they must learn what the words look like in mental pictures. And, modeling how to sit for children with ASD does not always allow them to see why they are sitting (Arwood, Kaulitz, &Brown, 2009). Pictures of sitting also do not provide the meaning for why a person is to sit or what happens after the child sits. Understanding the content of a picture is always based on how much language the child has to think about what he sees. Young children or children with ASD must learn the meaning of the visuals in the picture to be able to "see" the meaning of the picture. Most will learn the meaning of the visual content through shapes. Shapes of written print do not change their visual form and, therefore, for many individuals with ASD and related disorders, they are easier to see. See *Figure 7.1* to see an example of shapes of printed ideas.

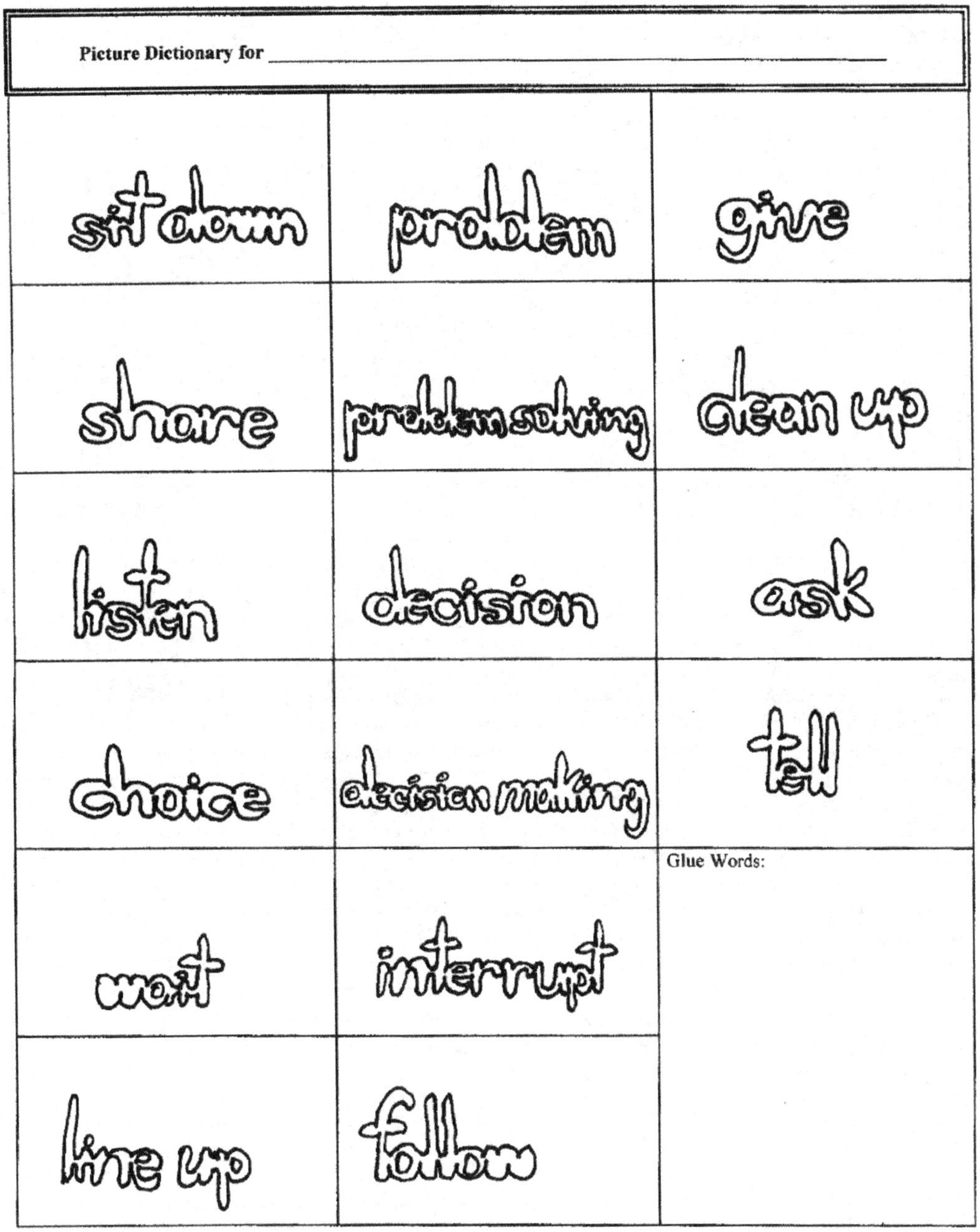

Figure 7.1. Picture dictionary of shapes.

Notice that in this picture dictionary, no meanings are associated with the words. Instead, the printed words are visual-motor patterns of shapes. In order for the shapes to have meaning, there has to be concepts. Drawings are conceptual. *Figure 7.2* shows the meaning attached to the shapes through pictographs.

Figure 7.2. The concepts and the shapes.

These types of words in the picture dictionary require multiple pictures. Pictures are concepts. Concepts provide more knowledge or choices. As the child acquires more pictures, she is able to think about more choices of how to behave. Knowledge is power; power is the ability to make choices based on knowledge. So the more knowledge a child has about what is okay or not okay to do, when to do a behavior, how to do a behavior, what behavior to choose and why, the more power the child has in making choices on the way to empowerment. Increasing the number of mental pictures provides the child with more choices about how to think and to behave. Learning to think provides more choices, more empowerment.

Activity: What is power?

An increase of knowledge or power is an increase in meaning. Conceptual meaning or thoughts provide more information about choices. The ability to make a choice in behavior increases the power a learner has for functioning in society. In other words, a learner with lots of choices or power has more choices for behaving in society. *Figure 7.3* shows a young child learning to make choices in a preschool setting.

Figure 7.3. *Child makes choices of action in a pre-school setting.*

The cartoon provides one scenario for what the child might select to do. The options for other choices are shown as different cartoons in a pull-down type of menu. Each selection provides the child with different behaviors of what the child looks like with each choice (Arwood & Brown, 1999). In this way, the child is learning several things about behavior:

- Behavior is always a choice based on one's thinking.

- Thinking about behavior provides choices.

- Each choice results in different behaviors.

In the case of *Figure 7.3*, the child is given pro-social options, meaning that whatever choice the child makes, her behavior will be acceptable. Options are choices that are real. For example, the child may choose any of the different choices of what to do and still fulfill the educator's expectations of the classroom.

Activity: What are behavior options?

Sometimes adults give children a choice that is not an option. For example, an adult says, "Will you please read the next page?" The adult really means, "Melinda, it is your turn to read. Read the next page." The child does not have the option not to read, but she does not always know the adult's intent. So when the educator asks the question, "Will you please read the next page?" Melinda says, "No. I want to go now." Melinda provides an honest answer. It is only when Melinda has enough language to think from her teacher's perspective will she realize that the educator was being polite and that the question was not really a request but an order. Educators and parents are the adults. They are responsible for giving only real "options." Real options provide the learner with success in being pro-social.

Here are some rules about choices:

- Limit choices to those that are real choices. All choices are acceptable (see *Chapter Three*). So if the adult wants to limit the choices a child can make, provide only real choices. For example, offer a child the choice of wearing pants or shorts only if it is okay to wear either pants or shorts. If it is snowing outside and the child chooses to wear shorts, then the child will either be coerced into wearing pants that punishes the child for making the choice of shorts; or, the child will be cold if he wears shorts. In this way, only draw what the child should do (more about this later in the chapter).

- Provide choices for as many situations as possible. Providing the child with choices gives the child the opportunity to gain more knowledge and, therefore, to gain power. Such power or knowledge may be provided through cartoons that are drawn or spoken orally.

- Provide the thinking that goes with the choices. Remember that choices are thoughts about what the child looks like completing a task. Draw the child and the thoughts that go with the behavior in a horizontal cartoon. Add choices through a pull down menu of other cartoons. This provides the child with the knowledge that there are multiple ways to think about choices.

Activity: What are some rules about providing options?

Making choices is about acquiring knowledge about different ideas or choices of a situation; selecting the choice that works the best considering all possibilities; and, then acting on a choice. To be empowered, children must be able to understand multiple ways to think about an idea in order to have the flexibility (*Chapter Eight*) to problem solve.

Activity: How does providing choices help a child learn to be empowered?

Problem Solving

The simplest problem to solve is one that is a simple choice, e.g.: Juice or milk? From these simple choices, a child's knowledge increases. As a child's knowledge gradually increases, the child develops more and more meaning, in the form of concepts, to be able to make acceptable choices. These concepts are cognitive in nature. Therefore, as the child learns more about the people or agents, their actions, and the objects, the child's ability to think about the world around the child also increases. With the increase of concepts, the child also learns about how to relate to others. Knowledge about the world around the child is cognitive (concepts) in nature; and, how to interact with others in a child's world is social (relationships) in nature. Therefore, learning to think about the choices requires cognitive as well as social development. The cognitive portion is about the conditions or concepts of the situation whereas the social concepts are how to consider others in making a choice. In this way, the child is learning to be a thinking person who makes social choices as part of problem solving. Problem solving involves the use of thinking to make a choice and/or decision.

Activity: How does thinking affect problem solving?

Learning is a process (defined in *Chapter Ten*) of acquiring meaning through the neurobiological system. Learning is not teaching. A child cannot be taught to problem solve or to think flexibly. *A child can learn to problem solve and think flexibly to make acceptable behavioral choices if given the appropriate opportunities to acquire the concepts for making choices.* Such opportunities are provided through situations that involve offering a learner with knowledge about what others (agents) think (actions) and about the rules of their world. Such situational learning is contextual. Contexts are relational in that they show a learner how to think about others in the same space. *Figure 7.4* shows a child what he might think about what to do when another student asks for his book.

Figure 7.4. Thinking about choices to solve a problem about a book.

By providing the child with the choices of what he could do in a specific situation, the child is learning about the relationship between his actions or behavior and the actions or behavior of others in his space. Moving from one set of picture options to another set of picture options shows the child the relationship between his behavior and the behavior of others around him. These various choices also allow the child to see how his behavior is a choice. The child is learning how his behavior relates to others or affects others. Making choices lead to problem solving.

When a child learns to think about others and what others do, the child moves from making simple choices to beginning to problem solve. Problem solving means that the answers are not obvious but that the child must think through different options of real choices of what he could do.

Activity: How does making a choice lead to problem solving?

The following case study demonstrates an application of how choices lead to problem solving.

Argus. Argus is a 10-year-old child with ASD. He has developed a lot of language structures. He is able to read silently, and he appears to enjoy telling anyone who will listen about what he reads, whether or not others want to hear Argus' thoughts. Sometimes Argus talks and no one listens. Sometimes he tells about the print in a recent book in a monotone voice, suggesting that the print meant very little to him. Unfortunately, most adults like the continuous spewing of words whereas peers do not see a lot of meaning or relational thought when students like Argus continue to talk. Socially, the peers are correct. Argus' ability to spew words covers up the other thinkers, taking the other students' mental pictures away. Talking when others are not involved is preoperational (3-7 year old behavior) and is not high enough to share life with someone else. In other words, Argus is in his own picture but others are not in his picture.

When a person like Argus fills space with a behavior such as non-stop talking, talking about his own ideas, drumming with pencils on a desk, making raspberry sounds, and so forth, the other people in the same space are not considered. Argus does not know he has a problem because he does not see others' thoughts, needs, or desires. Argus is an extension of the world around him. At best, he is an agent doing his own thing. He is not functioning as an agent in relationship to others who are also agents. A child like Argus is able to produce a lot of products but is not able to function well enough to problem solve. He can make choices, but the choices are simple choices without solving a problem. To be able to problem solve, Argus must learn about others in his world and be able to understand their perspectives.

Activity: What is problem solving? How much knowledge must a thinker have to be able to solve problems?

Martin. Martin is 10 years old. He is also diagnosed with ASD. He wants to learn to solve some simple problems. He wants to know how to ask another student to come for a sleepover. He knows that other students do "sleepovers." He knows that he likes to do things that others do. So he wants to invite another to sleepover even though he has never been invited to a sleepover.

Martin has a problem. It is not a procedural problem; it is a social problem. If Martin's problem were a procedural issue, the adults could give him the rules about inviting a student for a sleepover and Martin could then solve his problem by doing what the adults suggest. But Martin does not really have friends. Martin does not know what a friend is. Therefore, even with the rules for how to invite others to a sleepover, Martin does not know who to invite. Besides it is not appropriate to invite someone who is not a friend.

The concept of friendship, like agency and any other social concept, is learned across time, over many opportunities to layer more and more meaning. The concept of friend layers onto a person becoming an agent in relationship to others. "Others" have different roles and functions. Friends are one type of other agents. The first attempts to understand who a friend is and who is not begins to be apparent around six years of age. The child has learned to play with others in a group and to talk about others. A six-year-old has also learned that others affect what the learner does, so most six-year-olds have "fickle friendship" knowledge (Arwood & Young, 2000). Fickle friendship looks like this: If a classmate plays with her, the six-year-old thinks that the classmate is a friend. If the same classmate chooses not to play with the child the next day, the child thinks he is no longer a friend. Friendship for six-year-olds is defined as those who do things with them. This thinking about the meaning of friends comes from the assigned meaning of adults. Adults continue to assign meaning to help children learn more sophisticated meanings of concepts such as friend. Martin needs more conceptual development about ideas like "friends." Also, Martin needs to learn to think about choices and how choices affect others; how others think when Martin makes a choice, and how his behavior affects others' thinking. Caroletta depicts how friendship and the thinking of friendship develop across time and experiences.

Caroletta. Caroletta, at age six, is showing some disappointment in how Megan acts as a friend. So the adult assigns more meaning, "Megan wants to play with a jump rope, not swing. She is still your friend; she just has something else she wants to do today." By the time Caroletta is seven or eight, she realizes that others make choices to do what they want to do but that they are still friends. By eight or nine years of age, Caroletta knows that friends also have interests, desires, and wants that are separate from her own interests, desires, and wants. Friends have common interests, but friends also have different interests. Caroletta is also beginning to fit in with others who have common interests or desires.

Activity: What is a six-year-old's friendship based on?

By seven or eight years of age, Caroletta is beginning to realize that she is separate from others and that others also are agents. She is also developing some friendships with Megan, Rachel, and Sydney. By the time she is 10 years old, Caroletta wants to spend time at home with her school friends. Caroletta wants to invite Megan, Rachel, and Sydney to come spend the night so they can play games, talk, eat snacks together, and go to sleep (maybe!). At school, the girls talk about the fun they had at their sleepover. Martin thinks he would like to have fun, too. He does not realize all of the layers of developing friendships developing that went into Caroletta's sleepover.

The concept of a sleepover emerges from other concepts: Friends who have something specific they want to do together out of school, an idea that what they do together is fun, and the desire to spend time with others refined and built over many experiences over time. Many times children and youth with ASD express a desire to have a sleepover, have a friend, have a job, go to college, have a girlfriend, have a date, and so forth; as if these social relationships were objects that can be possessed. They express the desire to have these "things" without understanding the meaning of the social reasons for engaging in these activities that involve others: jobs, college, dating, and so on. Pro-social development does not occur from learning or memorizing rules (*Chapter Ten*) or from possessing "social activities." It requires learning about how to be social in relationship to what others think and do. Developing social relationships with others is part of the cognitive development necessary to be empowered to function with others in activities that involve others. Learning to think about others and how choices affect others is part of the pro-social development.

Activity: How are social relationships learned?

To solve social problems such as having a friend to invite to a sleepover requires learning the knowledge about being an agent, about being an agent in relationship to others, about understanding what others think, and about how to make choices in relationship to others' needs. Like all concepts, these social concepts must be acquired over time, in a scaffold of layers of knowledge overlapped with multiple experiences to make appropriate choices. These concepts are learned as part of the development of agency and continue to expand into an understanding of the other agents, resulting in problem solving about social relationship problems as an extension of learning to think and making choices about oneself and others.

The following case study is an example of how a child grows up without the thinking to use language to solve social problems. Thinking and language levels may be arrested at any chronological age. The methods used to help this adult become empowered are the same methods used with younger children, just adapted for the age and situation.

Case Study. Howard is 27 years old. Howard was first seen as a 15-year-old who had just been diagnosed with an ASD. He had been viewed as cognitively impaired up to his teen years when the school realized that Howard displayed "moments of smartness." For example, he could drive the family farm equipment, but he could not follow simple requests at school. He displayed no aggressive behavior. His adaptive behavior was quite good. He dressed himself, handled his own hygiene needs, and often imitated what he saw others do, only if it was socially acceptable. This meant that even though his language was limited, his thinking was making choices between right and wrong. Over eight years (15-22), he developed a lot of language from going to a private clinic, and he began to hold jobs as well as relate to members of his family as well as others. Once he began to hold jobs, he could no longer make the several-hour treks to receive help with his language and thinking, so his family stopped bringing him to the private clinic where he had worked to develop the language.

The family recognized that Howard wanted the same type of relationship he saw his parents have. Howard began to seek out women who would provide him with that relationship. Unfortunately, he did not have enough knowledge about other people and relationships to recognize what a healthy social relationship consisted of. His parents had a healthy long time marriage and he wanted a relationship that looked like their marriage. But, he did not have the language for what he saw in that relationship because he did not have the concepts about healthy relationships. For example, he would say he wanted to get married and would find a woman who wanted to get married. He did not realize that the reason why his parents were married was that they had a relationship that was based on values and beliefs. Howard acted as if finding a woman was like buying an object. His first "girlfriend" type of relationship was based on money. The girl wanted him to give her his salary. He did. When the salary was not enough, then he would ask for money from his parents.

Howard tried to make this relationship with the same woman work several times. He knew the girl was seeing other men and so he tried to buy or possess the girl. After several problems with trying to "possess[15]" this social relationship, Howard began to look for another woman he could marry. Soon Howard was engaged with another woman in, yet, "another" unhealthy relationship that continued over a two-year period. The parents realized that Howard did not understand what relationships were about and felt that Howard needed help. But, Howard would not follow his parents' suggestions about the

---

[15] To possess a relationship means that Howard tried to own the person; controlling her work, her friends, her time, her thinking and so forth.

relationship. He had knowledge about what his parents looked like in their relationship. He had learned enough language to be able to socialize on a superficial level, but he did not have enough knowledge about social relationships to understand the meaning of others who would take advantage of him. The parents asked Howard if he would go for more language help.

The purpose of the language help was for Howard to learn the concepts that would underlie words like "marriage" or "healthy relationship." Howard agreed. The following information about this relationship was provided by Howard and his mother in an attempt to find out which concepts Howard knew at a concrete level of understanding (shared and rule-based) and which ones he did not understand at that level:

- This second, two-year relationship with Veronica began when Howard started a job through vocational rehabilitation. Howard spent a lot of his SSI (Supplemental Security Income) money on Veronica, buying her what she told him to buy – about $500 in just one month. As a result, he did not have the money he needed to pay his bills.

- Veronica was not always truthful. Her values were not always healthy for maintaining a relationship with Howard. For example, Veronica slept with someone else. Howard was "okay" with Veronica's choice, but his parents were not. According to what the mother reported, others had told her that Veronica had sex with a guy friend of Veronica's girlfriend. So others besides Howard were affected by Veronica's choices. According to his parents, it seemed like this relationship with someone else was designed to hurt Howard. The girlfriend invited the guy friend over, then the girlfriend left, leaving the guy friend alone with Veronica in the girlfriend's bedroom. When pressed to admit the truth later, Veronica accused the guy friend of having "raped" her, but she didn't press charges or tell the police.

- Afterwards Veronica told everyone at work that she was pregnant. She told Howard she wanted a baby with him. Veronica did try to have sex with Howard, but he did not comply. Howard was very explicit about what he and Veronica did and did not do. (It should be noted that Howard does not have enough language to match the complicated pictures of being able to "lie" or to understand others' lies.)

- Veronica told everyone at work that she and Howard were getting married, but he hadn't asked her. In their small town, it was common knowledge that Veronica was shopping for a wedding dress.

- Howard was demoted at work, because Veronica kept following him around the worksite and waving to him, and if he didn't see her and wave back, she chewed him out. Before this he was given the better job of driving a forklift, but when he was spending more time looking for Veronica than monitoring his safety driving on site, he lost the job.

- Veronica told Howard that she would not go out with him any more if he did not get a tattoo of her. Howard wanted to get a tattoo at Veronica's request, but his parents would not take him to the city to get the tattoo.

- Veronica would call Howard 40-50 times a day. If he didn't pick up the phone, she would leave whiny, pleading, messages … or cry … and then yell. Literally yell at Howard that he was an "M……F…." and that she hated him and he shouldn't be so bad. Then, Veronica would talk sweet to him and ask him to "please" (repeated 10 times) call her back.

Howard's parents described Veronica as manipulative, controlling, abusive, and very immature. But no matter what his parents told Howard, he still said that he (a) loved her, (b) she was his only friend and (c) he couldn't break up with her. It should be noted that the parents were trying to get Howard to understand what Veronica was doing by "talking" to him. Howard did not learn much language until he was about 15 because he could not use sound to learn concepts. He only began to learn language when the educator wrote and drew with an emphasis on visual language, a representation of visual cognition. Howard was able to learn language through visual-motor patterns for which he could form mental pictures. Learning systems typically don't change. Therefore, years later, in order to explain to Howard about this social relationship with Veronica, he would need to see the concepts drawn and written.

Brown worked with Howard for about two hours at their first appointment. She drew out the information they talked about. Howard kept justifying why he needed to stay with Veronica: "She is trying to change," "but she loves me," "but she doesn't mean it," "but she needs me," and so on. These phrases were borrowed from Veronica and were sound patterns without pictures. The talking with drawing did not provide enough overlap of the social ideas that Howard could see mentally. (The talking was probably interrupting the formation of mental pictures.) So Brown wrote and drew about what he said and about his parents' relationship. *Figure 7.5* shows the drawings and writings about what Howard said and what Brown wrote and drew.

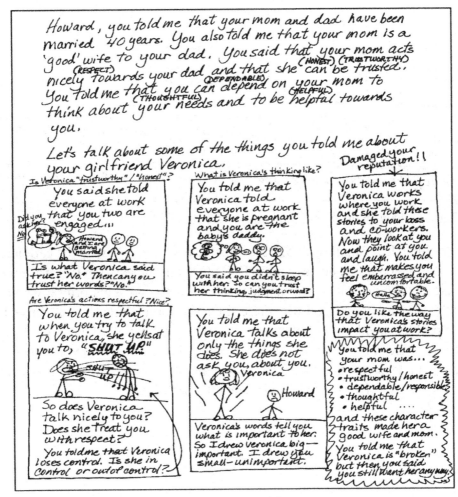

Figure 7.5. Brown does the writing and drawing.

Then Brown drew out many reasons why the relationship with Veronica was a series of choices. *Figure 7.6a* shows many of the reasons why the relationship between Veronica and Howard would not work to create a healthy social relationship.

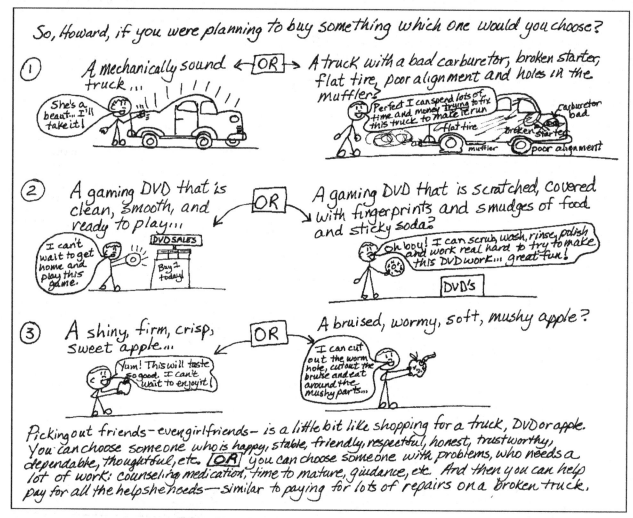

Figure 7.6a. *Reasons why the relationship is not healthy.*

The reasons included "Would you buy a car that had a known flaw in the carburetor, exhaust system, engine, etc.?" "Would you buy a gaming DVD for your play station that was knowingly scratched, dirty, etc.?" "Would you buy the apple that knowingly had a big bruise, with a big worm eating its way out?" Howard understood why these situations with "things" made sense, but he could not see how these problems with things related to his girlfriend. That is, when given the analogy, "Why would you accept a girlfriend like Veronica who you know lies to you, takes your money, tells you what to do, yells at you, tells you she is mad at you one minute and tells you she loves you the next, then says she is mad at you?" He could not understand the problem.

Brown now asked Howard to write out the problem. When he wrote out what Veronica's behavior was, he was able to see the problem. His writing was not borrowed from Brown but represented his own thinking. See *Figure 7.6b*.

I love My self so I dress up Nicely. I want an honest Person in My life. I want other people to respect Me by talking nicely to Me. I take care of my self by being with people I can trust.

Veronica has a personality disorder. She needs to change. Veronica lies to Me and to others. Veronica is dishonest. Veronica yelled, "shut u p" at Me in a loud voice which is disrespectful to Me. Veronica can't be trusted because she can't control her self and I can't control her.

Yes Howard, you are in love with the person you *want* Veronica tobe. You are *not* in love with Veronica for who she really is.

Figure 7.6b. *Howard writes about his relationship with Veronica.*

Brown then suggested that they write out what Howard was going to say (*Figure 7.6c*) when he called Veronica to break up with her … and he followed through!

So Howard, write out what you plan to say to Veronica when you phone her.

1. I'M not ready for a relationship.

2. So I don't want to be boy friend and girlfriend any more.

3. I'M breaking up with you!

4. Good - bye!

After you say, "Good-bye" then you just hang up the phone.

Figure 7.6c. *Howard writes about what he will say to Veronica.*

Howard learned his language with lots and lots of writing, learning to socially problem solve, even when he could talk about the issue also required lots of writing. Writing creates the movement of the hand to form shapes that he could see and attach the concepts to. Howard could solve the problem he could see through the shapes made by moving the hand while writing.

Activity: How could Howard talk about a problem but not problem solve it?

Learning to think about others and to problem solve social issues requires the same methods of learning to think as are needed to learn language in order to be able to read, write, view, think, speak, listen, and calculate. Problem solving requires having sufficient knowledge in the way a person learns concepts. Concepts are social and cognitive in nature, and their meanings refine over many layers of experience receiving additional meaning. Problem solving requires the ability to see multiple choices with their possible outcomes. The ability to understand that problems have multiple choices for solution also requires refining the meaning of the concepts in the problem.

Activity: Why does problem solving require conceptual learning?

Refining Thoughts

Providing a learner with choices over time allows the learner to develop a variety of options when faced with a problem to solve. The more options a thinker possesses, the more choices the thinker is able to utilize for problem solving. This acquisition of knowledge to make the best choices is the result of acquiring concepts. The acquisition of concepts about what, when, where, why and how to behave empowers a learner to think about problems and to solve problems based on past choices. The tool that the learner uses to sort through the concepts is language. *Language mediates thought in the process of learning to behave.*

Activity: What is the main tool for learning to problem solve?

When the learner is able to acquire this type of social knowledge in relationship to others through everyday interactions, the learner grows up to be socially competent. However, for individuals with ASD and similar challenges, the ability to put meaning to behavior from what others say and do is often not possible. So in our culture, individuals with ASD must be explicitly taught what people think about when they see them do certain behaviors. Explicit teaching in this sense means that individuals with ASD must be provided information about social problem solving through the way that they acquire concepts.

Conceptual learning may be improved through the following visual-motor methods:

- Cartoon what the behavior looks like and what the others look like when they see the behavior. *Figure 7.7* shows what others think when a child, Jason, picks his nose.

Figure 7.7. Jason thinks about picking his nose with his finger.

In the next strip, *Figure 7.8,* Jason remembers what others think and, therefore, makes a different choice.

Figure 7.8. Jason makes a different choice based on Figure 7.7.

- Write about the behavior, with or without cartoons. Most children and adults with ASD learn concepts better when the drawings are paired with writing. *Figure 7.9.* shows the rich language that goes with the picture for *Figure 7.7. Figure 7.10* shows the language of the pro-social choice.

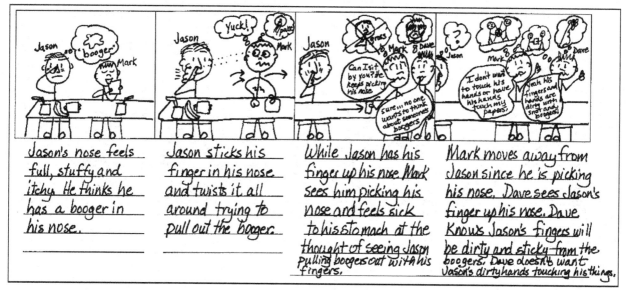

Figure 7.9. *Words explain the meaning of the picture concepts.*

Figure 7.10. *The written words help explain a better choice of behavior.*

- Use oral language to talk about what others think. The written words in *Figures 7.9 and 7.10* may be given orally as well as with writing and with signing.

- Encourage the learner to do as much of the drawing and writing as possible. When Howard wrote his own thoughts, the movement of his hand created his conceptual meaning. In this way, he understood the pictures, the words that he had seen and spoken and the words others had spoken.

Activity: What type of methods will help persons with ASD learn to think about their own as well as others' behaviors?

Educators and parents play an instrumental role in not only helping children develop the concepts necessary to make acceptable choices of behavior but in helping them develop the concepts necessary to make those choices through problem solving. The acquisition process is a scaffold that requires constant and consistent feedback from the adults about the child's behavior within the child's environment. In this way the child's thinking refines. The child becomes empowered as an agent who becomes a person capable of pro-social behavior. The empowerment comes from the power of knowledge about what choices are acceptable and what others think about the various choices of behavior.

Activity: Why is power of knowledge about choices so important in learning to behave?

Control vs. Power

Although the words power and control are often used interchangeably, control and power are not the same. *Control* is what an adult does to make sure that another person's behavior is acceptable. Control refers to the use of any force or power necessary to limit somebody's actions regardless of what the person thinks, believes, or wants. Parents control newborn babies by doing everything for them. But within three days, babies begin to show a difference in the crying behavior to inform parents what they want: to be fed, to be comforted, to be given water, to be changed. As soon as children begin to show behavior that is different (differentiated behavior), parents begin to let go of the control; instead parents begin to listen while modeling and showing acceptable behavior. Parents also give feedback on what is not acceptable behavior.

The process of providing feedback can be exhausting when dealing with a child who does not respond to parents' assigned meaning or for a child who has what seems to be infinite ways to reject the parents' input. Both of these types of situations occur in families who are raising children with different ways to perceive the world. The first urge is to quit listening, quit engaging, quit assigning meaning, and move to control. Control the child, control the behavior, control the classroom, and so forth. This control is different than power. Power refers to learning to make choices from knowledge. Control, on the other hand, offers little knowledge but a lot of discipline – rewarded and punished behavior from an adult's perspective.

Activity: What is the difference between control and power?

All three authors were educated in ways to "control" behavior. Arwood began working with children with ASD in the late 1960s. She was trained in specialized programs designed by followers of behaviorism, and she became so good at that type of training that she supervised and trained others. But there was something lacking in the children in these programs – learning to think. Under stimulus control, children would sit and perform tasks, their backs rigid and their utterances rote. In other situations, they were off topic and often inappropriate. The older these children were, the more obvious it was that they could learn these tasks under stimulus control but all of the generalization programming in the world did not create children who were thinking and problem solving about everyday activities so that they could learn to live independently. Today, after 40 years in the field, some of the same types of discussion often occur; for example, "The child's behavior is so out of control ... we have to get the behavior under control before we can work with meaningful activities."

From a safety standpoint, yes, making sure children don't hurt themselves or others is paramount. But there is a huge difference between controlling behavior for immediate safety and helping a child learn to be an agent, with power to make safe and acceptable choices of behavior. Helping a child learn to be an agent (*Chapter Six*) is a huge step toward safety. For example, Karen's parents brought her across the United States to work with Arwood in Portland, Oregon. Karen was a six-year-old with severe autism. As soon as Arwood began to work with her, Karen began to show some natural rejection of the activities by pushing away the pencil and paper. Arwood accepted the rejection and pulled out some novel toys to wind up, knowing that movement would engage Karen's learning system (remember that most children with ASD use movement to learn to visually think). Eventually, Arwood introduced a picture with multiple agents involved in an event (see *Figure 7.11*).

Figure 7.11. *APRICOT I. Picture.* Used with permission (Arwood, 1985).

Arwood began to label the picture, draw about Karen and Arwood thinking about the picture, and writing the words they talked about. Karen would sometimes pause and either flap her hands or rock, two forms of self-stimulation. Every time Karen engaged in these self-stim behaviors, Arwood would guide her hand into a hand-over-hand acceptable movement such as writing. Karen's behaviors communicated the need for Arwood to provide more meaning in the way that Karen learns concepts – through movement.

Activity: Why is it important to use the visual-motor system for children with ASD to learn to behave?

During the work, Karen's posture relaxed, and she began to show a more natural look, even with an occasional hand flap or rock. Karen was learning how to be an agent, to be listened to by Arwood, and to be given appropriate ways to behave doing activities that would provide Karen with flexible options of literacy – learning to view, think, listen, read, write, calculate, and speak.

Karen's parents were perplexed. Karen was not being "controlled." So the parents said, "Let's show you what Karen can do." They pulled out a set of two cards that were side by side on a ring. The adult could turn one of the cards at a time. On the right side of the card might be an object such as a tree. On the left side, the card was a color such as red.

As soon as the cards were pulled out, Karen's back became rigid as if a pole was running down her back. Karen's father pointed to the first set of cards and said, "What is this?" Karen responded with an unnatural tone of voice, "red tree." The dad then flipped the color card, and Karen said, "Green tree." This went on through several colors. Then Dad changed the object card, to "hand", and the pairing of a color with an object continued. Some of the combinations like green tree or even red tree (fall colors) worked, but many combinations were not semantically accurate. For example, there are few "black trees." Karen's behavior was under control, stimulus control. She had learned to respond with specific behaviors to specific stimuli. This training had taken several years to develop, and the parents had a lot of time and money invested in this process. The parents were wary about using any other approach than the one that could show their child compliantly responding to adults' commands.

Activity: Why does learning to respond with specific behaviors to specific stimuli not result in improved thinking?

Training is not the same as conceptual learning or thinking. Conceptual learning is power when the knowledge provides thinking choices. Training a person to do what an adult wants increases the adult's thinking but not necessarily the child's thinking. Training provides a low level of pattern learning that is sub-cortical in nature. In other words, patterns are formed in the limbic or sub-cortical levels of the brain/brain stem that does not include the higher levels of the cerebral cortex. Pattern development is a low level of learning. Learning to respond to training stimuli with imitated patterns or associated skills does not include the higher levels of thinking that humans are capable of developing. Learning to behave involves acquiring concepts for learning to be empowered, to make choices, to problem solve. Training of patterns does not provide for making choices, or solving problems to be empowered; but training results in reactive behavioral responses.

Without thinking as a way to make choices about her "self" and about problems related to herself and others, Karen will still grow bigger. Her behavior will become more aggressive as Karen works to get others to meet her needs. For example, as a small child, she did the tasks that were given her. Then, she would wander around the room during "down time;" spinning, flicking, engaging in many self-stimulation behaviors. But, as she became bigger, her self-stimulation behaviors would result in her body running into others, knocking over objects, falling through space which looked like she was running away, self-injurious hitting, flaying arms that hit and hurt others, etc. Karen did not learn enough about the thinking behind her behavior to become an agent, a person who has choices of how to behave. Empowerment requires a lot of knowledge in the form of social and cognitive concepts about being an agent in relationship to other agents, what other agents think and do, and how one's own behavior affects others' behavior and thinking. Language is the tool for this development of learning to be empowered as a social agent. Lots of language drawn in real time with written language often in a hand-over-hand method helps develop the thinking behind pro-social development for empowerment as an agent.

Summary

Chapter Six provided the reader with the methods for increasing agency. This chapter provided the reader with methods for how to help learners acquire the ability to make choices of acceptable behavior for an increase in power. The tool for these methods is language. *Chapter Eight* will provide the reader with strategies for using language as a tool to prevent unwanted behavior while increasing conceptual thinking about behavior.

Important Concepts in *Chapter Eight*

Readers should be able to explain each of these behavior principles upon completion of this chapter:

1. **Language represents thinking.**

2. **Language mediates behavior.**

3. **Language names behavior.**

4. **Language interprets behavior.**

5. **Language assigns meaning to behavior through words.**

6. **Language helps think about others in relationship to one's own behavior.**

7. **Language adds meaning to thinking for higher order problem solving.**

8. **Language provides the tool for thinking about others.**

9. **Language helps thinkers make acceptable decisions.**

10. **Language improves thinking and, therefore, results in more socially appropriate behavior.**

CHAPTER EIGHT
Language to Behave

Use your words, not your hands.
See with your eyes, not your hands.
I wonder what my hands do
When I think with my hands.

As children learn to be powerful agents, making choices is a matter of language. Language represents thinking for both the adults and the children. Without language, children are limited in many ways. Language is a literacy tool. Literacy is more than producing products related to reading and writing. Literacy is thinking, viewing, speaking, listening, reading, writing, and calculating. Without language, children lack the ability to show their thinking through their literacy. When children's language is limited, so is their thinking, which results in a lack of *productivity.*

Some children produce lots of language structures but without the underlying conceptual meaning. In other words, some children talk a lot but many of their structures are borrowed from what they have heard or read. If questioned about what they say, many of these children do not have a depth of understanding that supports their language structures. If their language lacks depth of thinking, then these children are also limited in their thinking to be social and to learn to behave. If children possess language structures without the underlying meaning, they lack cognitive development or *semanticity.* Without conceptual meaning, children continue to grow older, but they lack sufficient pro-social behavior to live as independently as possible. When children lack language, they lack the ability to be pro-social or *flexible* with their thinking.

To plan goals, to see the consequences of one's actions, and to solve problems according to expected outcomes, children must be able to think about the past, the present, and the future. Language is the tool that allows children to learn to think about ideas that are not in the here-and-now. Language allows learners to think about others and about ideas that they cannot see, feel or touch. This ability to think about ideas that are not immediately viewed includes thinking about others and how one's behavior affects those not present. This language function called *displacement* allows a person to think about consequences to behavior that cannot be seen.

Thinking clearly about one's own behavior while including others' needs results in very *efficient* language – language that helps a person problem solve and make acceptable decisions that results in learning to behave.

This chapter will present methods that increase language function (productivity, semanticity, displacement, flexibility, and efficiency) to help children learn to behave.

Productivity

Productivity refers to the ability to use language in a variety of ways to communicate complex choices. With learning to behave, children learn a variety of ways to communicate their needs – hitting, biting, talking, writing, throwing objects, and so forth. If a behavior is productive, the child is able to "get needs met." Whether the child is attempting to satisfy basic physical needs such as hunger or trying to obtain a toy to spin one more time, the child's behavior is productive. The child's behavior tells others what the child understands. If the only thing the child's learning system is able to decipher is the sensory input, the child's productive behavior could be any motor output such as crying, hitting, screaming, yelling profanity, and so on. However, if the child is learning to decipher the meaning of others' behaviors, words, and thoughts, the child learns to behave according to what the child conceptually learns. Instead of learning to hit or bite, the child learns to use more acceptable behavior such as words to meet the child's needs. Productivity is the ability to use whatever patterns or concepts the child has learned to use to meet needs. Some children can only meet their survival needs through hitting, crying etc. while more advanced thinkers are able to produce their language in a variety of ways to represent more in depth thinking.

Activity: What is productivity?

Learning to use language for thinking (conceptualization) is called productivity. Since children with ASD and related social communication disorders are not able to decipher the typical sound-based input of speakers' voices paired with what they see,[16] adults must provide ways for these children to learn to use language in the way that individuals with ASD learn to conceptualize in order to be productive in ways that are pro-social. The following methods help increase productivity:

- Increase the numbers of ways to talk, write, read, draw, listen, speak and calculate about the same idea. For example, when a child reads about an idea, then talk about the same idea, draw about the idea, write about the idea, then refine the thinking, drawing, and writing so that the ideas become more productive…that is the child has greater depth of thinking about the same topic.

- Provide additional meaning for words or phrases that have limited productivity. For example, if a middle-school child says, "I don't care" in response to an adult explaining why others do not like it when he makes vegetative noises like raspberries in the classroom, that means he does not understand the relationship between his behavior and the thoughts of others. Words like "I don't care," "I'm bored," "I socialize when I want to," "I hate X," "This sucks," "I'm tired," "I think this is stupid," and "I hate my parents" lack depth of thinking about others and what others think or feel. To increase depth of meaning, expand the child's ideas to include who, what, where, when, why, and how. Expanding the child's thinking by adding information about who, what, where, when, why, and how helps develop more in depth thinking, increasing

---

[16] For an explanation of the different types of sensory patterns that form concepts for language use, see Arwood & Kaulitz (2007), Arwood, Kaulitz, and Brown (2009), and Arwood (2011).

productivity. In other words, the child is using these phrases such as "I am bored" because the child does not have enough conceptual development to come up with something to occupy the child's thinking.

Adults, sometimes, interpret the child's words from an adult perspective and try to add meaning to "I don't care" or "I am bored" with adult thoughts such as "my child is so bright that he doesn't do his work because he is bored. I know he is bored because he tells me he is bored." In reality, unless the child shows behavior that is independent of others interpreting and advocating for him, then most of these statements are borrowed and do not represent the actual level of thinking. Most children with ASD and related disorders have learned to produce these utterances for predictable responses from adults. That is, in response to these types of phrases, adults immediately jump in to try to convince children that they really do care, that they are not bored, that they can always choose to socialize, that they do not hate X, and so forth. The adults are trying to help shape or control the children's thinking. But to empower their thinking (see *Chapter Seven*), the adults need to bring in more depth, that is the "who, what, where, when, why, and how." So when the child says, "I don't care" or "I am bored," it is time to add meaning through cartooning, oral cartooning[17], drawing, and writing to help the child know the meanings of "caring" or "being bored." *Figures 8.1-8.3* show what "being bored" means and the words that go with the picture of being bored.

Figure 8.1. Being bored empties his thought bubbles.

---

[17] Oral cartooning is saying what the pictures of a cartoon would say. For example, "I see that you your mental pictures are empty and therefore you say you are bored. But, you may not have pictures in your mind for a lot of reasons. One reason you may not have pictures is because you need more information about what you could do during this time...etc."

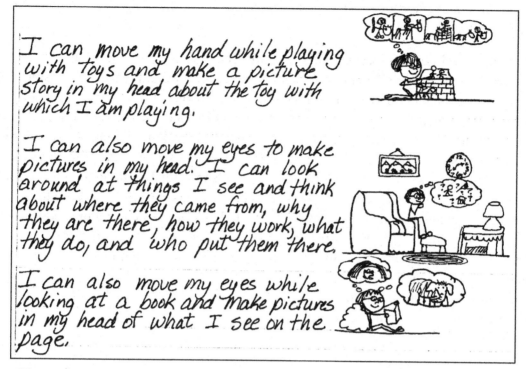

Figure 8.2. Filling my thought bubbles through appropriate movements.

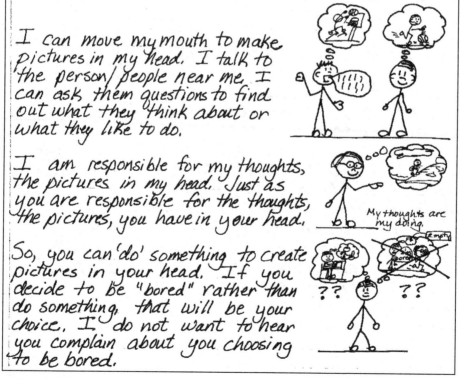

Figure 8.3. Being responsible for my thinking.

Activity: Why does adding depth through increasing a variety of ways to add language help a child learn to be more productive?

- Create a dialogue through drawing and writing about ways to be a productive thinker or learner. *Figures 8.4-8.5* show the simple behaviors for Rocko, an 11-year-old who shows a lot of behavior that appears aggressive, belligerent, oppositional, and noncompliant in nature. Rocko was originally treated for behavior problems, but his thinking was not only not rational at times but showed a lack of developmental socialization, which resulted in an additional diagnosis of autism spectrum disorder. Each box shows a choice of behavior that he makes using his language. He has lots of language but lacks the social meaning of his language structures. The drawings, with the writing, help provide Rocko with the language he needs for learning to behave.

Figure 8.4. The meaning and rules of simple behaviors.

Figure 8.5. *Deciphering the meaning of words with pictures.*

- Provide pictures and language for what a productive agent or learner looks like, sounds like, etc. For example, many students learn the words for name calling and devaluing themselves as well as others without understanding their choices. *Figures 8.6-8.7* provide examples of drawings with Rocko who often used words against himself as well as others.

Figure 8.6. Matching pictures of behavior to ages of development.

Figure 8.7. Drawing out the pictures that go with the child's spoken words.

- Write explanations of words as "because language" so that a child sees the meaning of the words he says. This writing is especially important when the child's words do not match his behavior. For example, Rocko is in a classroom, but he is not "cognizant" of the other people in his classroom. He does not think about the teacher or her perspective. He is able to draw pictures of what he sees, but he is struggling to learn the meaning of the drawings since he does not easily write his ideas. When he is able to write, he avoids referring to himself because he does not see himself. Therefore, he is seldom responsible for his behavior.

Writing should be the best way for Rocko to learn concepts since he learns best with the shape of written ideas. But, to learn to write in school, Rocko was taught to put sound to words and he does not learn from the sound. Therefore, he misspells words and struggles to get accurate patterns down on the page when he writes. He often does not do work in school even though he tells others that he works hard. His language sounds manipulative as he orally always has a reason for not doing his work. So in therapy, he often draws and the educator writes. Once he is able to see the written words, he is able to change his drawing or mental picture and even his own writing. See *Figure 8.8*. Note that Rocko is given "because" reasons for the behaviors that goes with words such as "boredom." Also note that the session begins with what he says about the work at school. By starting the session with his words, he can see where his words match or don't match the pictures. The idea behind improving Rocko's thinking and writing is to help him think about being an agent who is more pro-socially productive Remember that being productive refers to the ability to use language in a variety of ways to represent a variety of thoughts.

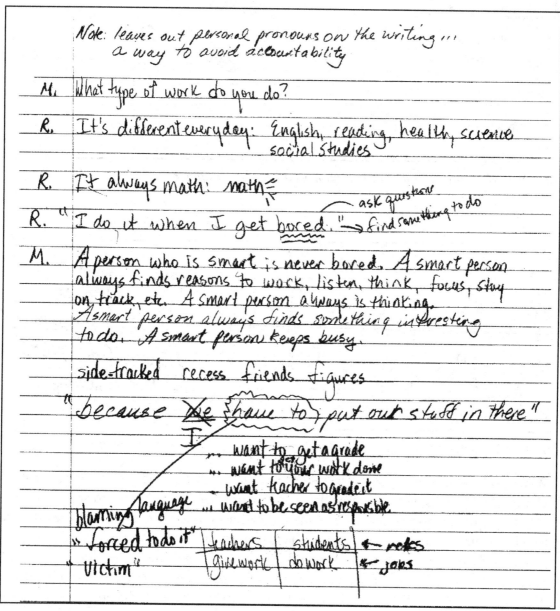

Figure 8.8. Writing about school work.

Activity: What are some ways to improve productivity through language methods?

Semanticity

Children are as capable of thinking with productive language as they are able to learn to acquire meaning from their world. This ability to acquire depth of conceptual meaning is called *semanticity*. Semanticity occurs through adults adding more and more meaning to what children do so that the children learn more conceptual meaning. Meaning is added through the use of language. The following methods are used to add meaning for better semanticity.

- Use rich language. "Rich language" refers to an increase in meaning that will form mental pictures. *Tables 8.1a and 8.1b* show words that do not create mental pictures and some examples of rich, meaningful words. Also there are examples of words that work well for creating richer meaning.

Table 8.1a. Brown's List of Do-Not-Use Words

Words That Are Not Rich	Usage Examples	Rich Words That Better Describe the Desired Action
Get	"Get the book."	Buy, borrow, check out, bring …
Go	"Go to the store."	Walk, run, drive, bike …
Goes	"It goes over here."	Put it, place it, set it, stand it …
Got	"I got it."	Carried, brought, caught …
Went	"I went to Spain."	Traveled, journeyed, flew …
Put	"Put it over there."	Place, carry, load, pull, arrange …
Come	"Come to the table."	Walk, saunter, stride, stroll …
Came	"She came over."	Slept, stayed, played …
Take	"Take it to school."	Pack, carry, bring, push …
Took	"I took the mail in."	Carried, lugged, packed …
Is	He is nice. (What is nice?)	Dresses, talks, plays…nice
Are	They are there. (Doing what?)	Standing, waiting, looking … there
Was	She was okay. (Meaning what?)	Felt, heard, saw … okay
Were	We were late. (In what way?)	Arrived, scheduled … late
Had	It had water.	Contained, kept, stored … water
Have	I have marbles.	Collect, play, receive … marbles
Has	She has horses.	Owns, rides, shows … horses

Table 8.1b. List of Rich Words

"Said" Words	Verbs of Motion ("walk/run")	Verbs of Purpose ("sit or stand in a single motion")	Verbs of Sight ("to see")	Verbs of Touch	Character Traits
asked	amble	bow	behold	brush	bossy
blurted	bolt	crouch	examine	collide	conceited
bawled	canter	cower	eyeball	crash	confused
called	climb	cringe	gaze	finger	curmudgeon
chattered	crawl	droop	glance	grab	closed-minded
cheered	cruise	lounge	leer	graze	determined
commented	dart	lunge	look	heave	evil
composed	fly	kneel	notice	hit	fair
declared	gallop	nestle	observe	hold	fearful
drawled	glide	perch	ogle	hug	frank
exclaimed	hobble	pose	peek	massage	industrious
giggled	hop	roost	peep	nudge	intelligent
hissed	jog	slouch	peer	press	just
mumbled	jump	squat	scan	poke ram	kind
murmured	leap		squint	rub	kindhearted
panted	limp		spy	scratch	loathsome
pronounced	lope		stare	shoulder	lonely
raged	lumber		study	slam	loving
reminded	march			slap	loyal
replied	pace			tap	open-minded
responded	saunter			thump	materialistic
screamed	scramble				optimistic
shrieked	scurry				pessimistic
snarled	slide				risk taker
spat	sidle				serious
sputtered	skip				stern
stammered	step				sweet
stated	stalk				trustworthy
	stagger				temperamental
	stride				timid
	stroll				vicious
	trudge				zealous

- Use complete ideas. Complete ideas include the "who, what, where, when, why, and how" about what people or agents do in an event. For example, when talking and writing use language to help create meaningful mental pictures. *Figure 8.9* shows how Rocko draws and writes about what his day looks like and what his behavior looks like when he is involved with various activities. Notice that his ideas are complete and include a number of time-based words such as "before," "once," "later," "next," "so" "since," "while," "during," "then," "when," and "because" that he is learning to use to connect his ideas. Increasing the meaning of these concepts helps Rocko increase his understanding of how ideas connect for greater meaning or semanticity. It should be noted that the educator drew and wrote about the organization of Rocko's entire school day so he would follow the teacher's rules and do activities the way the teacher expected, not by "Rocko's rules."

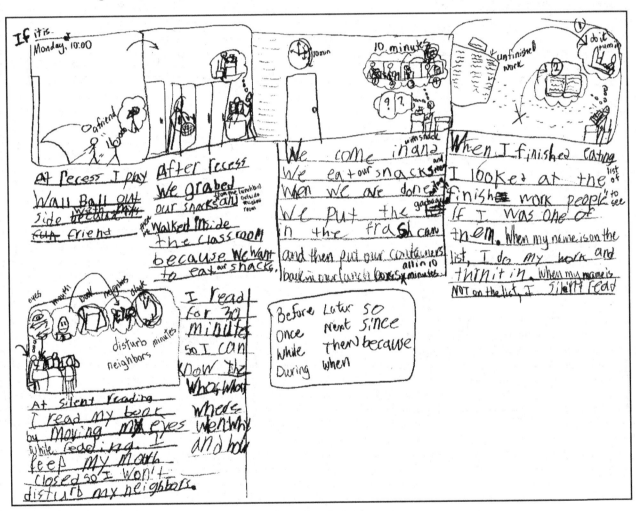

Figure 8.9. *Drawing and writing about the school day.*

- Add more meaning (semanticity) through the use of multiple ways to show a specific language function such as greeting, acknowledging someone's presence, and so forth. *Figure 8.10* is an example of giving a teen diagnosed with ASD multiple meanings for specific language functions. Language function represents a person's thinking. Because this student worked on thinking or conceptual learning, his IQ score increased by 30 points from 60 to 90 in nine months by working on language for one hour, once a week during this time frame of nine months. Semanticity is a language function that is directly related to thinking.

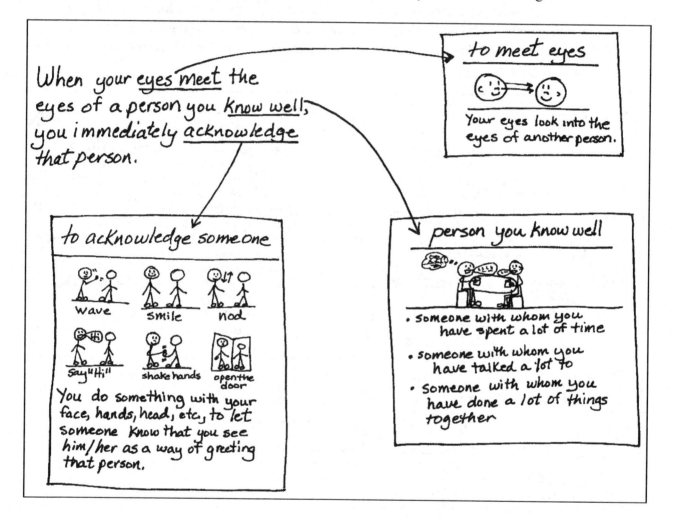

Figure 8.10. Increasing the meaning or semanticity through language functions like greetings.

- Semanticity has to do with meaning that matches thoughts with oral language and behavior. Sometimes adding more meaning to behaviors helps students see their choices of behavior and why or why not they chose a behavior. *Figures 8.11-8.14* again showcase Rocko, who often says he is sick, sleepy, worried, or mad. In fact, "I am mad" is one of his most frequent expressions. Being mad does not have specific behaviors or mental pictures to go with the words. But he does yell, hit, run away, slam doors, make faces, stomp feet, and so forth. So this sheet shows which of his behaviors go with his word "mad;" and, which behaviors do not match with the words and what others think. So *Figures 8.11a-8.11c* show that Rocko is learning to match his mental pictures, with his behavior, with others' expectations. This ability to refine his thinking by adding more meaning is semanticity.

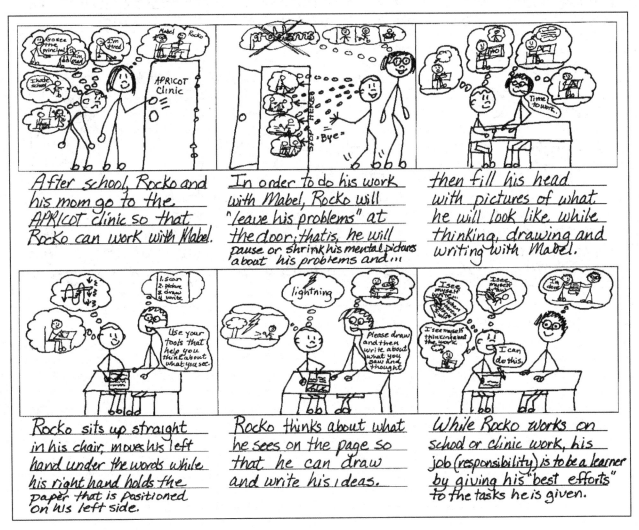

Figure 8.11. Rocko's responsibility as a learner.

Figure 8.12. *Rocko's activities as a learner.*

Figure 8.13. *Rocko's behaviors are choices.*

Activity: Why is matching mental pictures with words a way to increase semanticity?

- Use the rules to explain the meaning of ideas. For example, in *Figures 8.11-8.14*, Rocko often says inappropriate things without thinking about others' feelings. Some of these inappropriate sayings are imitations of what others say. For example, he began walking around the school saying, "All I want for breakfast are roasted Latino babies." This imitation of others' words without meaning suggests a lack of semanticity. To increase semanticity—what the rule is, how the rule plays out, and what others think—all need to connect.

Figure 8.14-15 are work pages from helping Rocko understand how his best effort means to follow the rules and directions

Figure 8.14. Best effort means to follow the rules or directions.

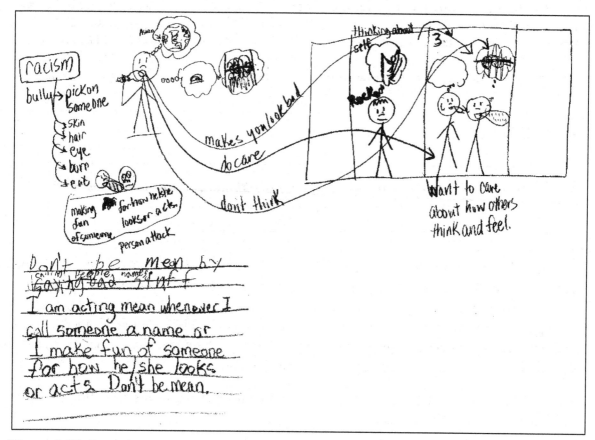

Figure 8.15. Learning to act at an appropriate level means to think about others.

In *Figure 8.15*, the cartoon on the right refers to the four stages of development of concepts. The first box is empty because that is the lowest level such as hitting or biting. The second square refers to Rocko's level of functioning where he name calls or bullies others because he is the only one in his picture. The third level is where Rocko is able to think about how others think and feel. (More about these stages is found in *Chapter Nine*.)

Activity: What are some methods used to increase semanticity?

Flexibility

As children learn more language that is productive with underlying depth of meaning, their behavior becomes more flexible. Listed below are some ways to increase *flexibility*, that is, to help children and adults learn to think about possibilities of choice of behavior that affects others. When individuals are able to think about others, they have more acceptable behavior choices. This means that the learner who exhibits a lot of language has more flexibility to understand meaning from a variety of perspectives. The following methods will help develop more flexibility.

- Use pictures and writings to help children understand the many behaviors that could mean specific concepts. For example, Rocko, the 11-year-old introduced in some of the previous figures, called others snobs but refused to work in small groups or be part of a team. Because his language represents his thinking about himself and not about others in relationship to him, the rules about others and how he fits in the group with others are difficult for him. *Figures 8.16 and 8.17* show how he is writing out what a "group" means in terms of understanding the concept "snob" and how those meanings refer to the concept "team." The writing gives Rocko the language he needs to understand the meaning of spoken words that he hears and repeats without adequate understanding. The movement of his hand creates the shapes of mental concepts or ideas. Writing creates the actual thinking for Rocko.

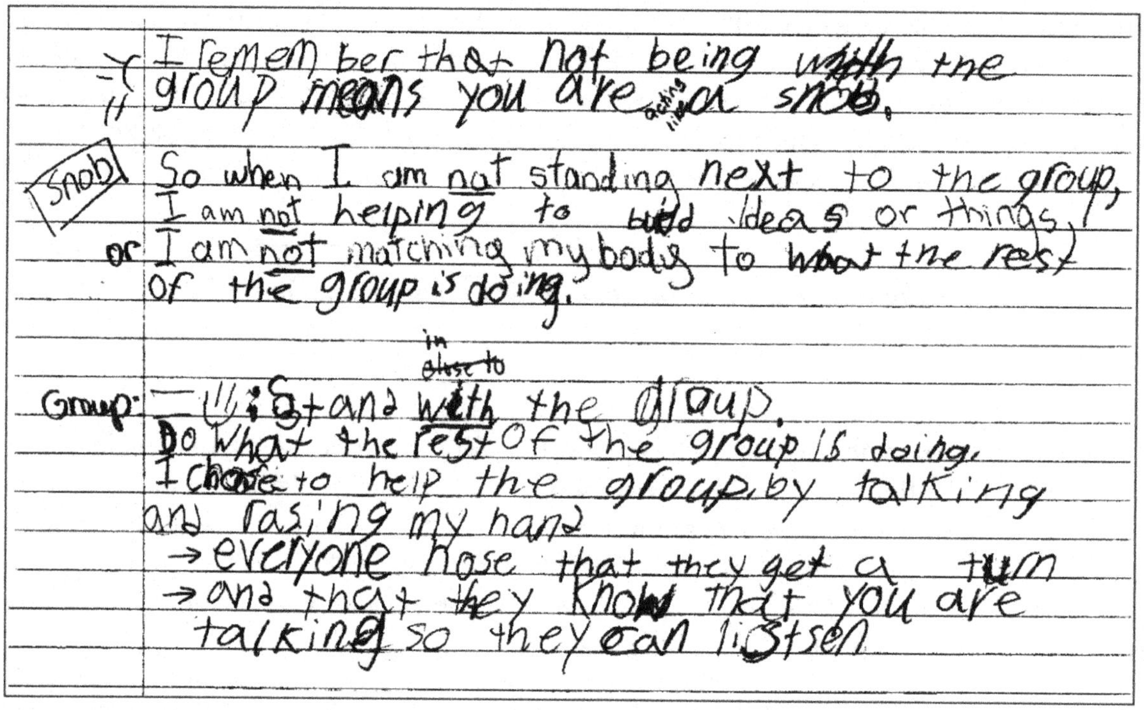

I remember that not being with the group means you are [~~acting a~~] snob.

[Snob] So when I am not standing next to the group, I am not helping to build ideas or things, or I am not matching my body to what the rest of the group is doing.

Group: — 1. Stand with the group. [in close to] Do what the rest of the group is doing. I chose to help the group by talking and rasing my hand
→ everyone nose that they get a turn
→ and that they know that you are talking so they can listsen

Figure 8.16. Writing about "group."

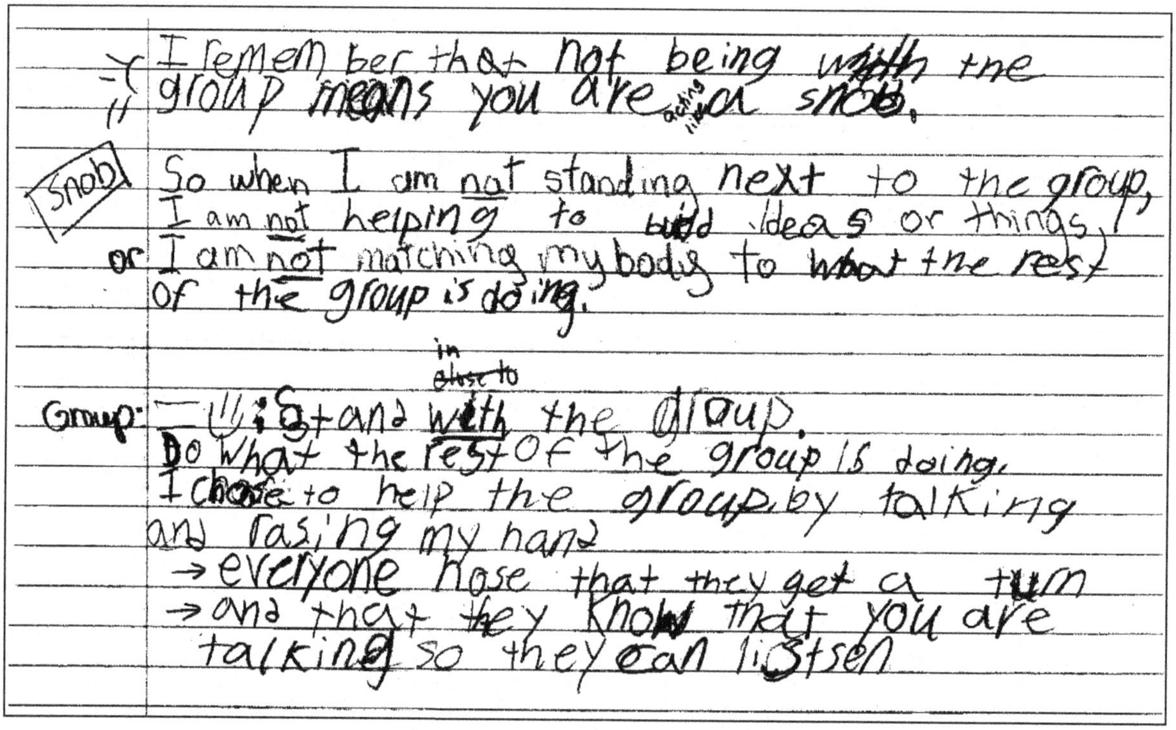

I remember that not being with the group means you are [~~acting a~~] snob.

[Snob] So when I am not standing next to the group, I am not helping to build ideas or things, or I am not matching my body to what the rest of the group is doing.

Group: — 1. Stand with the group. [in close to] Do what the rest of the group is doing. I chose to help the group by talking and rasing my hand
→ everyone nose that they get a turn
→ and that they know that you are talking so they can listsen

Figure 8.17. Writing and then drawing for the concept meaning of "team."

Rocko's writing is legible when he understands the meanings, but his writing is very difficult to read when he does not have the conceptual meaning. He has to have the concepts to be able to use flexible language. Language names thinking. When he has the thinking to go with the language then his behavior matches both his thinking and his language.

- Use a lot of different ways to interconnect concepts. The overlap of concepts increases semanticity or meaning. Overlap with pictures, rules, and writing interconnected helps create flexibility since the meaning is seen in a variety of examples. *Figure 8.18* shows Rocko learning about groups and teams (*Figures 8.16 and 8.17*) in even more ways than the previous examples. Most of these examples are helping Rocko begin to see that his behavior affects others and that his language has meaning (ideas or mental pictures) that also affects others. In other words, the educator is trying to move Rocko from thinking only about himself to thinking about others.

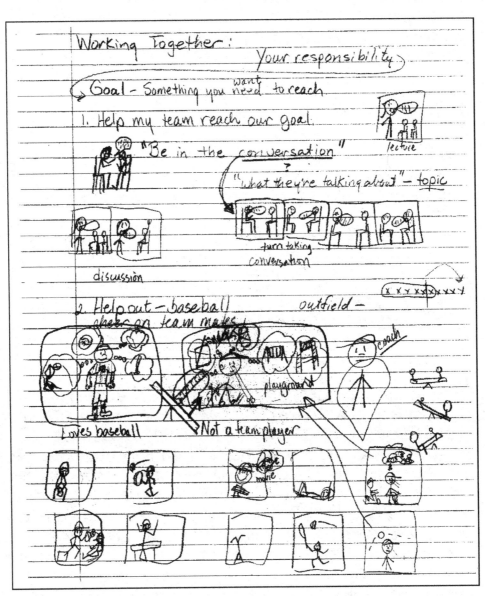

Figure 8.18. *Rocko learns what working together means.*

Activity: Why does improving semanticity help develop a child's ability to flexibly respond in appropriate ways?

- Translate everyday phrases into behaviors based on what others think about the behaviors. *Figures 8.19a and 8.19b* show Rocko understands "goofing off" in relationship to playing baseball on a team. The picture dictionary includes the words that he uses but does not understand about supporting a team.

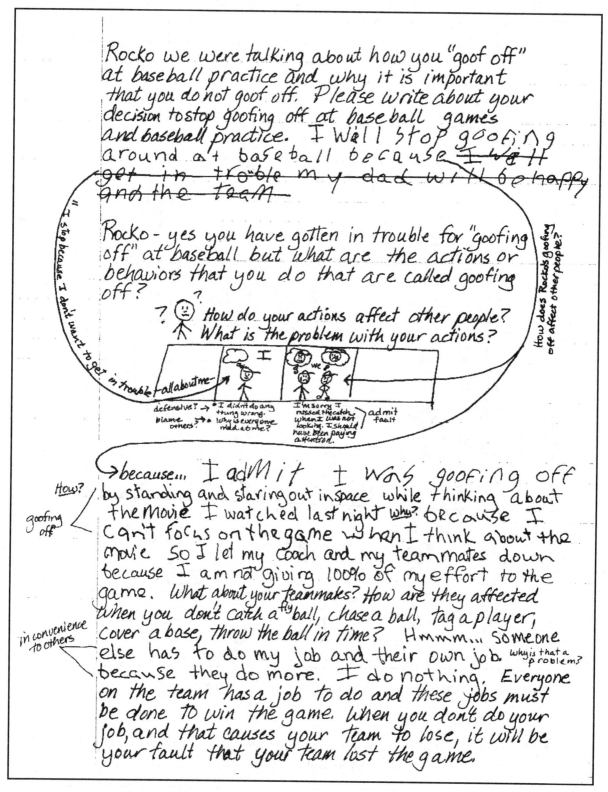

Figure 8.19a. Rocko learns about the term "goofing off."

Picture Dictionary for _____		
dependable	trustworthy	reliable
considerate	thoughtful	Glue Words:

Figure 8.19b. Rocko is learning about what behaviors mean.

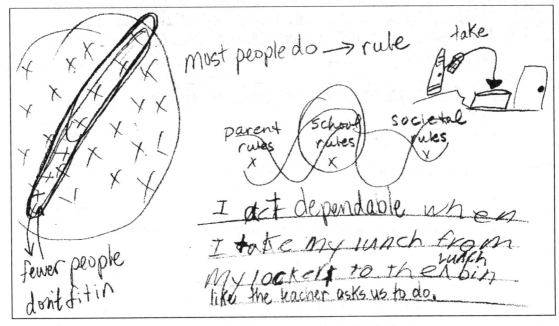

Figure 8.19c. Rocko uses the words to write about his behavior.

- Increase what the learner understands about behavior, rules, and words. To be flexible, a learner must be able to view a problem or situation from multiple perspectives. But most students with behavior issues do not think about their behavior in relationship to others (more about this in *Chapter Nine*). So it is important to help a student "view" or "see" what others think in order for him to begin to see how to "fit in" with others' expectations. *Figure 8.20* shows an example of how writing and drawing help Rocko see how he fits into a group or team.

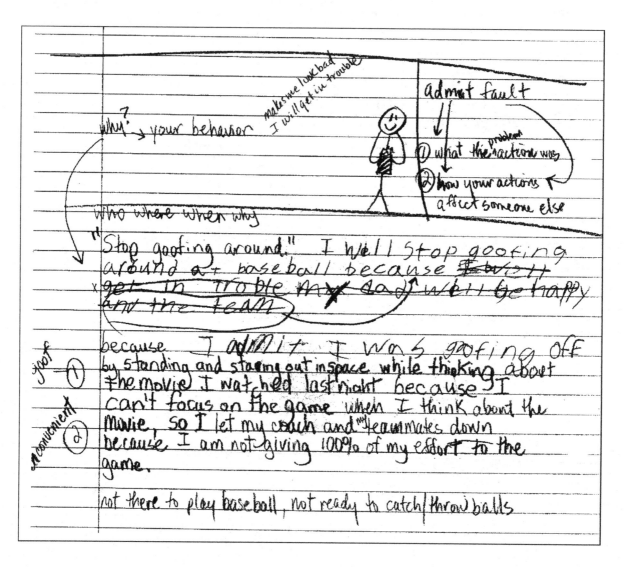

Figure 8.20. *Rocko learns about how his behavior affects others.*

Activity: How do the methods for flexibility play into social development?

Displacement

Probably one of the most important functions of language is displacement. *Displacement* in language acts as a tool to help a person learn to think about ideas that are not in the present. Displacement refers to the ability to think about one's actions with regard to others, their actions, their thoughts, and all of the consequences of one's behavior in relationship to others' behaviors. The following is a list of ways to increase displacement.

- Use materials that are developmentally appropriate for the child's age and level of language development. (*Chapter Nine* provides more information about development.) For example, babies show little displacement because they are dependent on the adults to survive. Their thinking is about their sensory needs and they learn behaviors that help them get those needs met – crying, fussing, limited word usage, and so forth. Children between 0 and 2 years of age will survive based on what others are able to provide. Appropriate input would be sensory in nature for this age where the child does an act and the adult assigns meaning physically as well as verbally to the act. However, for children who are older and who cry or fuss, then the additional information about why the children are expected to behave in more developmentally appropriate ways should be provided through rich oral language, drawings, writings, cartoons and so forth.

Activity: What is displacement like at the sensori-motor level of thinking?

- Use people as agents in as many materials as possible. As children grow older, they move farther and farther from dependence on others until they are independent and are able to take care of their needs as well as the needs of others. Language represents this type of displacement. Therefore, helping a child learn about being an agent means that materials should be based on the use of people. For example, a young child may laugh at monsters because they look funny or unusual, but an older child understands that monsters are not real. Understanding what is real and not real and understanding what others do or don't do is all part of understanding that an agent is about a person. For example, a child sees a movie and is scared, because others say they are scared but he does not know whether the monsters are real or not. His lack of understanding is due to the fact that he does not know whether monsters exist or not. This is because he does not have the semanticity or deep meaning for "monsters" and does not have the understanding that just because he sees monsters in a book or in a movie does not mean that monsters actually exist. *Figure 8.21* shows Rocko having monsters in his head as an excuse for not doing a task.

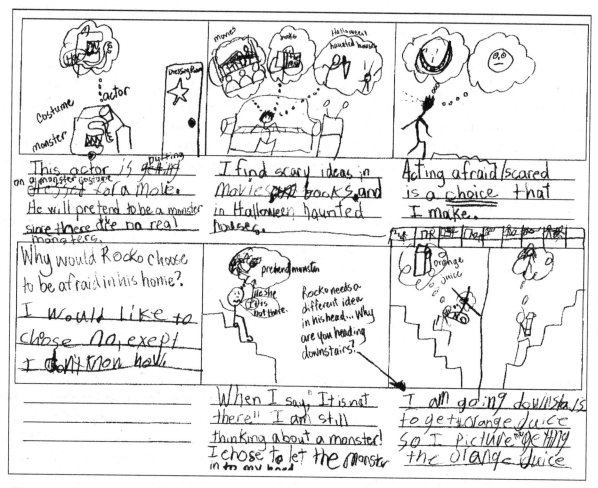

Figure 8.21. *Rocko thinks and chooses what he will think about.*

- Use language that emphasizes people rather than fiction or personified objects. Many children use all sorts of language about the visually unusual – dinosaurs, monsters, made-up characters, robots, and so forth. This type of language is too displaced from reality for many individuals with ASD and related disorders. When this type of language is used, draw the learner thinking about these ideas (thought bubble) rather than socially relating to others as a monster, robot, character, and so on. *Figure 8.22* provides an example of a child thinking about pretend rather than pretending agency.

Figure 8.22. *Child thinks about pretend.*

Activity: Why is displacement important in learning to socially behave?

Efficiency

When a language user is able to be productive with language so as to think flexibly, the thinker is also able to use enough meaning (semanticity) to be more than in the here-and-now (displacement). That is, the learner is able to be more independent or displaced. This also means that the thinker is able to communicate the learner's own needs as well as understand others' needs. Such understanding of others' needs requires language that shows the child's efficiency in thinking.

Efficiency is a test of reasonableness. When presented with a problem, a person who responds quickly and with little misunderstanding is developing enough language to be efficient. Efficiency occurs in language function when a thinker is able to quickly analyze options and respond with the behavior that a reasonable person would produce. The following methods help a learner begin to use more efficient language thus showing more socially reasonable behavior.

- Turn expectations into rules. For example, if you expect a child to show more and more pro-social ability as the child grows older; put that expectation into a "rule." "Sharmin, I see that you were thinking about the other students when you asked if anyone needed help," (here comes the rule) "thinking about others tells me that you are growing up." In this case, the rule is that one thinks about others as one becomes older.

Activity: How is efficiency about learning to think about others?

- Be sure that expected behaviors are visible to the learner. Since most learners with ASD think with visual ideas, turn words into visual thoughts. For example, "Andy, I saw you and Philip on the playground together. What did you see?" In reality, Andy and Philip were on the ground punching each other. But what is it that Andy knows about the situation? Ask for the information that Andy is able to actually see. (*Chapter Nine* provides some developmental levels for the various stages of seeing one perform behavior.) Andy replies, "Nothin'." So put him into the picture. "Andy, draw what your eyes saw when you were on the playground." Sometimes children draw themselves center to the activity as if they are on the paper. And sometimes children draw what someone else would see. In Andy's case, he drew a picture of Philip on top of him and Phillip hitting Andy. See *Figure 8.23.*

Figure 8.23. Each child draws his perspective of the same event.

While Andy was drawing, Philip was drawing the exact opposite. When the two boys are put together with the two pictures, the teacher gives them the language for what they see. "When the two of you look like this, this is called fighting. So were you, Andy, and were you, Philip, fighting on the playground?" One boy then said "yes." The other boy said, "We looked like this."

Activity: How does learning to see others in the same picture, help a child learn to be efficient in language?

- Give strategies for making quick decisions and for thinking quickly. For example, many children and youth find themselves doing unacceptable behaviors when they are not able to think about whether the behaviors are okay or not okay. The learners can use strategies to keep from engaging in unacceptable behavior. "Mia, when you are with your friends and they ask you if you want to do something, you should have a clear picture of doing what they ask, what your parent looks like when you are doing the behavior, and what your parent looks like after your parent knows you did the behavior. If you do not have a clear mental picture of all of these parts of your friend's request, then you tell your friend that your mother told you to come home."

This strategy means that the learner does not have to explain why Mia will or won't do the behavior or activity. For this to work, the mother has to agree to the "excuse." When Mia arrives home, she is to tell her mom about the friend's request so Mom can draw and write out the options for better thinking and problem solving.

Mia must be given several examples in order to learn the concept of how to think about making choices offered from others such as "Your friend Sissy asks you to go for a ride. She says, 'Mia let's go.' What do you say?" Mia responds, "Okay." The adult asks, "Where are you going? With whom? When? How long? How will you get there?" What are you doing there?" Mia says she does not know the answers to any of these questions, so the adult draws and writes out what Mia's options are. Since Mia has no pictures for Sissy's request, Mia is to say she has to go home as her mother expects. These types of strategies are not really taking the place of thinking. They are to be used when the learner does not yet have the knowledge to have a visual mental picture of what is okay or not okay to do. The drawing and writing to the "who, what, where, when, why, and how" help develop the thinking for making choices about ideas that cannot be seen.

The more thinking that Mia is able to acquire, the more efficient her language becomes. For example, when Mia cannot answer the questions about others and what others would think, then she shows restricted language. Restricted language depends on the interpretation of others and sounds like this, "Uh, well, I don't know, well sometimes, well maybe." As Mia adds more concepts for higher order thinking, her language becomes more efficient and the listener is able to share in the meaning. For example, "I don't really see myself go with you for a ride, so I am going to go home. My mom asked me to come home after school. Thanks for asking me to go for a ride, maybe next time." The listener is able to understand the "who, what, where, when, why, and how" without asking lots of questions or guessing on the interpretations.

Activity: How does having a clear mental picture help a learner think about what is okay behavior?

Language methods that help increase displacement, semanticity, productivity, flexibility, and efficiency help a learner with better decision-making, choices, and problem solving for more pro-social behavior. The following case study highlights how to increase language function for better language of behavior.

Case Study. Ralph is a 9-year-old male. He has a visual thinking system that did not allow him to learn the alphabet with sound names in kindergarten. He struggled with academics until he was transferred to a different school where the first-grade teacher provided a visual way of thinking, reading, writing, and calculating. Ralph did well in first grade. Because he could do what was expected, his behavior seemed to work well in the classroom. The teacher provided Ralph with strong visual behavioral limits. She drew, used visually rich oral language, showed Ralph how to read and write using shapes, and helped him develop strategies for better literacy.

In first-grade, the teacher made sure that Ralph fit into the classroom by being successful but outside the classroom Ralph had developed a lot of oppositional statements. Many of these statements were developed in response to not being successful in Kindergarten. For example, "I can't" meaning "I won't" tactics were dominating doing anything that the parents or others outside school asked Ralph to perform. Parents felt they could not work with him so they sought outside school help. Getting additional help outside of school resulted in even more use of these tactics, including telling the adults that he "wants to be normal" and be like the other kids who don't "have to go to receive help." Ralph was pushing back, wanting to be an agent, but not under the control of others.

Even though he was not diagnosed with ASD or a related disorder, the school and parents questioned whether Ralph might have Asperger Syndrome. Whatever the reason for his differences in learning, his behavior did not show age appropriate social development. At 9 years old, Ralph did not show age appropriate perspective taking. He spoke about himself showing that he "acted in a self-centered way" but when asked about whom he was thinking about, he always said that he thought about others. That is, he was not aware that he acted in a self-centered way.

Here is a sampling of his behavior: He demands things to be done his way. One day, he ordered his mother to get him water. "I want water!" He pushed his water cup towards his mom to refill it, not looking at her. While she went to find the water, Ralph sulked and would not work. When she returned, he took a small sip of the water and left the cup up close to his body. Mom began to move the cup away from him so the cup of water did not spill while Ralph did his work. Ralph rose up and snatched the cup right out of her hand and slammed the cup down, spilling what was left. Everyone "dances" around this type of behavior, trying not to anger Ralph. Ralph is controlling others. The educators who work with him say he lives by "Ralph's rules." Ralph is able to tell the rules that his mother sets. He is also able to tell the adults the punishment if he breaks the rule. And he is able to tell the adults when he breaks the rules. But, his behavior shows that he does not think about others.

Most people would say that his behavior is intentional; that is, Ralph intends to be "bossy," to "break the rules," and so forth. The authors take a different approach to understanding what Ralph needs. Since Ralph is not able to comply, he must not have enough information to be able to be productive with his language. In other words, Ralph does not have the concepts necessary to understand the spoken rules, the breaking of the rules, or the punishment. His thinking is restricted, so his language is restricted to talking about himself, his needs, his wants, and his way of doing things. He lives in the here-and-now because he uses language that is restricted: talks about himself, that he is bored, that he will do an activity only when he wants to, when he needs water he expects his mother to get the water, and so on. In order for him to learn to fit in pro-socially, (fitting in is a typical social expectation for 9 year olds), Ralph needs visual ways to see the expectations of others, their thoughts, the outcomes, and how to make appropriate choices. This will equip Ralph with more thinking to support his language. His language will reflect more depth of concepts and his behavior will reflect greater pro-social development.

Figures 8.24-8.25 show how an educator helped Ralph resolve a problem by writing, to which some pictures were added to help clarify conceptual meaning.

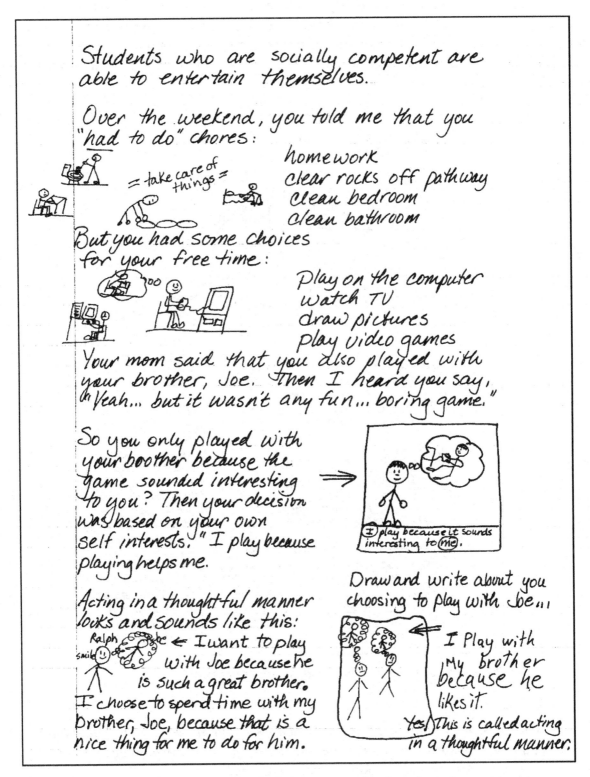

Figure 8.24. *Learning the language for how to act with others based on expectations.*

With writing, Ralph could see that he was only talking about his own needs, wants, and desires. Through the writing he could see that he sometimes can play with his brother because that is what a big brother does for a little brother. But sometimes Ralph must do Ralph's work. Then the behavior is retagged as "thoughtful" that adds more meaning for better conceptual depth.

The same methods were used with Ralph to help him learn the language that goes with what his behavior looks like. *Figure 8.25* shows a work page that helped Ralph see the behavior choices, the resulting options of outcomes, and the retagging of the meaning for his choices. In this way, Ralph learns about what others expect and is able to change his behavior from "Ralph's rules" to rules where everyone fits.

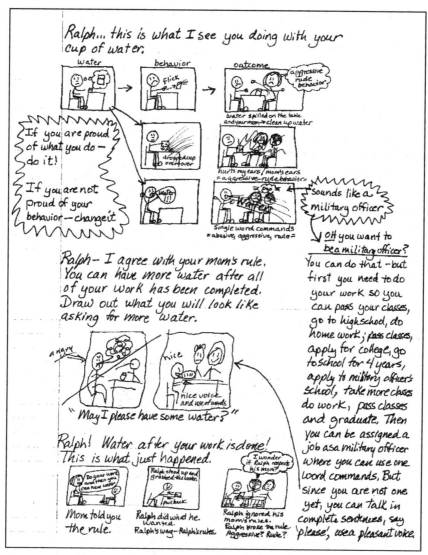

Figure 8.25. *Language for behavior and outcomes.*

Activity: Why does Ralph need to write and draw about his words to help him think in a more pro-social way? How does the writing provide the language for how Ralph thinks and acts?

Summary

Language represents a person's thinking. In order to possess language that allows a person to think about others in relationship to rules, expectations, problem solving, and decision making, a learner must be able to use language that represents that type of thinking. Language about one's own desires, needs, and wants shows a restricted way of thinking. Or language that does not take others' perspectives into consideration or shows limited ability to see a problem from the perspective of the others in the picture shows that the person needs more language functioning for higher order thinking or problem solving. Language limited to doing activities by the agent's own rules or expectations shows limited linguistic displacement, semanticity, productivity, flexibility, and efficiency. *Chapter Nine* provides developmental information related to agency, power, and language (*Chapters Six-Eight*).

Important Concepts in *Chapter Nine*

Readers should be able to explain each of these behavior principles upon completion of this chapter:

1. Behavior is the product of the neurosemantic learning system.

2. Everyone learns to behave based on acquiring the assigned meaning within the context of an environment.

3. Language is the tool for learning to behave.

4. Different levels of language show different behaviors.

5. Language and thinking match developmental expectations

6. Learning to think about self and others helps develop pro-social behavior.

7. Learning to behave is a process based on how a person learns to think.

8. Seeing is not the same as thinking.

9. Thinking with language helps to develop complex social behavior about problem solving, decision making, and prioritizing.

10. Behavior is as developmentally appropriate as society deems.

CHAPTER NINE
Developmental Behavior

I learn to see me.
I learn to be a person.
I even learn what is right and wrong.
I can only develop what I have learned.

A child can only learn the behaviors that the child is able to developmentally produce based on what the child "knows." In other words, verbal and nonverbal behavior is a mirror of what a child knows. If a child does not understand how the child's behavior impacts others, the child will not show an understanding of others' needs. For example, three-year-old, Joe, sees his hand touch the arm of another child. The other child falls down. Joe did not see Joe "push the other child down." Joe could only see hands touch the other child. At this age, Joe does not necessarily know what Joe's hands did or did not do.

A young child like Joe or some children with severe ASD see the hands, but they do not see that the hands are attached to them. They do not see their faces and, therefore, do not know that they are responsible for the "seen" hands pushing another child down. Until a child learns that he is an agent with arms and hands that he can move, he will not know that he is responsible for pushing the other child down. To be able to make choices about their behavior in relationship to others, children must first learn to be agents (*Chapter Six*). If they are not agents, they do not know that the hands they see belong to them and that they make the hands do things. All behavior like learning about how the hands work is a part of the developmental outcomes of the learning process.

Behavior is a product of development: language development, cognitive or thinking development, and social concepts or social development. The purpose of this chapter is to provide the reader with knowledge about how development pertains to learning to behave. This chapter discusses how behavior is a developmental product of a person's learning and thinking level. (*Chapter Ten* will provide additional information about how learning results in development.)

Language Development

Language is the tool for learning to behave according to societal expectations. There are basically three levels of language function: (a) preproduction with limited, if any, language structures and limited thinking; (b) preproduction with lots of structures but with restricted thinking; and (c) production of conversational language that shares thinking.[18]

---

[18] For more expansive description of these three levels, see Arwood (2011).

Table 9.1 shows the thinking and behavior that goes with each of these developmental language levels. Notice that with each level of language, the learner's behavior matches the thinking.

Table 9.1. *Development Levels for Language and Thinking*

LANGUAGE FUNCTION	THINKING	EXPECTED BEHAVIOR	LANGUAGE EXAMPLES
Preproduction, limited verbal	Sensory input and motor output	Hits, cries, spits, grabs, kicks, screams, throws objects, self-stims such as rocks or flaps, points, pinches, looks, reaches, takes, holds, carries, toddles, crawls, walks, smells, licks, tastes, chews, etc.	Mostly nonverbal, some differentiated sounds or vocalization
Pre-production, lots of language structures	Thinks about self ...	When stressed, may engage in behavior in a sensori-motor way (hitting, kicking, etc.). Compliant when not confronted or challenged. Follows others' models. Others maintain with this person	My book ... My class ... My crayon ... I want X. I'm bored. I won't ... It's your fault. He made me do it. I don't like X. I hate X. That is a stupid rule. The rule says X
Production of language	Thinks about others	Maintains with others; converses about others' ideas. Is able to share knowledge while accepting input from others. Uses shared conversation to work out differences. Shows ability to be flexible and to produce language in lots of different ways and in lots of different situations	Uses language to problem solve, to critically think, to plan, to make decisions

The connection between language and thinking is like a mirror. Examine the language or nonverbal communication; and the child's behaviors will tell you about the child's thinking level. Likewise, when somebody's behavior functions in a certain way, the learner is thinking at the same level. For example, if a 25-year-old is melting down and throwing objects at someone, he is thinking at the sensori-motor level of responding to what he sees, or smells; he is responding to basic sensory inputs. He is not thinking about what he is doing or what others are thinking.

Figure 9.1 shows different levels of behavior for an individual in the top strip. Below that strip, the educator shows Dennis what behaviors go with each developmental age. In this way, Dennis behaves the way he thinks. When drawing the pictures used in *Figure 9.1*, each frame represents the four thinking levels.

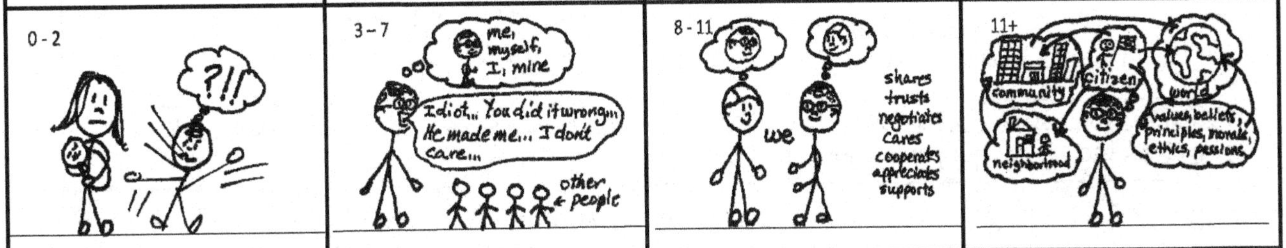

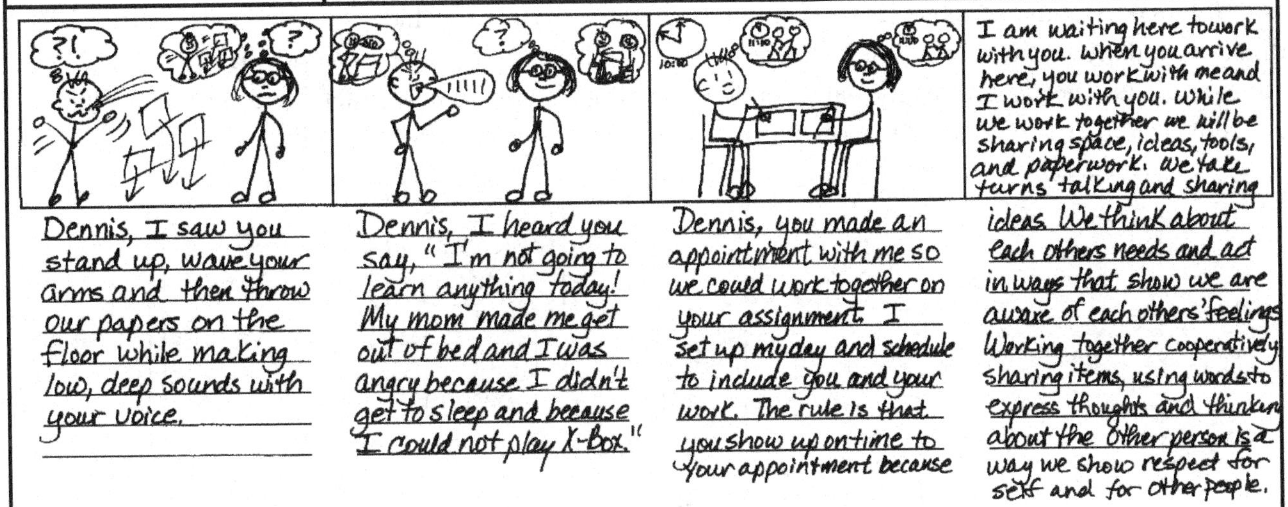

Figure 9.1. *Thinking drives behavior.*

Figure 9.2 shows the various cognitive developmental stages.

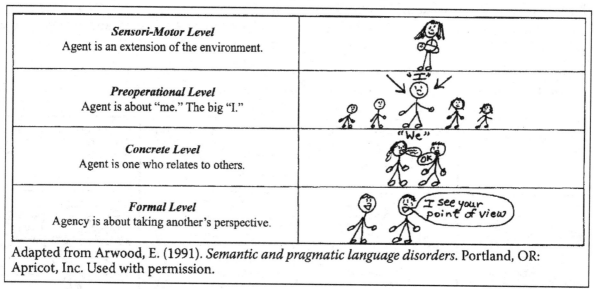

Adapted from Arwood, E. (1991). *Semantic and pragmatic language disorders*. Portland, OR: Apricot, Inc. Used with permission.

Figure 9.2. *Thinking stages matched against thoughts.* From Arwood, E. & Kaulitz, C. (2007). *Learning with a visual brain in an auditory world*, p. 106. Shawnee Mission, KS: AAPC Publishing. Reproduced with permission.

The stages in *Figure 9.2* relate to Piaget's (1952) stages, but the graphics show how individuals think about what they do as agents in relationship to others. A sensori-motor thinker does not think about self or others. A preoperational thinker thinks only about self. He or she is the center of the world. It is only at the concrete level of thinking that an individual includes other people in his or her thinking. Finally, at the formal level, the individual is able to think about concepts that include others, their safety, and needs. At this formal level, the individual is able to take others' perspectives. *Figure 9.3* shows another way to see a person in the way that he or she thinks about being an agent.

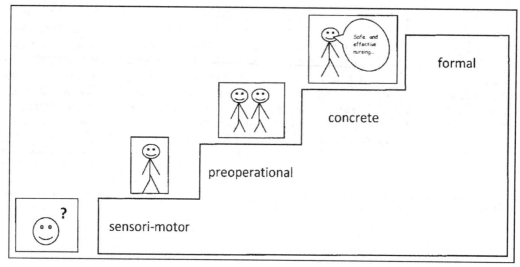

Figure 9.3. *Learning to be an agent.*

Activity: How does thinking about others relate to stages of cognitive development?

Figure 9.4 shows the developmental progression of how one thinks about being an agent.

| I am the picture. | I am in the picture. | The rules are about others I know. | I can think in visual mental symbols. |

Figure 9.4. *Drawing the child helps him see his own behavior.* From Arwood, E. & Kaulitz, C. (2007). *Learning with a visual brain in an auditory world*, p. 116. Shawnee Mission, KS: AAPC Publishing. Reproduced with permission.

In *Figure 9.4* the child is the picture. In fact, the first frame of drawing was done in response to asking a child to draw a picture about him watching TV. At the second stage of thinking, or preoperational thinking, the child is in the picture and the picture is all about him. He is center to the universe. In the third stage, the concrete rule-governed stage, the child thinks about others in relationship to himself and the rules about them. This is the societal level of expectations based on law and rules. Finally, in the fourth stage of formal thinking, the child is able to think in visual symbols not just about academics such as the solar system but about concepts that cannot be seen or touched such as "consideration," "respect," and "kindness."

The language matches these stages of thinking about self and about others. *Table 9.2* shows some of the language for each of the four thinking stages.

Table 9.2. *Thinking Stages of Language*

THINKING STAGE	LANGUAGE
Sensori-motor	Preproduction and limited, if any, language structures – nonverbal gazes, points, gestural signs
Preoperational	My books; my toys; my classroom; my students; my needs; you made me do it; you made me angry; I didn't do anything…the teacher sent me to the office; I am not guilty … the judge sent me to jail; I hate my parents; these are stupid rules
Concrete	We play chess sometimes when there is time for us to get together. There is this rule about staying on the playground; so, I won't leave the grounds because the teacher might worry about me. Sometimes my friend likes to go bowling but I have to be home by 10:00 or my mom worries if I don't get home on time. I forgot my book again, so the teacher told me to come to the office and explain why I forgot my book. Others want to eat lunch so I will sit down and not run around at lunch, so others can think about eating, not about me. I like to do my homework when I get home so I have time to play with my friends when they get home.

Table 9.2. Continued

THINKING STAGE	LANGUAGE
Formal	If I forget to bring the cake to the party, my friend won't have a birthday cake and she will be disappointed because I forgot; I must be sure to leave enough time to walk into class before the bell rings so that I don't disturb others. If I am late, then the other students look at me and lose concentration about what the professor is saying and I don't want to be responsible for them not doing well in class; I knocked over the fence when I was digging up the old bush, I need to go talk with my neighbor and let him know that I will replace the fence at my cost since I knocked it down; By showing up for my appointment on time, I am being respectful to others who have appointments after mine. I don't want them to take time out of their day waiting for their appointments because I was late to my appointment

As the thinking increases, notice how the language also increases, not only in structural complexity but in meaning. With increased thinking and language, the behavior becomes more pro-socially complex. When thinking increases, the individual has more choices about behavior, problem solving, and decision-making.

Activity: How does thinking and learning affect language?

Developmentally Appropriate Behavior

Behavior is as appropriate as society deems. Behavior is developmentally appropriate according to society's rules. "To be able to think about society", suggests that a thinker has at least a concrete level of thinking. So deciding what is developmentally appropriate behavior is not the task of children, but the task for adults who are able to think at the concrete level or higher. Adults must make the choices about behavior to help children learn what is developmentally appropriate.

The following section provides examples of adult roles in the process of children learning to behave and suggests some ways to help support developmentally appropriate behavior.

Activity: How is behavior related to developmental levels of language?

Avoid Mixed Messages. Mixed messages occur when society, a group, or an adult does not provide clear or consistent meaning for specific behavior. Children learn what adults teach. Adults must be sure to provide clear pictures of what is developmentally appropriate. For example, an adult who thinks about behavior as cute, funny, smart, loving, or any other adjective that reflects the adult's own personal bias or needs does not consider what is appropriate for the good of society. Therefore, this type of adult will not provide a clear message to the child of what is appropriate behavior. This is particularly troublesome because children learn to behave from the time they are born, not when the adult decides that it is time to learn to behave.

Here is an example of a parent who gives her son a mixed message. Nicholas is an adorable four-year-old child. It is 11:30 in the morning at a café that specializes in breakfast/lunch. Nicholas is giggling as he runs through the restaurant. Behind the boy is a woman in her thirties. She is smiling and laughing as she looks at the presentation of the restaurant's tables, occasionally straightening a condiment or pushing in a chair. Nicholas runs over to the counter customers and slides down under the counter. The woman walking around the restaurant continues to laugh as she drags Nicholas out from under the counter. Nicholas runs off to inspect the food on the author's table, peering over and breathing onto a dessert while laughing and gazing at the author's eyes. He then darts to the front of the restaurant, past customers dodging him while they carry food and drinks.

The amused boy, Nicholas, then runs past the author, slamming both hands straight into the door that opens onto a busy street. The author says, "This is not a playground. People come here to sit down and eat their lunches." The woman, still laughing as if she were playing a game of hide-and-seek with the boy, says, "He *thinks* it is a playground." The author says, "That is too bad. It is not a playground, and the boy or one of the customers might get hurt." At this point, the woman comes over to the author's table and says, "He's mine, and this is my place." She is the owner. She then takes the boy by the hand, and as they walk out, the boy begins some self-stim types of behavior, flicking around his eyes, hopping, flapping his hands, and leaning into the adult. The woman returns shortly by herself.

Nicolas lacked learning. Playing in the restaurant was a game that gave him several messages: It is okay to run around inside. You can do what you want as long as you have the power – the parent's restaurant. You do not have to consider whether your behavior affects anyone else if you are having a good time – a good personal time is all that matters. Whatever you do is okay as long as your parent thinks it is funny. Your parent thinks that you can do no wrong, and she will stand behind your behavior no matter what you do.

Mom's mixed messages are in part her way of coping with her level of understanding. Her comment to the author suggests that this mother believes she owns her child just like she owns the café. Her child is an object, a possession, which means that she does not separate his behavior from who he is. She either loves what he does or she is a bad parent. Her own developmental level of thinking is that of a preoperational thinker. Only she is in her picture. She is meeting her own needs – her emotional need to be okay as a parent, not her son's needs. She did not tell her son what was okay behavior or not okay behavior. Without a good understanding of limits, his agency was challenged. He did not know how to act as an agent. This lack of agency showed clearly when he left showing self-stimulation – he did not have enough meaning about who he was and what he did to understand the limits of his behavior affecting others or him. So he used self-stimulation as a way to stimulate the input that was not meaningful.

Activity: Why is it important for educators and parents to limit behavior according to others' needs?

What the woman owner thought was a fun game was annoying other people – one of the counter customers who was busy drinking coffee while she did some computer work had to move to allow the boy to be pulled out from under the counter and one of the authors had to move her food to keep the boy from putting his nose in it. In fact, the restaurant emptied out of customers while the boy's running around took place even though it was busy when the author first came in and it was the noon hour. Several customers ordered food at the counter, looked around, and then took their food with them. The boy's behavior was not acceptable at any time (see *Chapter Three*) and certainly not developmentally appropriate. Unfortunately, because the parent did not take the adult role to set limits and to send the child clear messages about what was appropriate, the child left looking more atypical than necessary. The parent's message was mixed: It is okay to behave this way and it is not okay to behave like this, so you have to leave.

Activity: What are mixed messages? Give an example of a mixed message.

Provide Clear, Developmentally Appropriate Messages. So what could this mother have done to set limits and help structure her son's behavior so it was developmentally appropriate? (These rules also pertain to what adults as educators can do in the schools.)

1. First, adults (like this mom) must understand that behavior that annoys others is not developmentally appropriate. The key here is "others." This means that it is a societal call – not the parent's call. If the parent doesn't know what is okay, a good rule of thumb is to look around and see if others must change their behavior to "deal" with the child's behavior. For example, the lady at the counter had to change what she did. The author had to say something and move her food. If others are affected in a negative way, then the behavior is not pro-socially acceptable.

Activity: Why is annoying behavior not developmentally appropriate?

---

2. Adults must consistently follow through with established societal rules. For example, what do people do in a restaurant? One unspoken but societal rule is that a restaurant is for sitting down and eating. If the child's behavior does not show him sitting down, the behavior is not developmentally appropriate. So Mom needs to give the boy the rules with language. If he does not attend to her voice by changing his behavior to meet Mom's expectations, she needs to draw and write out what the rules for a restaurant include.

Activity: Why is setting limits for what is developmentally appropriate necessary for children to learn society's rules?

---

3. If an adult gives the rules at least twice and the child does not follow through, it suggests that the child does not understand the spoken words. Instead of continuing to only talk to the child, draw out the expectations/rules to show what you expect and why you expect the child to

follow the rules. This helps provide input in a developmentally appropriate way for the child to learn the rules (e.g., *Figure 9.1*).

4. Adults' nonverbal behaviors must match their words. If an adult wants to establish developmentally appropriate limits for children to engage in appropriate behavior, adults must not laugh when the child(ren) does not follow the rules. If an adult is serious about the rules, the adult's face must also be serious. Likewise, when the children are engaged in appropriate behavior, the adults' faces must show pleasure, joy, and a pleasant demeanor.

Activity: Why does an adult's behavior provide meaning for what is developmentally appropriate?

---

5. Adults must be able to see the child's behavior as separate from their own needs – a child has a "who," which consists of personality, interests, desires, needs, and so forth. The child is okay, but the behavior may not be the behavior the adult wants. The child's "who" and the child's behavior are not the same. The child's behavior is a "what;" therefore, parents and educators must deal with the behavior separate from the love and caring they have for the child. Furthermore, children are not "what's" or possessions. Parents do not possess children and educators do not possess children (my classroom, etc.). Children are people who learn how to behave based on what concepts they acquire and their behavior must be separated from their "who." Adults must decide what is okay or not okay and be able to separate the behavior from how they feel about the child(ren).

Activity: Why is it important to separate a child's behavior from the child?

---

6. Adults are responsible for setting the limits for all children within society. Raising a child is about what is best for the child, not the adult. It might be easier not to confront Nicholas (the boy in the restaurant), but Nicholas will not learn to be a socially competent adult without rules, limits, and a good development of agency. To see Nicolas as separate from the adult's needs, Mom needs to ask herself, "What behavior is appropriate for a restaurant for adults?" The reason the question is for adults is that there are adults eating and the child's behavior must be acceptable to the adults. The same type of question would be asked in a child-dominated activity such as bouncing in the ball area of a pizza restaurant. One would not expect a full-size adult to go into the ball area as there would be no room for the children.

Activity: What are three things that Nicholas' mother could do to help Nicholas learn to behave in developmentally appropriate ways?

Thinking and Demonstrating Developmentally Appropriate Behaviors

Developmentally appropriate behavior is determined by what others need; not what the individual needs to do. Therefore, what others think determines what a person does. However, thinking and doing are not the same; yet, there is a reciprocal relationship between thinking and doing.

The child learns to think about what to do through the process of acquiring more and more meaning over time. The child will be able to "do" what the child is able to think about or understand. *Figure 9.5* shows the developmental stages in stair steps to represent the products over time along with a spiral to show how meaning scaffolds. Meaning starts with what a learner already knows, and then someone assigns meaning to actions that challenge what the learner knows. This challenge creates a drop or loop in meaning that requires the learner to add more meaning. The learner acquires more meaning from experiences, so conceptual meaning increases to the next level.

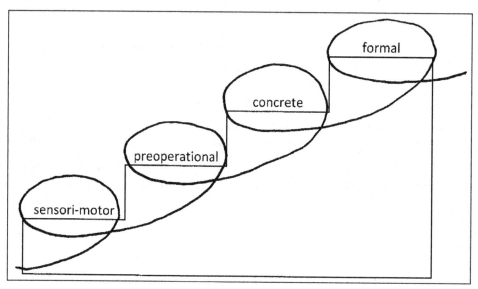

***Figure 9.5.** Thinking and doing.*

To learn the language of how to behave in a restaurant, Nicholas in the previous example needed lots of meaning added over and over in the way that is best for him to learn concepts. This overlap of meaning develops the child's personal boundaries of what is okay for him to do and what is okay for adults to do, and what is okay for other patrons in the restaurant to do that will not annoy or bother other people.

The same principles hold true for the classroom. The classroom is not the teacher's classroom but society's microcosm of what society values. The behavior of children should reflect the values of society. Learning to develop the language of how to behave requires that adults nurture, protect, and support children and youth, which is what society suggests that adults do to help children and youth grow up into healthy and productive citizens. This means that the classroom climate should invest in nurturing, protecting, and supporting – three values that encourage the development of agency while supporting pro-social development through learning the language for behavior. More about nurturing, protecting, and supporting will be provided in later chapters.[19]

---

[19] More expansive ways of setting up classrooms that nurture, protect, and support may be found in Arwood and Young (2000).

Activity: How are parents and educators alike in helping children and youth learn the language of behavior?

Developmental Language of Behavior

When children do not acquire the thinking about behavior in the way of neurotypical children, the adults must be ready to assign meaning in a way that helps the children acquire the language of thinking to behave in a pro-social way that matches the learner's thinking. In previous chapters, drawing with oral cartooning and writing was recommended for all children and adults with ASD[20]. This visual type of language must be developmentally appropriate.

The following recommendations are designed to help educators and parents make their oral, written, and drawn or pictured language developmentally appropriate.

1. *Look around. **What is the behavior of the majority?*** <u>Parents</u>: If it is a restaurant, the majority of patrons are sitting down, and that is the expected behavior. <u>Parents and Educators</u>: If it is a child's playground, the majority of children are swinging, climbing, running, and so on. Those behaviors are the expectation, not sitting and playing with a hand-held piece of technology. Since the playground equipment is for children and youth, adults should not be climbing up the slide. Just because there is no rule that says adults should not climb the slide, it does not mean the behavior is okay. "Getting away" with doing something for the sake of doing it is preoperational in thinking, that is, typical of a 3-to 7-year-old. Doing what fits in with society's expectations is actually a higher way of thinking than "getting away" with something or doing a task "my way."

2. *Use logic in setting natural consequences.* If a child does not do the behavior that is expected, what is the natural consequence? <u>Parents</u>: If a child does not sit on his seat at a restaurant but stands on it, what happens? The seat becomes dirty from the child's shoes; besides the child cannot eat his food standing. If he stands while eating, he will get food on the chair and floor, which someone else will them have to clean. Or someone might come and sit on the seat that has food on it and get her pants dirty. Or the child might fall and bump his chin on the table. <u>Educators</u>: If students are expected to sit while the teacher does her lesson, what is the logical expectation? Are they supposed to be thinking while the adult is presenting? What is the way most children think? Since most children think with pictures, the children are told to make pictures while they sit and watch the teacher's mouth and the teacher's hand draw and write. What is the consequence if the child is not engaged? If the child is engaging in an unwanted behavior, the other students will watch the child, and their mental pictures will go away and they won't be able to think about what the teacher is presenting. If the expected behavior is that the children retain the material, they will need to put the learning into their own language. They will need to write, draw, and put the lesson into their thoughts. So think about equipping children with dry-erase boards, picture dictionaries, and paper for drawing and writing whenever another student or teacher is talking, reading, and so on.

---

[20] It should be noted that most neurotypical children also learn concepts in visual ways. Therefore, these methods are appropriate for all thinkers.

3. *Use more pictured language.* Most instructions for parents and educators suggest using short phrases, simple vocabulary, and limited language. Since learning to behave is a thinking process, the child must have more language. <u>Parents</u>: Saying the same thing over and over does not add meaning, so change the way you say what you want. Use different words and look at whether or not the behavior changes. If the behavior does not change, begin to draw and write. Always write, whether or not the child is able to speak, read, or write. Writing consists of visual-motor patterns in the same form as the child's visual-motor system of concept thinking. *The lower the child's development, the more writing, the more drawing, and the more visual thinking or oral cartooning the adult must use to create adequate thinking.* <u>Educators</u>: One of the goals of education is to help children and youth learn to become productive members of society. To be like the other children and youth, a child must have enough language to think like the peers. This means that educators must create language that a child or youth can understand. For children and youth with ASD, this language is visual-motor in nature. Write! Write! Write! Use a document camera and/or poster paper so that the students can watch your hand move. Use lots of hand-over-hand assistance when monitoring to help children and youth learn the correct movement patterns to form shapes of ideas. Always think of meaning as the big picture, not the skills or parts, so that the children and youth are gaining sufficient meaning about the content to support their use of language for better literacy and problem solving (Arwood, 2011).

Activity: Why does a person need to use more language for a child who is functioning at a developmentally low level?

---

4. *Use "because language."*[21] Adults must set behavior expectations through the use of "because language," even for the lowest functioning students and children. Why do you want a child to sit? Why do you want the child not to run in the restaurant? Why do you want your children to sit on the carpet? Why do you want children not to interrupt in class? Unless an adult can explain why she is asking the child to behave in a certain way, the child will not learn the language to behave. The child will only produce the desired behavior when cued, rewarded, and or punished – in other words, when controlled. To independently learn to behave in an acceptable manner, the child must have the necessary thinking and be empowered. Remember that neurotypical children learn language easily and, therefore, use their own language to assign meaning to what others expect. For children who do not develop language function (thinking) the way others do, others must give them the language for what they see and do.

5. *Set limits (create rules) for desired behavior.* All behavior is okay, so all behavior has a set of rules of when it is okay to do a given behavior. Explain the desired behavior so the child learns the limits of the behavior. <u>Parents</u>: If you do not expect your child to learn how to care for his belongings, when will the child learn? For example, at the end of a task, always help the child put away the materials, clothes, dirty plates, and so on. Use a hand-over-hand method to help the child become the agent who is in charge of the child's space. This type of action helps the child learn to be an agent, to be pro-socially competent. If the child pulls back, calmly use

---

[21] See Arwood and Young (2000) for explanations about "because language."

language to explain why you are doing what you are doing. For example, "We will put the dishes into the dishwasher so we can wash the dishes. Then when we want a snack this afternoon, we will have clean dishes for our snack." "Toys, clothes, and so on, "get broken" when left out and about, and if they are broken, you will not have them to play with, to wear, and so on." The child needs to learn the value of people, their things, and their actions. Only through learning about people, their things, and their actions will a child learn to behave. <u>Educators</u>: The school is about so much more than teaching academics. The school consists of adults who also must nurture, protect, and support children. That is the role of adults in our dominant culture. So making the classroom into a "pseudo-family" (Arwood & Young, 2000) is important. Children spend a bulk of their daytime in that pseudo-family, so they must feel like they are competent. To ensure that all children are included in the limits of the classroom, the educator must provide all children with success for completing tasks, which means teaching them about how they learn best and providing them with meta-cognitive strategies about learning. (*Chapter Ten* will provide more information about how learning is accomplished.) There are lots of ways for children to learn the limits of their behavior and others' behaviors. The suggestions listed in this chapter will provide educators with an excellent start for helping children learn when to use what behavior and why.

6. *Emphasize social concepts, not social skills.* Social skills are learned patterns of behavior that do not necessarily include an understanding of the behavior. For example, a child learns how to change topics. He has practiced the skills and can perform them with mastery. Another student begins a conversation with, "Hey, what are ya doing at lunch?" The student with social skills says, "That is not a good way to start a conversation. To be interesting, begin with something interesting about yourself." He has developed social skills, but his skills lack pro-social development. In other words, the child has learned to demonstrate psychomotor social skills. The child has learned through imitation, practice, and reward the correct behavior of how beginning a conversation. Unfortunately, he has not learned the social concepts about people who want to do something with him. <u>Parents</u>: Social "niceties" or etiquette show gracious behavior. Saying "thank you" when someone gives you something is a nicety. It is also a learned skill. However, saying thank you can have a lot more meaning behind it, such as when to say thank you, different ways to say thank you, or using thank you as part of a way to show appreciation for others' efforts. Therefore, it is more important to explain why a person says thank you than just saying thank you. <u>Educators</u>: There are a lot of programs for teaching social skills. If students do not show social skills, it is because they do not have the underlying social concepts. It is more valuable in the long run to teach social concepts, a variety of ways to greet a person, to say thank you, to acknowledge others, to share ideas about doing something with others, and so forth.

Figure 9.6 shows an example of work with a student who shows his skills. On the left side of the paper, the teacher helps draw out what he typically does when he is upset or mad. On the right side, the student draws what he feels like, which is scribbling in dark, non-referential ways – a sensory response.

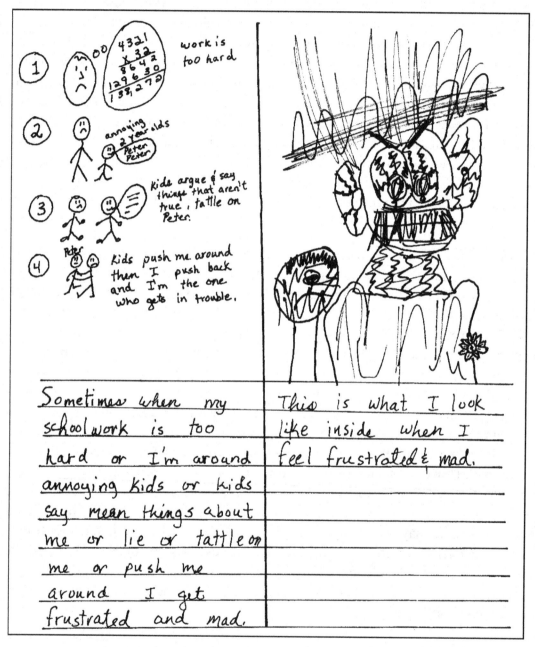

Figure 9.6. *Student draws his feelings.*

The student's behavior does not change. He continues with meltdowns because he has not learned the concept of who he is in relationship to what he does. The teacher does a couple of more drawings with him, comparing for him what he does and what he feels. But this language is at a developmental language that is too high for this student. Finally, the teacher draws him as an agent in a cartoon. This works for him and his behavior changes. He needed the social concepts, not the rules about social behavior. *Figure 9.7* shows the cartoon of his behavior.

Figure 9.7. *He is able to see himself as an agent.* These drawings, *Figure 9.6 and 9.7* were provided by Lyn Larfield, who was a Speech-Language Pathologist from Vancouver, Washington. Used with permission.

Activity: How does developmentally appropriate language help a student reflect learn the language of how to behave?

See or Not See, Understand or Not Understand, Problem Solve or Not Problem Solve

Whether or not children are able to see what an adult sees, understand what an adult understands, or problem solve at the level of an adult is based on the developmental level of the child's language. The previous section presented a variety of ways to align the child's thinking with the child's development of language to help him learn the developmentally appropriate level of the language to behave. This section of the chapter provides examples of developmental issues related to behavior that is dependent on language. These issues have to do with seeing, understanding and problem solving. *Chapter Ten* will provide the reader with a better understanding of why conceptual learning is based on the neurobiological learning system.

See or Not See. Earlier in the chapter, the authors provided the connection between language and thinking for learning to behave: Behavior represents one's thinking, and language represents one's thinking. So learning the language of behavior is as good as one's thinking. This notion of learning to think in order to behave in acceptable ways seems straightforward, but there are some developmental issues related to thinking to pro-socially behave.

The first issue has to do with being able to interpret the world that one sees and hears. Individuals with ASD and related disorders use visual-motor ways to create concepts, not sound (Arwood & Kaulitz, 2007); therefore, adults must provide them with visual-motor ways of seeing the world. Everything that one would say with sound must to be translated into the pictures of the movement of the lips or the hands for writing and drawing.

The concern is that most educators and parents think that as long as they provide ideas in the form of a "visual," the person with ASD will be able to understand what they see. Unfortunately, this is not true. Being able to interpret one's world is a developmental issue,[22] based on how well the learner is able to process the visual; that is, how much conceptual meaning (language function) the learner has for what is on the page. *Table 9.3* shows the various stages of seeing based on "knowing."

Table 9.3. Seeing and Knowing

COGNITIVE STAGE	THINKING	SEEING	LANGUAGE
Sensori-Motor Stage Neurotypical age: 0-2 Any time a person no longer thinks about behavior ... kicking, hitting, spitting ...	Features of light and shape ... patterns of sensory input	Parts, edges where light reflects, movements of light or edges, patterns of shapes or light edges ... 2D acquisition (see *Chapter Ten*)	Points, gestures, picks up some vocalizations, some patterns that represent meaningful relationships among people, their actions, and objects
Preoperational Stage Neurotypical age: 3-7 Any time a person or child thinks about self as center to the rest of the world ...all about self	Thinks in complex patterns and simple concepts acquired from own experiences. Recognizes agents, actions, objects related to self as patterns. Child is developing concepts related to what he physically knows and experiences	Sees features of people, their actions, and objects. Sees objects, people, and their actions as part of events, provided the child has the language names for these items. Easily sees stick figures on black-and-white pictures that relate to the child. Pictures must show the whole child and the objects related to the whole child so child is able to put himself into the pictures	Names for people, their actions, and their objects within events related to self – simple sentences related to content of the child's environment. Child's language reflects living in the present with the world revolving around the child

---

[22] See Arwood, E., Kaulitz, C., & Brown, M. (2009). *Visual thinking strategies for individuals with autism spectrum disorders: The language of pictures* for a more complete description of the developmental levels of visuals.

Table 9.3. *Continued*

COGNITIVE STAGE	THINKING	SEEING	LANGUAGE
Concrete Stage Neurotypical age: 7-11 Any time a person or child is able to think about others outside of the person's or child's own needs … rule-governed, fitting into society	Thinks about others and self as "we" interacting together according to rules	Sees the content of pictures or photographs with language or 3D	Language is conversational and person is able to follow the flow of others' comments and then add to those comments with new language
Formal Stage Neurotypical age: 11 plus	Thinks about concepts with ideas that symbolize, such as the ability to think about ideas that cannot be seen, touch, or felt, such as "liberty," "freedom," "government," "love," "justice,"…	Sees whatever the person has language for – is able to think about the whole, not just the parts of a visual graphic	Language shows that the person is able to step into the shoes of someone else and think as if the person is another person

Note that in *Table 9.3* a child must be able to think with enough language to be at a concrete level of thinking to be able to use a three-dimensional photograph for learning new concepts. At a concrete level of thinking, a child is able to use language to maintain a conversation. In other words, all materials have a language and thinking level. Photographs require a lot of language to be able to see the meaning of what is in a photograph. Language provides the third dimension of being able to see. So showing a child a picture of what the adult has language for does not mean the child sees what the adult sees in the picture. The visuals must meet the developmental thinking needs of the child to be usable for learning to think at a higher level. So, materials and methods must be at the level of thinking for children to learn concepts. Social concepts such as being an agent in one's own picture is actually an easier level of thinking than learning to memorize social skills based on rules. Rules are at a concrete level. Rules include what others know in relationship to what a child does. The child must have the language for thinking and doing to follow a rule. For example, a child is able to learn a variety of ways to meet someone easier than a child is able to learn the rules for when to greet someone. By giving a child a variety of ways to meet someone, the child is learning the social concept about what to do when the child sees another agent. Rules for greeting has too many variations such as when to say hello, what to say to someone you know or don't know or have seen recently or not, what to expect the other to say, and so forth. There are too many rules and it is developmentally too challenging for a person to learn all of the rules necessary to pro-socially think.

Ideally, thinking with social concepts begins at the preoperational level. Put the person in his or her picture with a variety of ways to see the world. *Figures 9.8-9.10b* show an example of how to help a child learn appropriate behavior through learning the language that goes with the social rules about what to wear. Notice that there is a lot of language that overlaps the thinking and the concepts (drawings) about the thinking so as to create more meaning for the child.

Figure 9.8. *Simple because language for choice.*

Figure 9.9. *More complex language for learning the social rules for selecting clothes.*

You wear your holey and/or stained clothes when you are playing with the dog, rolling or falling on the grass, digging in the sand or mud, or when you are climbing the play structure or the trees in the back yard.

You wear old pants and shirts (the ones with the holes and stains) when you play in a way that could tear or make your clothes dirty, so you do not ruin your new, nice looking clothes.

You wear your fancy dresses—the ones with bows, lace or ruffles—or your fancy, new tops and pants, when you go to parties, to church, to recitals or to appointments since you will be with others who are dressed up and you will be sitting or playing quietly, so your clothes will stay nice and clean.

You wear your new, fancy looking clothes for celebrations and special occasions like birthdays, holidays, weddings and funerals, where it is important to look clean and tidy because you want the other people at these special events to feel comfortable and to enjoy being around you.

Figure 9.10a. Learning how others think about what clothes are selected.

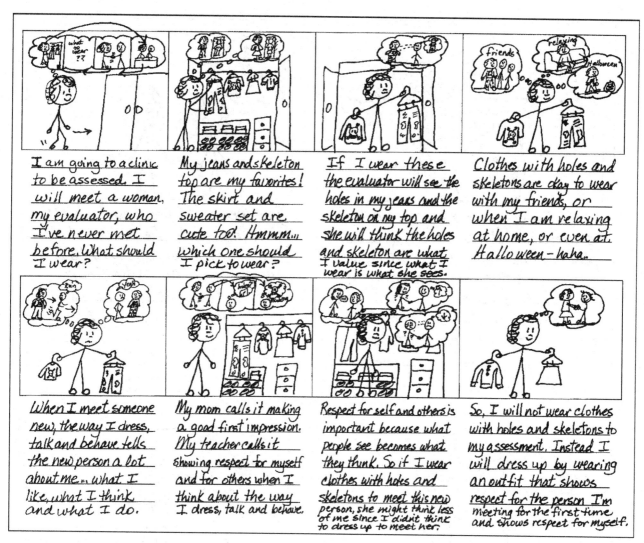

Figure 9.10b. *Learning how to see society's expectations for rules about what clothes to wear.*

Each of *Figures 9.8 to 9.10b* show a progressively higher level of language needed to learn to think with more progressively complex social concepts.

Activity: How does learning the language that goes with the social behavior help a child learn to behave?

Understand or Not Understand. Whether or not a child is able to understand depends on the child's ability to take the adult's point of view. *Table 9.4* shows the levels of thinking that allow us to understand what others think.

Table 9.4. *Different Perspectives about Understanding*

THINKING	THINKING ABOUT SELF IN RELATIONSHIP TO OTHERS	EXAMPLES
Pieces of ideas: Sensori-motor	Hands, eyes, mouths, feet, toes	Poke, tickle, hit, kick, spit
Agents, actions, objects related to self: Preoperational	I see others – they affect me	She made me mad; Those hands picked up the TV; I am not bad. I did not steal the TV
Others and me in relationship to each other: Concrete	We are together on a task according to the rules	I took the TV but I did not know it belonged to somebody else; I was speeding and so I got a ticket
Thinks about the good of society: Formal	Symbolizes ideas that cannot be seen, touched, felt	Stealing affects everyone in society, it robs people of their safety as well as their property

From the examples in *Table 9.4*, it is evident that most children who have behavior problems are functioning at the first two levels of thinking: sensori-motor or preoperational. This means that most students who are eligible for behavior supports or services in special education do not have a concrete level of thinking or language to be able to understand the rules. Therefore, it is better to increase language learning through increased thinking than to teach the parts or skills of behavior or rules for social behavior. Learning to think conceptually allows a person to make better behavior choices, which functions as both a preventive and an intervention measure given that better thinking is necessary for better behavior.

Activity: How does an individual understand another's perspective?

Problem Solve or Not Problem Solve. Probably the greatest mysteries for those with ASD and related social disorders include: multi-tasking, taking others' perspectives, and simultaneously prioritizing concerns so as to problem solve. People with ASD often do not see themselves in a social setting because they have not developed agency at a conceptual level of seeing themselves in relationship to what others do and think. Therefore, in making decisions that involve what others think or do is very difficult. Since most multi-tasking and prioritizing involve others' thinking, people with ASD often struggle with the decision making in those situations. For example, deciding to attend a 5:00 p.m. reception is either "Yes, I will" or "No, I won't." But that really isn't "a problem." The problem comes as a result of numerous decisions that need to be made quickly regarding the reception: Do I have anything that is appropriate in my suitcase to wear? What is the dress code? Where is the reception? How long will it take me to get from my 4:00 presentation that is over at 4:30 to the reception? Will there be food at the reception? I usually eat around 5:00 – will the food make up my dinner? If I go to the reception and want to eat, will there be some place to sit so I don't have to stand

and eat? Will there be enough to eat? Will I want to leave and go get dinner? Who will be there? When I walk into the reception who will I see? Will I recognize those people? Will I have to sit some place? I only want to go if I can sit by someone I will recognize. Who wants to sit by me? Does the reception begin at 5:00 or should I be there at 5:00? Will they serve food at 5:00? Are you asking only me, or will there be others? How many people? What type of food will there be?

If the reader is "tired" of all of the questions, think about this: The authors actually listened to an adult diagnosed with autism go through these questions in response to being invited to a reception. And there were more questions. The invitee did show up at the reception and immediately began the "out loud" questions to work through the process of what to do. He expected others to answer the questions but he also did not wait for answers to many of the questions leaving the listeners somewhat perplexed by what he wanted from them. The questions were ways to use his mouth to "motor" through the shapes of pictures to connect his behavior to the event. He almost immediately obtained a plate of food and went to one of the cocktail tables where people were inviting him to stand. He had lots of invites as he was the keynote speaker at the conference. Then he began to talk his way through what he was doing at the reception. "I decided to come. One has to eat, so I am here. There is lots of food, so I am eating. This is like my dinner. Another plate makes this dinner. This is like dinner. I eat to nourish my body. Everybody has to eat. So I thought I would come to the reception. The reception is nice. Lots of people. Who is here?"

This person did not connect the publishers as the hosts to the fact that he is an author and wrote for the sponsoring publishers, which is why he was invited to the reception. As soon as he had eaten his second plate of food, he left. There was no social chitchat or discussion about current affairs in autism or about his presentation even though the other people at the cocktail table tried to engage him in that type of discussion. The reception presented too many social decisions that he had to make while he was "doing the reception," which taxed his thinking about anything else. Developmentally, he was able to create enough language through his talking and others responding to create a successful situation, but his functioning at this social gathering was at the preoperational level. That is, he was dependent on others to create a reception for him. He did not "do" the reception as someone who contributes to helping all attendees fit into the reception.

Activity: Why did this presenter have difficulty socially conversing with others at the reception?

Case Study

Problem solving occurs over time and requires the use of lots of concepts with language to be able to prioritize, make decisions, and solve problems. The following case study highlights the issues presented in this chapter and provides suggestions to help develop problem-solving conceptualization.

1. **Provide numerous solutions as choices to all behavior situations from the time a child is an infant.** This suggestion underscores the need to provide lots of language about everyday situations in the way a child learns concepts. Katie is a 9-year-old diagnosed with ASD. On the morning of her language assessment, she changed her outfit nine times before her parents could get her out of the motel to the authors' clinic. The parents called the clinic to say they were

going to be late. It was suggested that the parents draw out the event like a cartoon so that Katie could see herself in the picture doing what was expected along with the written words. In this way, Katie would be receiving information about the situation, which would help Katie make solutions to her problems. The parents felt that they could get Katie to the clinic without doing the drawing. They arrived 2-1/2 hours late. Katie could not make the decisions, and all clothes were options. To help remove some of the clothes from options, the parents needed to provide only two choices and a cartoon of what Katie would think when she made a selection with the words written below: "I am selecting this outfit to wear because _____." See *Figures 9.9-10b.*

2. **Provide choices through the "because language."** For Katie, the "because language" might be: "I am selecting this outfit because it is purple and purple is my favorite color." By seeing what she knows and by being in the picture, Katie is learning to think (make sure there are thought bubbles) about making choices. See *Figure 9.10* as an example of how Katie is helped making choices about what she wears and why she wears the clothes she picks. Once she has mental pictures or concepts for her clothes choice, she will do better at making a choice in the future.

3. **Be detailed in explaining what the child sees and does.** Tell the child specific ways he can use his voice, eyes, face, hands, arms, body, legs, and feet. Give three to five logical reasons for using the specific behaviors. See *Figure 9.11* for an example of the details that go into thinking to learn to behave.

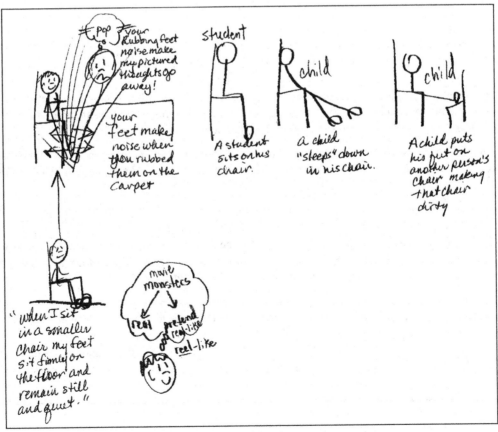

Figure 9.11. A child learns to sit and to look like a learner.

The child in *Figure 9.11* needs the information about his body to make a picture of what he looks like so that he can see himself as an agent sitting as a learner. With sufficient language, he is able to act like a learner. The language for these drawings is sometimes quite extensive. *Figure 9.12* provides an example of oral language for Karen, a 10-year-old.

Karen, because you are a learner, you will use your body to help you think and learn.

Karen, you will use your hand to hold the pencil so you can draw the ideas you think about. Then, Karen, you will use your hand to write about your drawn ideas. Karen, when you use your hand to write and draw with the pencil, you will remember the ideas you saw, thought, and drew.

Karen, you will use your hand to give your finished work (turn in) to the teacher, so the teacher can see Karen's, your work and find out what you, Karen, knows, so the teacher can give you, Karen, a grade on your work.

Here are some more rules about how you will use your body to help you learn:

Karen will use her hand to get the teacher's attention. Karen will put her hand in the air (raise her hand) when she needs help from the teacher. Karen will raise her hand to ask the teacher questions about her work. Karen will put her hand in the air to ask if she can use the bathroom. Karen will put her hand in the air to answer the teacher's questions.

Karen will use her eyes to see what the people in the classroom say. When the teacher is talking, Karen will watch the teacher's mouth move and make a picture in her head of what she sees her saying.

Karen will use her eyes to watch the teacher's hand draw and write so that Karen can think the meaning of what she sees. Karen will use her eyes to see what most of the other students are doing with their bodies (eyes, hands, and feet) so that Karen can make her body do the same activities that the other kids are doing.

Karen will make her body ready to learn. Karen will put her bottom flat on the seat of the chair; Karen will put her feet flat on the floor; Karen will rest her back flat against the back of the chair; and Karen will put her hands down on the table top. When Karen's body is in her chair, she will be ready to see what is said, so she can think the pictures of what she sees.

Karen will use the sound that comes out of her mouth (her voice) for talking to another person. Karen will use her soft, quiet inside voice when she is inside the classroom, the hallways, the library, the cafeteria and the bathroom. Karen can use her louder, outside voice when she is out on the playground playing. When Karen is watching someone and sees that person's mouth moving, that means that person is using his/her voice. When Karen sees a person using his/her voice, Karen will keep her mouth closed so that her words do not fall out of mouth at the same time as the other person who is speaking. Karen can use her voice to speak when the other person's mouth stops moving.

Karen will use her face to show what she is thinking. Karen will turn up the corners of her mouth to show that she is happy, friendly, and learning. Karen will look to see how her face moves to match the meaning of what she thinks and feels.

Karen will use her feet for walking to the gym, cafeteria, and recess. Karen will use her feet to stand on when in line to leave the classroom. Karen will use her feet to for running and walking while playing. When Karen is working on her classroom assignments, Karen will keep her feet flat on the floor so they are quiet. Moving feet make noise and noise makes the pictures in the head go away! So Karen will keep her feet quiet while working in the classroom so that her classmates can keep their pictures in their heads so they can see, think, draw and write.

Karen will use her toes inside her shoes to help her think. Karen can wiggle her toes, when her feet are resting flat on the floor, to help her head pictures move so that she can think. Karen will use her fingers to help her learn. Fingers are for holding pencils, for turning pages in a book, for picking up work papers, for handing in papers, for handing out papers, for hanging up coats, for eating lunch. While seated in her chair listening to the teacher talk, Karen can wriggle her fingers to help her think. Karen will make sure that her finger wriggles are quiet so that the people sitting by her can think.

Figure 9.12a. Learn how to use one's body through the use of language.

4. Use the constituents of who, what, where, when, why, and how with all events (school academic, social, behavioral, and at home) to help develop thinking concepts with functional language, not skills.

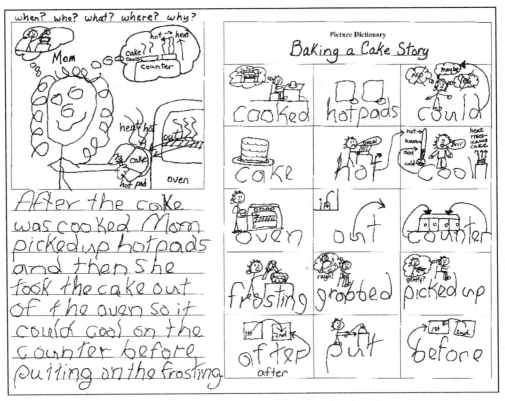

Figure 9.12b. An example of Kelly thinking about baking a cake.

Educators as well as parents fear confronting children like Nicholas, Katie, Karen, and Kelly. What educators and parents need to realize is that children will not shut down or melt down when they can mentally see or understand what their choices are and then are able to put themselves into the pictures with other people. Given the language through writing and drawing, these children are literally able to see how to do the tasks. And, learning to think helps the children become pro-social agents.

Activity: How does language help individuals learn to think about how to behave?

5. Translate the world from a sound-based spoken explanation into a visual world that is explained through the movement of the mouth, the hand (writing), and the seen concepts of drawings. Most people learn how to behave from being told about the world. For individuals with ASD, the world must be translated into what is seen and written. Individuals with ASD must see the edges of the movement of what people, their actions, and their events mean. That is why writing is so important. Individuals with ASD cannot see their own movements in a role play, but they can see what others do when the written words are attached to those movements. The written words do not change shapes or meanings and therefore provide consistent meaning to develop the concepts. *Figures 9.13a-c* show written sessions with Katie and an educator.

Limited sound (oral language) is used as they write back and forth to allow Katie to create the visual language of her thoughts through the written language. In this way, Katie's mental pictures develop the language or name of what Katie sees. She is able to understand and problem solve with enough visual language.

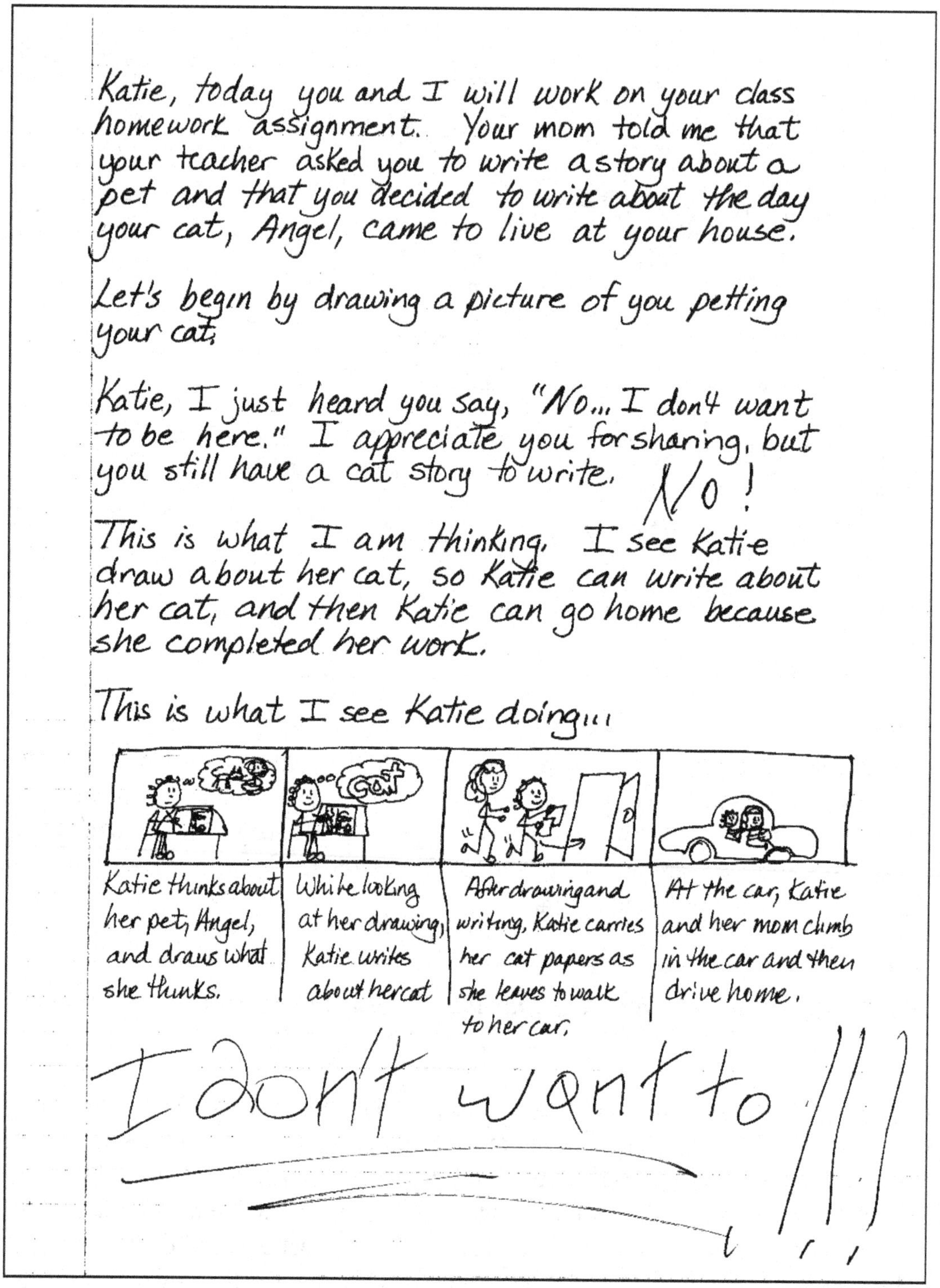

Katie, today you and I will work on your class homework assignment. Your mom told me that your teacher asked you to write a story about a pet and that you decided to write about the day your cat, Angel, came to live at your house.

Let's begin by drawing a picture of you petting your cat.

Katie, I just heard you say, "No... I don't want to be here." I appreciate you for sharing, but you still have a cat story to write.

No!

This is what I am thinking. I see Katie draw about her cat, so Katie can write about her cat, and then Katie can go home because she completed her work.

This is what I see Katie doing...

I don't want to!!!

Figure 9.13a. *Katie is learning how to behave.*

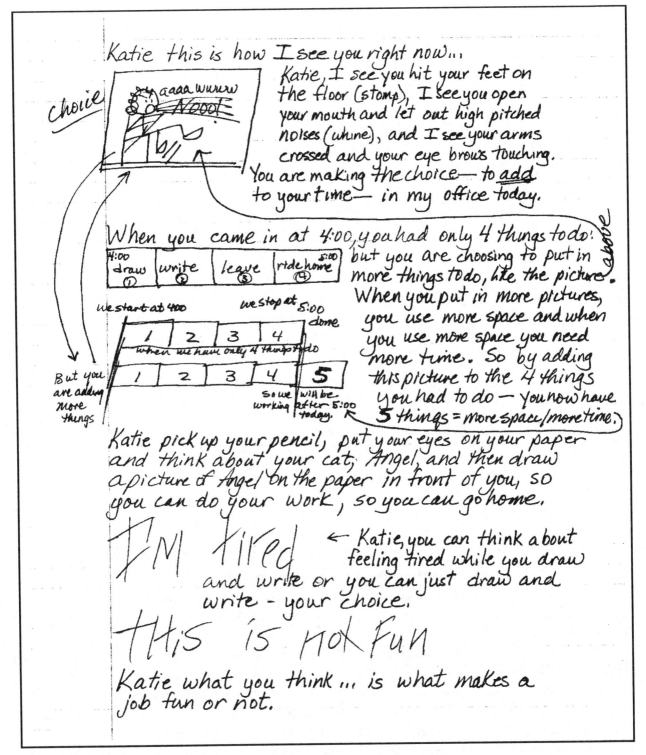

Katie this is how I see you right now...

choice

Katie, I see you hit your feet on the floor (stomp), I see you open your mouth and let out high pitched noises (whine), and I see your arms crossed and your eye brows touching. You are making the choice — to **add** to your time — in my office today.

When you came in at 4:00, you had only 4 things to do:

4:00 draw ①	write ②	leave ③	ride home ④ 5:00

but you are choosing to put in more things to do, like the picture. When you put in more pictures, you use more space and when you use more space you need more time. So by adding this picture to the 4 things you had to do — you now have 5 things = more space/more time.

we start at 4:00   we stop at 5:00 done

1	2	3	4

when we have only 4 things to do

But you are adding more things

1	2	3	4	5

So we will be working after 5:00 today.

Katie pick up your pencil, put your eyes on your paper and think about your cat, Angel, and then draw a picture of Angel on the paper in front of you, so you can do your work, so you can go home.

I'M Tired   ← Katie, you can think about feeling tired while you draw and write or you can just draw and write - your choice.

THIS IS NOT FUN

Katie what you think ... is what makes a job fun or not.

Figure 9.13b. Katie matches her behavior with her written language.

Figure 9.13c. *Katie learns to match her behavior, with her feelings, with her thinking.*

Activity: How does Katie learn to problem solve?

Summary

Behavior is as developmentally appropriate as society deems. To "fit into" society, children and adults need to learn the rules for behavior as social concepts, not skills. In this way, they possess the language necessary for thinking and the requisite thinking to form the language for helping them behave. To assign developmentally appropriate meaning to a child's behavior, the adults in the child's environment must be able to see the child's behavior as separate from the child; evaluate the child's behavior as society would think (not as the adult thinks); set limits (create rules) for desired behavior based on healthy boundaries; and use logic in "seeing" natural consequences for behavior. The adults must translate the sound-based culture into a visual-motor set of concepts for decision making and problem solving for children with ASD and related disorders.

Important Concepts in *Chapter Ten*

Readers should be able to explain each of these behavior principles upon completion of this chapter:

1. The brain learns to see how to behave.

2. The brain learns to think for making choices and decisions.

3. The brain only sees and hears patterns.

4. The brain learns language as a tool for thinking.

5. The brain learns concepts or thinking.

6. The brain knows only what it is able to process.

7. The brain requires novel stimulation.

8. The brain learns more than simple input and output.

9. The brain learns to be literate through the acquisition of meaning.

10. The brain learns ideas (concepts) as basis for literacy and problem solving.

CHAPTER TEN
Neuroeducation and Behavior

The brain sees everything I know.
But the eye only sees the patterns.
To see what I know,
I need to be able to learn what I see.

Viewing behavior as a set of skills, separate from the human learning system, provides an objective approach to teaching somebody to respond, imitate, and practice input. Inputs are simple at first; a verbal or nonverbal cue results in a change in behavior. But over time, the human brain recognizes more and more inputs from the past, and the complexity of processing the input increases. With an increase in processing complexity, the human is able to do more than respond to others' inputs. With increased complexity, the brain begins to overlap simple patterns into complex circuits that create networks. Such circuits allow for concepts to layer in complexity to form networks; and, the networks allow for complex patterns of language to name the concepts. Learning to think or conceptualize formulates the mind which parallels the way the brain functions. The brain literally learns to think.

As the brain learns to think, more complex ways for the learner to perceive the world also emerges. Simple inputs become more than a set of skills. Complex processing of overlapped and recognized past input results in higher thinking or concept development and language function. This chapter will provide the reader with a translation of the neuroscience of the brain into a neuroeducational understanding of behavior. Understanding that the brain is responsible for learning to think and to behave helps educators and parents develop methods that parallel how the brain functions for more effective strategies to promoting pro-social development for all learners.

Neuroscience and Learning

This section will translate the neuroscience of how the human brain processes sensory input to illustrate how we learn to behave. The only way a human can learn is being able to receive the various sensory inputs or stimuli. The early inputs do not consist of words, pictures, or objects. Instead, they are in the form of sensory particles – pieces of the sound wave, pieces of the electromagnetic light wave, and so forth.[23] Therefore, when they are first born, infants do not hear words or see people. Infants must learn the meaning of what they see and hear.

---

[23] This chapter will focus on the eyes and ears since these are the distance senses used by humans to communicate with others. The other senses integrate with sight and sound but are not capable of forming units that can be communicated across time and space. In other words, smell, taste, and touch create meaning but only for the person who is close enough to smell (like some children who smell others) or taste (biting) or touch (like scratching).

Activity: Are babies born able to hear words and see people?

At the beginning of the learning process, a neurotypical baby's eyes and ears are able to see light and hear sound. But, light does not make people and pictures visible; and sound does not make words understandable. Sensory input is the first stage toward developing the learning system[24]. This first stage in learning is simply the reception of light particles by the eye and/or reception of pieces of the sound wave by the ear (Arwood, 2011). Thus, it simply consists of the physical ability of the eyes and ears to see and hear.

Activity: What is the first stage in developing the learning system?

Senses. The receptor organs, eyes and ears, pass the signals via cranial nerves through multiple layers of cellular structures that compete for recognition of past and present incoming input. These layers of cellular structures are located in the sub-cortical regions of the central nervous system (brain and spinal cord). The outcome of these messages is in the form of patterns: patterns recognized as sensory input. These sensory patterns of input make up the second level of the neurosemantic language learning system (Arwood, 2011). These patterns consist of the properties of vision or hearing.

Activity: What is the second stage in developing the learning system?

When the neurobiological structures are able to recognize the sensory input as patterns, the human body responds. To sound, the child turns his head. To light, the child's eyes focus. These patterns continue to overlap to form more meaningful responses. Thus, the child's eyes see "shininess," and the child's hand reaches for what the child sees. At this second stage of learning, the child does not know that the shininess is part of the properties of the object that belongs to Mom or that the object is named an earring. The child also does not know that what attracted the child is called "shininess."

With more overlap of sensory patterns, the child becomes able to imitate the sounds and sights modeled for the child. By 18 months of age, most children show even a walking pattern that is similar to that of their parents. Later, the child's parent crosses her legs and the two-year-old will try to do the same (Garfinkle & Schwartz, 2002). Speech patterns are imitated and refined by the same imitation and practice of tasks. The parent says, "Do you want some juice?" and the child says, "Juice?" Patterns for speech or for matching movements are typically easy for children to imitate. Such imitation is not based on thinking.

---

[24] The learning system was introduced in *Chapter Two*. This is a more complete explanation of the learning system as it pertains to behavior.

Activity: What is the second level of learning like?

Methods that directly teach these patterns provide children with clear and specific models for imitation. Once the child is able to produce a specific pattern, it is important to repeat or practice the pattern. The repetition keeps the input being rehearsed for continued output of patterns. If the patterns are not repeated frequently, then the patterns will be dumped from the processing system of the sub-cortical part of the pattern. Only retained motor patterns such as used for muscle memory to ride a bike can be retained for long periods of time. This is why educational tasks that are rote memory types of input to output are quickly forgotten during weekends or time away from school. It should be noted that patterns are easy to teach because the brain only uses patterns.

```
┌ ─ ─ ─ ─ ─ ─ ─ ─ ─ ─ ─ ─ ─ ─ ─ ─ ─ ─ ─ ─ ─ ─ ─ ─ ─ ─ ─ ─ ─ ┐
                    The brain only uses patterns!
└ ─ ─ ─ ─ ─ ─ ─ ─ ─ ─ ─ ─ ─ ─ ─ ─ ─ ─ ─ ─ ─ ─ ─ ─ ─ ─ ─ ─ ─ ┘
```

That is correct! The brain only uses patterns. This means that educational programs, materials, and voices are all patterns to the human brain. And the brain wants patterns.

Activity: What does the human brain process?

Patterns. Because the brain only uses patterns, imitation of modeled patterns is additive. That is, more sensory input results in more and more patterns. The output is always a form of behavior. Educational programs that rely on teaching the output as the targets of controlled stimuli or cues through methods of direct modeling, imitation, rote learning, practicing, and repeating are relying on the basic patterns of learning – input becomes output associated through rewards that are reinforced. If a learner is not able to do anything more with these simple patterns, the learner grows bigger and the patterns continue to dominate. Such patterns might include moving the arms and feet through space, much like a six-week-old baby does during diaper changing. But, when a 12 year-old produces these same movements, these behaviors are interpreted as hitting and kicking. Patterns can also include touching and tasting, also known as pushing and biting.

When a child produces patterns without the underlying thinking, there is no intentionality and no agency. For example, the movements of a 12-year-old with severe autism who has no verbal (vocal or non-vocal) language system are random outputs to input. The behavior has limited, if any, conceptual meaning. Sometimes the 12-year-old sits when she is fed, but as soon as the feeding stops, she stands up, and her body falls through space, meaning that she is on her tip toes as if horizontal to the wall. She is moving through space to reach another stopping point without thinking.

Activity: Does the imitation of patterns require thinking?

Continuing to teach imitated patterns maintains the lowest level of learning – imitation. Remember, patterns emerge as the result of sensory input. Therefore, this level of learning does not require thinking. For example, teaching a child with severe autism to sit down on a verbal or nonverbal cue tells the child nothing about why she is sitting, what she is to do while she is sitting, how to think about sitting, when to stand after sitting, why her parents or educators want her to sit, and so on. And, the same methods "to get the child to sit" do not help the child learn to think. These are the same methods used with animals (Grandin & Johnson, 2005). In fact, those who train animals have to teach a "release cue" so that a dog knows when no longer to sit.

The truth is that children sit so that they can make mental pictures of what they are hearing, seeing, doing, and so on. Children sit so they can think about something they are doing that they can't do when they are standing, running, walking, and so forth. But this type of complex learning is beyond the pattern level of learning. Thinking requires the acquisition of concepts.

Activity: Do simple methods of imitation provide thinking? Why or why not?

Concepts. Learning to think is more than repeating imitated patterns. In the neurological pathways, the patterns continue to overlap through a complex system of inhibiting past messages (patterns) while integrating new messages (patterns) to create circuits of function. These circuits connect the outermost part of the brain or cerebral cortex to the lower levels of memory and recognition. It is in these circuits that the information from the sensory systems becomes complex messages. For example, looking at a word on a page may activate several parts of the brain, whereas saying the name of the word activates more parts of the cortex, and drawing the object of the word on the page requires even more parts of the brain to be activated. With each different activity, the brain learns more.

Such complexity is far beyond simple imitation. Such complexity demonstrates the brain's flexibility[25] and allows for increased learning or productivity[26] by the brain for higher thinking and problem solving. With an increase of complexity of the brain, behavior also increases. Instead of simple imitation, the learner is able to think about choices of behavior for responding to input.

Activity: What is conceptualization? How do concepts help a person think about behavior?

---

[25] Note that flexibility is one of the linguistic principles (displacement, productivity, efficiency, semanticity) of the language system previously discussed in *Chapter Eight*.
[26] See *Chapter Eight*.

Figure 10.1 (also *Figure 2.1*) shows a graphic of the learning system for a neurotypical learner.

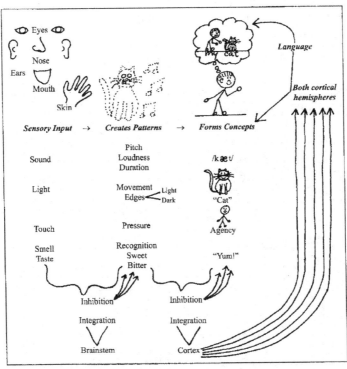

Figure 10.1. *Neurotypical learning system.* From Arwood, E., & Kaulitz, C. (2007). *Learning with a visual brain in an auditory world*, p. 22. Shawnee Mission, KS: AAPC Publishing. Used with permission.

As illustrated in *Figure 10.1*, there are four levels within the learning system: sensory input (1st) forms patterns (2nd), patterns form concepts (3rd), and language represents the concepts (4th). Structures of language match the patterns of the world around us. For example, children who hear speakers of English learn English patterns or structures. But the conceptualization behind language is language function or thinking. Learning to think allows a person to behave according to the thinking. **So behavior is as good as a person is able to think and represent thinking with language.**

With children who have compromised or neuro-atypical learning systems, there may be a breakdown in the learning at any of the four levels. For children diagnosed with ASD and related disorders, the primary breakdown happens in the conversion of patterns to concepts. As a result, they are capable of taking in sensory input[27] to form patterns. Patterns continue to increase. But if the patterns do not form concepts, they have to create new patterns as a way to stimulate the learning system.

Educators and parents typically see this creation of new patterns as "self-stimulation." For example, the child flaps his hands in front of his eyes so the eyes see different visual inputs over and over or the child engages in maintaining the input of patterns. To neurotypical adults, this is repetitive behavior. To the learner, this behavior creates new patterns over and over. The patterns keep coming in and keeping the lower brain activated. In this way, the learning system stays awake, but the patterns are not creating neuronal circuits that form concepts. If concepts were being formed, the child would

---

[27] Some people show co-morbidity with sensory impairment, such as being deaf and having autism.

be using concepts, not patterns of behavior. The child would be thinking, "I've seen this toy already, I need a new toy." Unless the child is able to convert the patterns into the concept of an object, "toy," the child's brain will continue to see the spinning of the object as new patterns over and over. In other words, the patterns appear new each time so they are never seen as old and, therefore, converted to concepts. *The brain loves new patterns, so the repetitive behavior continues.*

Figure 10.2 (also *Figure 2.2*) shows what happens when the neurosemantic learning system cannot easily convert patterns into thoughts or concepts.

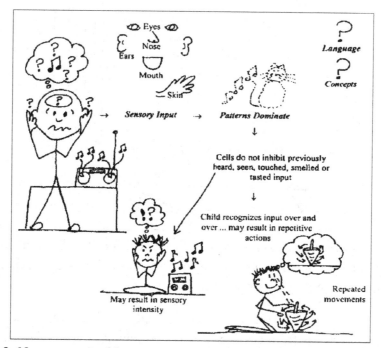

Figure 10.2. *Neuro-atypical learning system of a child with ASD.* From Arwood, E., & Kaulitz, C. (2007). *Learning with a visual brain in an auditory world*, p. 24. Shawnee Mission, KS: AAPC Publishing. Used with permission.

Activity: What does self-stimulating behavior provide a child's learning system?

Language. When the learner's patterns convert into thoughts about people, their actions, and their objects (earliest concepts), the learner begins to name the thoughts or concepts with language. Language is the tool used to represent thinking. Language is a form of verbal behavior, but underlying those words, sentences, nouns, verbs, and so on, is a brain that finds meaning out of the overlapping and layering of concepts or ideas. Just like an educator can teach a child to imitate the act or behavior of sitting, an educator can teach a child to imitate word patterns. Some children with ASD are able to imitate verbatim long sets of patterns such as the national anthem, a TV commercial, a poem heard once, the call of an ice hockey game, every dinosaur label in the dictionary or on the internet, dialogues, paragraphs read from a Harry Potter book, and so forth. These imitations are simple outputs. The outputs are patterns, not concepts. Therefore, there is little thinking underlying these imitated patterns.

Activity: What does language represent?

These imitations of patterns often confuse educators and parents. On one hand, their students are doing well on academic requirements, worksheets, written and spoken patterns, speaking patterns. On the other hand, the same students show behavior that is socially immature and lacks sufficient problem solving to be able to stay alone or live independently. When there are a lot of imitated or borrowed patterns, the learner is not using language as a representation of thinking. The learner's thinking may be at a considerable lower level than what might be expected for a person who reads, writes, and talks a lot. The quantity of surface patterns used for word calling print on a page or for speaking lots of borrowed phrases in pace of functional natural language represents restricted thinking.

Activity: Why do patterns sometimes look meaningful?

```
The brain creates thinking.
```

Thinking cannot occur through simple sets of patterns arranged to form greater skill sets. Arranging skill sets into a hierarchy of patterns is just that – more patterns. If the goal of intervention is for the learner to provide more patterns, then methods designed to arrange patterns of imitation and copying into greater skill sets work. If the purpose of the learning is to create better thinking for problem solving and learning the depth of concepts, then methods must provide opportunities for individuals to learn concepts. Conceptual methods capitalize on what is known about the neurosemantic language learning system (Arwood, 2011). The likelihood of success for better thinking and literacy increases with an increase of concept development. The following section presents methods that are grounded in knowledge about the neuroscience of learning.

Neuroeducational Methods for to Improve Pro-Social Behavior

Children, diagnosed with severe autism and related social communication disorders, often show behavior that is based on pattern thinking; but their brains do turn the patterns into conceptual thinking. Therefore, their behavior is often randomly based on sensory input – smells, tastes, touches, sounds, and sights. They smell ears, taste people's skin, stretch another person's skin over the person's neck, pick up tiny bits of debris as they walk along, fall through space, self-stimulate when there is nothing new to see, pick at their fingers, chew on their digits, bang their heads, rock back and forth, spin objects, and so forth. Their behavior is simply a representation of how well they learn patterns. Even higher functioning individuals with social communication disorders will spew rules, talk about non-social debris such as why the light is on while everyone else is talking about their activities over the weekend, or calculate many mathematical problems without being able to explain why they calculate the problem a specific way.

All of these behaviors tell us that these individuals learn patterns well. When patterns can be turned into concepts, the concepts form both social and cognitive or academic knowledge. With only pattern thinking, a learner may exhibit these types of restricted thinking examples: They do not know that pulling skin hurts themselves or others. They do not know that the differences in visual patterns along the walkway are really plants with flowers. They do not know that it is impolite to put one's body so close to another person's ear so as to smell the wax in his ear. They may not know that doing tasks the way the learner wants to do it is not always a pro-social way to interact or consider others; and, the list goes on. At the pattern level of learning, the child learns from moving the child's body in response to sensory input. Such movements must be meaningful or the child's brain would disengage. Brains under repetition of similar stimulation disengage (Bookheimer 2004).

```
The brain needs novel stimulation!
```

Children with ASD repeat a lot of patterns over and over as if the patterns are new. The question for the educator is: How can the patterns be turned into concepts?

The majority of learners use sight and/or sound to create concepts, but sight and sound inputs do not work for those who are restricted in one or more of the developmental domains: language, thinking (cognitive concepts), socialization (social concepts), motor movements (muscle development and movement), and physical development.

What other neurosemantic options are there? In addition to seeing another person or hearing another person to learn what the world means, a learner's neurosemantic system can make conceptual meanings from movements associated with the eye (Arwood, 2011; Arwood & Kaulitz, 2007). The eye moves to increase the space of patterns of light (Hubel, 1988). And such movements of the eye or hand or mouth create the outline or shape of what the eye sees (Arwood; Arwood & Kaulitz). For example, when a blind person uses his hands to move around the raised shapes of Braille, his visual cortices are activated (Sadato, 1996). Much like a Helen Keller phenomenon, the hand shaped around the edges of another hand creates visual thinking, shapes of objects, shapes of people, shapes of their actions, and so forth (Arwood & Kaulitz, 2007; Arwood, 2011; Grandin and Panek, 2013).

```
The brain sees shapes through movements.
```

Activity: How does the movement of the hand and/or mouth create concepts?

Create Shapes. The notion of concepts being shapes rather than words, sounds, or photographs helps create effective methods such as bubbling words. *Figure 10.3* shows a picture dictionary example of bubbling words related to complex behavior such as "being trustworthy."

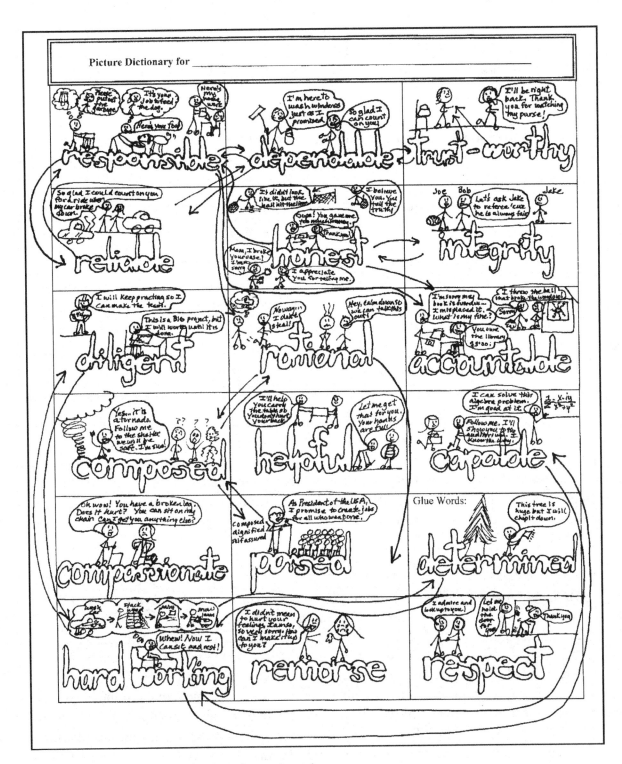

Figure 10.3. *Seeing the shapes of complex ideas.*

In previous chapters, the reader was encouraged to use hand-over-hand (HoH) methods to create shapes for learning to think about choices for agency and empowerment toward pro-social development. Taking the child's hand and writing hand-over-hand creates shapes, the shape of the movement to make configurations, similar to finger spelling hand-over-hand or watching the mouth creates shapes of ideas.

The brain only learns the way that the sensory system provides. If the child is not learning to comply with the sound of a voice telling the child what to do, and if the child is not learning to match the child's body to what the child sees others do, the child only has the shapes of the visual system by which to acquire thinking or concepts.

> ## The brain learns concepts through sensory input.

Activity: How do brains learn concepts?

We have, at least, five senses, but only two provide information from a distance – sight and sound. Thinking about ideas that are away from the body requires a distance sense. The movement of the eye provides the brain with the ability to scan the shape or outline of light reflecting off an object and the hand or mouth can create the same types of shapes.

> ## The brain creates meaning from sight and sound.

When light reflections do not provide the right type of patterns for forming concepts, as for children who are deaf, movement can be used to create the same visual shapes. Movement patterns of the hand and mouth will create shapes for learning to think just like light and sound patterns. And, as previously stated, individuals who struggle with social communication disorders are not using sound for learning to think. They are using visual concepts, made from the light bouncing off edges of planes to form dimensional sight or space and from the movement of the edges of those planes to see the dimensions of space.

Activity: How does a person learn to think about ideas when they do not use sound or sight?

Write. A child with ASD must have writing from day one. When a person writes in real time or as hand-over-hand movements, the learner is able to watch or feel the movement of the hand. In this way, the child is learning the shapes that are concepts. If parents or educators try to provide behavior "training" for a child with severe ASD or related disorders without providing the shapes of what the behaviors mean through the movement of writing and drawing, they have put that child into a state of learning deprivation. In other words, writing in real time so the child is able to see the movements as a mental shape creates meaning. In this way, educators and parents can use writing to assign meaning to behavior so that a child "learns" what sitting down is supposed to represent – sitting down represents what the child thinks about what he or she is doing. Knowledge about neuroscience about the hand and how the movement of the hand develops the brain is significant in learning (Arwood, 2010; Merzenich, Tallal, Peterson, Miller, & Jenkins, 1998; Merzenich et al., 1999) for providing opportunities for individuals who think outside the typical sight-and-sound way of teaching individuals to behave. The case study later in this chapter highlights the use of writing for learning to think.

> The brain sees patterns so writing can be visual.

Activity: Why should all behavior work with individuals with ASD show writing?

Make Ideas Visual. Many educators and parents realize that individuals with ASD are visual learners. But many do not understand how to maximize the benefits of visuals. Not all visuals are the same (Arwood, Kaulitz, &Brown, 2009) (also see *Chapters Eight and Nine* of this book), and just making input visual may not result in creating concepts. Hand-over-hand movements to outline the shapes of the pictures on a page helps a child with ASD see the shape of what others "see" on the page. Or hand-over-hand touching a face (for a person who is blind) is "seeing a face." Watching the face move helps a learner create shape concepts about what the face movements mean. Writing or moving and seeing helps a person with a visual brain learn in an auditory culture (Arwood & Kaulitz, 2007). Why these methods work is self-evident within the understanding of neuroscience. The following provides examples of the evidence for four applications of neuroscience to education:

1. *Seeing in 2-D.* The brain only sees in 2-D. If the reader thinks that the reader sees in 3-D, it is because the reader has developed language to assign meaning to all of the edges of the planes that the brain sees. Therefore, for learning new concepts, it is better to use a paper and pencil to draw stick figures. In this way, the input is simplified, provided that there is sufficient overlap of information, like a cartoon, to show that the 2-D people think, walk from one space to another, and so forth.

> The brain only sees in 2-D.

Activity: Does the brain see in 3-D? Why or why not?

Photographs and video clips are more difficult than line drawings or stick figures because there is more information in the background that requires more cognitive development. Likewise, pictures that lack the people and their actions are also more difficult because the brain must provide the language to fill in the missing people. Remember that all learning stems from the person as an agent. Also, people are identified by their actions. Therefore, a drawn object or a photograph of an object is more difficult to think about than a cartoon of a stick figure doing actions. The case study in this chapter will also highlight cartoons that are 2-D.

Activity: Why are cartoons easier to understand than photographs?

---

2. *Seeing contrasts.* The brain sees black on white as the easiest contrast. Therefore, using pencils on white paper creates easier meaning for the learner to decipher than using crayons, colored

pencils, and so forth. Adding color to categorize items by function such as circling all people with a blue pencil or writing all names of people in blue adds meaning, but drawing pictures in colors adds more dimensions for the brain to interpret and therefore, complicates the process.

> The brain sees black and white as easiest contrast of light.

Activity: Why is a pencil and paper easier to see than a digital photograph?

---

3. *Seeing across quadrants.* The brain sees four quadrants at the same time; two quadrants above eye level and two below eye level. Each of these is divided in half, by the right eye seeing half of each side and the left eye seeing half of each side. This means that where the educator or parent puts the paper determines what the child may see. In fact, when ideas are broken into parts such as letters and the paper is put in front of the child, the child sees those letters differently in each of the quadrants. Without the sound of the meaning of the idea attached to what the child sees, the child cannot create the meaning from the parts. So a p letter is also a q and a b and a d, depending on where on the page the letter appears. Instead of using letters and sounds (an auditory task) use the shape of ideas to create meaning.

> The brain sees in four quadrants.

Activity: Why does the brain see four quadrants?

However shapes of ideas are like drawings; and, drawings create sufficient overlapped meaning, especially when the drawings cross quadrants with the same image such as a person. For example, cartoons overlap the same person doing a variety of concepts across quadrants allowing the brain to create overlapping patterns for concepts.

4. *Overlapping the concepts.* The pictures of a cartoon help create meaningful relationships (semantic relationships) across overlapping frames. The brain needs to create neural circuits for concepts to be available. It is thought that these circuits are a result of many overlapping and related intercellular patterns (e.g., Baars & Gage, 2010; Pulvermuller, 2003). This means that the child will learn more from using multiple overlapping pictures than single pictures. Furthermore, these concepts layer in depth for greater cognitive meaning overtime. The brain is arranged in networks of layered cellular structures.

> The brain needs related, overlapped patterns to create concepts. The concepts increase in meaning through layered networks within the brain.

Activity: How do cartoons help create the kind of meaning that will create concepts in the brain?

Seeing Ideas

People are ideas. These ideas or people are agents. Agents do activities. Therefore, seeing a person means that the learner must be able to see what the person does. But the brain only sees 2-D and, therefore, only sees the literal action. For example, a person who is walking is seen as shapes that move – the legs go up and down and the feet touch the floor one at a time. We do not see walking. "Walking" is the language that represents the concept of what we see. So use literal language to help a child overlap concepts or ideas for better thinking for pro-social development. In the following example, Char continues to talk when the teacher is talking. Char cannot see rules such as "Don't talk" or "Don't interrupt." But, Char can make mental pictures from visual language.

What Literal Language Sounds Like:

"Char, when you open your mouth, your words fall out. When your words fall out, your words cover my space. When your words cover my space, then my pictures go away because I only see your words. When my pictures go away, I cannot think. When I cannot think, I cannot do my work. When I cannot do my work, then I have to stay after the students go home to do my work. When I stay after the students leave so I can do my work, then I cannot pick up my daughter from her school. When I cannot pick up my daughter at her school by 5:00 or when the clock looks like this (draws clock), then the teacher at my daughter's school has to wait with my daughter. When my daughter's teacher waits with my daughter, then that teacher cannot go home to see her family. Her family is waiting at home, and when they do not see the teacher walk into their home when the clock looks like this or 5:30, then they begin to think that maybe she is hurt because she was in a car accident …(add as many layers as needed)

So for me to do my work so I can walk out of the school, climb into my car, drive to my daughter's school to pick up my daughter so that my daughter and I can drive home and walk into our home by 5:30, I want you to keep your lips closed so your mouth is shut so your words do not fall out of your mouth and fill my space and make my pictures go away.

Literal language creates the visual patterns of mentally seeing ideas in space, moving in space to create the concept of what an agent does. This type of language works well by itself for some. For others, it helps when this type of literal language is put with a cartoon that shows the pictures of the words, thus enabling the learner to see how the shapes of written shapes matched with the movements of the mouth. In this way, the educator or parent is providing the conceptual meaning (drawings) of the movement of the hand (writings) with the overlapped movement of the mouth (speaking), which helps create overlap of visual concepts from the shapes of the motor movements.

The brain sees overlapping visual-motor patterns to form visual ideas.

To be able to see people do things, the learner must have the language to interpret the brain's overlapping patterns. Language provides the interpretation of the patterns as concepts or thoughts. These thoughts or cognition represent the learning by the brain of the perceived and interpreted world. Behavior reflects what meaning a person has been able to interpret from learning about the world.

Activity: How does language represent thinking?

Learning Concepts. The brain creates overlapping visual-motor patterns to form the thinking about what the learner's world means. Other people assign meaning to what a learner does. With sufficient overlapped meaning, the learner is able to verbally and nonverbally represent meaning through gestures, acts, utterances, and so forth. For each behavior the learner produces, others assign meaning. Overlapping patterns that connect the learner with his world begin to overlap into concepts. The first concepts are about the child's own self, an agent who does something.

Eventually, around three years of age, a child is able to talk about the world in relationship to himself. The child is central to the child's thinking. This is the point at which all new concepts begin their journey of adding meaning over and over to form more complex conceptual meaning. For example, the complex concept of "respect" might mean nothing more than a rule said by a parent to a 3-year-old, "Mommy says to respect." But with more layers of meaning, the brain integrates past messages about "respect" with new inputs and the neuronal circuits become more complex connecting "respect" to other meanings such as "being kind," "considerate," "fair," and so forth. These layers of meaning are forming language networks in the brain.

Concepts cannot be taught, but educators and parents can set up opportunities for concepts to be acquired by assigning meaning to and interpreting behavior to create the overlap and layer of meanings. Trying to teach concepts like "respect" does not make sense given the notion that the brain learns these concepts through multiple varied experiences that occur across large amounts of time. However, providing multiple ways to use these concepts with assigned meaning through visual-motor explanations and graphics layered with other related concepts works. (See the case study later in this chapter for an example.). Over multiple experiences with similar content, a learner acquires the concepts of even the most difficult concepts like respect. This is why the authors really encourage the readers to use the same content to read, write, talk, refine the processes for improved content and then start the process all over again.

> The brain learns concepts.

Activity: How are concepts learned?

Use Relationships (Context). Most of the curricula schools in the United States follow a developmental framework; the child is expected to master grade one before grade two and so forth. Small pieces of the final outcomes are taught in a systematic, hierarchical sequence: first-grade math, then second-grade math, and so forth. The assumption is that skills (patterns) build to form skill sets. However, if the learner is not able to use language to assign meaning to these lessons, the learner is not able to achieve depth or underlying conceptual meaning to the skills. For example, social skills training results in behaviors that do not always represent social concepts. A child learns to greet others and continues to greet all people, whether or not the child has already greeted the person at the same event within the same time period. "Hello, I am Jake. What is your name?" Ten minutes later, "Hello, I am Jake. What is your name?" To be able to use the skills or patterns as concepts, the learner must have language that connects the context to the conceptual meaning.

Individuals diagnosed with ASD and related social communication disorders do not create concepts from these types of skill lessons. Since they learn concepts best through visual-motor types of patterns (visual patterns with movement access), it is important to present the visual patterns for concepts in relationship to each other. For example, in the following case study, Barry is given several ways to write, talk, and draw out what he sees and what others see in their thought bubbles to help him see the relationships in an event among the people, the child in the case study, and the actions and objects within the context of an event.

> The brain processes the overlap of patterns to form thinking concepts.

Activity: How do individuals with ASD learn to think?

If concepts are acquired by overlapping lots of patterns in multiple contexts over time, what about practicing patterns? The input of patterns must be novel for the brain to recognize them as something to be processed. This is why multiple opportunities are so important. When an idea or concept is used in a variety of ways, the input is novel. However, each time when the pattern is repeated over and over, the brain hangs onto the patterns as long as there is repetition, but *the thinking stops during the practice* and the cortical part of the brain actually begins to disengage or shut down (Bookheimer, 2004). *This means that practice is not as important as conceptual opportunities to use thinking.* For example, musicians or athletes will practice but they say they never practice the same way twice. They always think about what they are doing just a little differently every time and that enhances the finished product e.g., the musical piece is played more precisely every time, the basketball is thrown at a slightly different angle, etc. Thinking about what they are doing and why engages their brains while they are working on the muscle memory of repetition.

> The brain disengages with practice.

Activity: Why is it important to maintain multiple ways to use ideas?

Social-Emotional Concepts

As we have seen, the first stage of the learning system is sensory in nature. That is, a child's eyes, ears, skin, mouth, and nose receive input as raw data. These receptors continue to bring in new sensory input until the input begins to overlap and the neural messaging system recognizes that the input is old. So an infant may feel intense pressure when given an injection with a needle, but any crying is more from not recognizing the input than feeling any pain. "Pain" and other names for the sensory feelings are concepts. Concepts are learned. Learning of concepts occurs over time as the neural system continues to process past input into recognizable input into old or past input.

The learning or acquisition of concepts requires overlapping experiences in multiple situations where words assign meaning to a variety of activities. The brain learns the meaning associated with all concepts, including those that refer to feelings, also known as emotions. For example, teaching a child to say "happy" in response to a face with a smile does not help her learn the meaning of the concept happy as it refers to many different situations, different faces, different people's perceptions, and so forth. In reality, imitated or cued responses about these concepts lead to the learning of skills or patterns, not concepts. To learn emotions or other social concepts such as respect, the learner must have multiple opportunities to "see" what the concepts mean (see *Chapter Eleven* for an explanation of how emotion is learned).

Activity: How do emotions represent concept learning?

The following case study highlights the neuroeducational methods presented in this chapter.

Case Study

Barry is a 10-year-old male with a primary diagnosis on the autism spectrum with ADHD as a medical issue related to attention and focus. Furthermore, Barry is being considered for a behavior classroom since he is showing defiance, noncompliance, and other symptoms related to a conduct disorder. What makes him different from many students with ASD is his behavior. Barry shows behavior that others assume he understands. In other words, others think that because Barry talks a lot (has a lot of language structures or patterns) he understands his actions or behaviors. Remember that behavior reflects knowledge. So if Barry's behavior is not what adults expect, it means that he does not understand what they expect. Barry talks a lot, but his behaviors say he does not understand what it is that he does that affects others or affects his own outcomes!

When assessing Barry's language in relationship to his behavior, it is apparent that Barry is always in his own pictures. He perceives the world as revolving around him. He constantly insists that he doesn't do anything "wrong," and his language does not include others in his pictures. Barry is able to tell the rules about what is right when questioned or sometimes as a piece of narrative. Therefore, adults think he understands those rules. But Barry's behavior does not match what he says. This means that for Barry, most of the time, the rules are just imitated patterns of what others told him was okay or not okay in similar situations.

Figures 10.4a-10.4d are pieces of lessons with Barry that took him through several layers of concepts within a context so that he became able to not only repeat rules but to understand what they mean. Then he was able to increase his thinking though language development so that his behavior is more compliant. Eventually, he learned to use the language to plan his world.

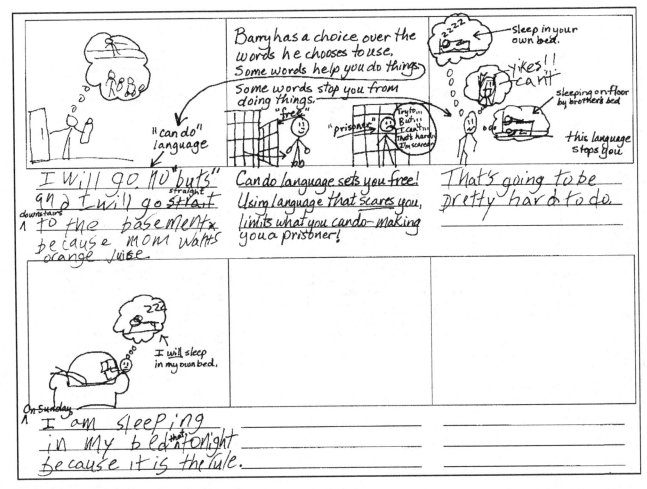

Figure 10.4a. *Barry learns the rules.*

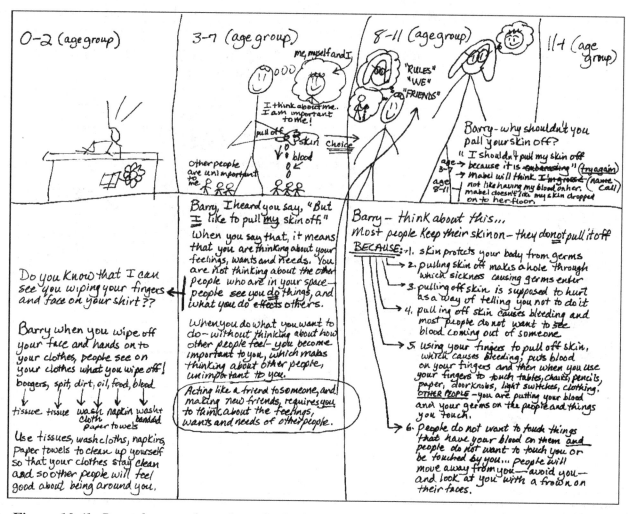

Figure 10.4b. *Barry learns what others think about the behaviors for the rules.*

I ˢᵃm an explorer...
I 'm an explorer...

Think about what you read on Monday...

aeiou
↑

Write about what you read...   Anton Was aⁿ explorer
who ĩ̶n̶ lookᵉᵈ t̶h̶r̶o̶u̶g̶h̶ through magnifyinglasses and then make
lenses and some magnifyed up to 300 times
b̶e̶t̶t̶e̶r̶ better than a plain human E̶y̶e̶. His lenses were
so good that the king and queen of
england, the ruler of Russia came to see
the lenses.

Your written summary shows that you understand
the gist of the story and many of the visual details.
Your summary is missing the auditory details! Names,
places and dates. Draw pictures that show what you wrote.

You can use the who, what, where, when and why/how
questions to figure out which auditory facts are missing...

When did Anton explore with magnifying glasses?
What did he explore?
Where did he explore?
Why did he explore?
What did he look at while using the magnifying glass?
Where did the magnifying glass come from?
How did he know to explore with the magnifying glass?
What do lenses have to do with magnifying glasses?
How do lenses work?
When was Anton born?
Where did Anton live and explore?

Figure 10.4c. *Barry learns to use language to think and plan about what he does.*

Figure 10.4d. *Barry also learns to think about academic content.*

Summary

The methods described in this book are based on the translational works of one of the authors, Arwood, who uses neuroscience as research evidence of how children and adults learn. This chapter explained why understanding how the brain learns helps create better methods for providing learners with social concepts and language function, not skills and patterns, so as to improve their behavior. Including this information in this book helps provide the rationale for why the methods work. Adults often try to explain behavior in terms of emotions; *Chapter Eleven* explains how emotion is language-based whereas feelings are part of the early sensory part of the neurosemantic learning system. *Chapter Twelve*, in turn, discusses what happens when conceptual learning is anti-social and results in bullying types of behavior.

Important Concepts in *Chapter Eleven*

Readers should be able to explain each of these behavior principles upon completion of this chapter:

1. **Emotion is language-based.**

2. **Sharing emotions is part of pro-social development.**

3. **Social-emotional development parallels cognition or thinking.**

4. **Feelings and emotions are not the same; feelings connect to sensory input.**

5. **Naming feelings requires language.**

6. **Stages of thinking should parallel stages of social development.**

7. **All concepts are socio-cognitive.**

8. **Thinking with emotions is the result of learning to be social as an agent.**

CHAPTER ELEVEN
Behavior of Emotion

I feel, but I don't know the name.
I say I am mad,
But my teacher says I am angry.
I see red, but my counselor says I am blue.

In *Chapter Ten*, the authors provided an explanation for how emotional words like "angry" or "sad" represent social, language-based concepts. Since learners acquire social concepts over time, it is important to provide multiple opportunities across various events to acquire the language of emotion. Behavior represents feelings. Language names the feelings as emotions. The purpose of this chapter is to provide examples of how to help children and adults develop the language for their behavior of emotion.

Social-Emotional Development

Social development has to do with how to become part of the surrounding culture. Being an agent (*Chapter Six*) of a culture means being able to discern as well as use the emotions of an agent in that culture. Therefore, emotional development is a part of social development. To be social includes the ability to represent one's feelings through the words of emotion such as being able to use the word "angry" or "sad" in thinking about others' feelings or one's own feelings.

Methods to teach social-emotional development follow the beliefs of the educators. Since the behaviorist approach is most prevalent in the U.S. educational system, the most prevalent way of dealing with social-emotional development, represented by words such as "angry" or "sad," is to teach those types of products or words as a series of learned skills taught through imitation and practice.

Activity: What is the typical way that U.S. educational systems think about emotions?

For example, the adult says the name of the emotional word that goes with a specific picture of a person's face or situation and then expects the children to imitate the word. The teacher provides ample practice for the child to name the emotional word that the educator associates with the picture of the person's face. In this type of teaching, emotions are responses to certain input and can be taught as skills. This approach to teaching social-emotional words sounds like this:

The educator has a picture of a person with a facial posture that could be angry. The educator points to the picture and says, "She is angry." "Angry. What is this? Angry. The girl is angry. Say, angry." The child imitates and says, "Angry." The educator then gives an opportunity to practice, "You tell me. What is the girl?" The adult expects the child to say angry. The child must infer that what she sees in the face of the girl is the word "angry."

Sometimes the adult teaches that a particular face means one of these emotions. For example, "See the frown. The boy is angry. What is the boy?" If the child does not respond, then the adult adds, "The boy is angry. You tell me. The boy is angry." The child is rewarded for imitating the words that the adult teaches. Or, sometimes children are taught that certain facial postures have emotional words tied to them. For example, this face is angry. In this way, the adults are hoping to teach the child to use words to express "anger" rather than inappropriate behavior. The adult might say, "When you are angry you can say, 'I am angry.'" But, these types of pairings between facial postures and emotions do not help children learn to think about their behavior in response to their feelings.

These types of lessons often continue for years. Sometimes, the lessons progress into situations where the learner is expected to come up with a statement such as, "She feels sad." The adult then uses a cue and says, "Why does she feel sad?" The learner is expected to answer, "She feels sad because Mary hit her." After practicing these types of tasks, many students are able to say the correct rule or response to the cues or pictures, and even tell the adults what the adults want to hear. But, too often, these same students are seen doing something they shouldn't be doing such as hitting someone, using a rote apology followed by the same behavior such as hitting another child. Saying what others think or feel in a situation is a form of practicing skills, not learning concepts.

Activity: How does teaching words that go with emotions allow a person to learn words but not concepts?

These types of social skill tasks assume that if a learner is able to respond to a picture of a face with an appropriate word, the child understands emotions. Or, if the learner is able to say or write a "because statement," the child understands all of the relationships that connect the learner to the rationale for the learner's behavior. Or, if the learner is able to practice phrases or words, the child "knows the meaning." And, the adult might be heard saying, "Jane is learning emotions. She knows what sad, happy, and angry are." However, skills are patterns and simple patterns are not concepts.

Even though there may be variations in the exact words spoken by the adults, the methods remain the same: The adult provides the pattern or skill and the learner responds with an expected verbal behavior about what the adult might feel. But what a child feels is separate from what the adult is teaching as "emotion." Emotions are language-based concepts, not skills.

Activity: How does a model that rewards products deal with emotion?

Since language represents concepts, the language of emotions is about concept acquisition. In the previous chapter on neuroscience, the reader learned that concepts such as emotions are not skills but the layering of meaning over time. The acquisition of all concepts, including those of emotion, occurs as long as the brain is alive. This means that an emotion such as anger is acquired through multiple experiences of learning how to connect sensory input to internal states, not by practicing the skill of saying words. Further, learning how to decipher what others feel based on visual cues related to body posture and facial postures is part of the language learning of concepts of emotions, not the practice of saying words to others' thoughts about what visuals mean. Learning the names of emotions is a language task; learning concepts is represented by language. Skills or patterns are imitated and memorized but do not represent the learner's feelings or thinking.

Activity: What do words like angry or sad represent?

Learning Emotions

Based on neuroscience, the language of emotion is a layered process of language acquisition where the learner is given the opportunity to connect feelings with words to represent underlying concepts. Therefore, teaching words like "angry" and "sad" without acquiring the underlying concepts is not very effective. Emotions are learned over time from an association of what a child feels (sensory input or internal state for past input) paired with the words (language concepts) to name the feelings. Language of emotion represents the learning of the concepts. **Emotions** consist of language for concepts of bodily states of thinking and feeling.

Activity: How are emotions taught in the schools? What are emotions?

If emotions are language-based, then what are feelings? Feelings are not emotions. Feelings are responses to outside stimuli or internal states of feedback and inhibition of the sensory input. A young child feels pressure to touch, not pain. A young child sees light in response to visual input, not a table. A young child feels temperature change in response to skin reception, not cold. A young child orients to the sounds of the world; not the word "Jeff." A young child tastes sour, not a lemon. Words like "pain," "table," "cold," Jeff, and "lemon" are concepts that the child learns over time. Words like "angry," "happy," "sad," "hurt," "disappointed," "frustrated," "anxious," "fearful," "joyful," "glad," "anticipated," "excited," "love," "cheerful," "optimistic," "irritated," "disgusted," "shame," "contentment," "surprised," "rage," "envy," "sympathetic," and "nervousness" are also concepts. They must be learned over time in relationship to other concepts, through multiple experiences, and with lots of language. Emotions are not memorized responses to pictures of what others experience or feel.

To learn about emotions, the child must learn to *think* about the differences in feelings in the way that society assigns meaning to those feelings with words. For example, if the people in a child's environment often talk about being "anxious," the child will learn to be more anxious. The word "anxious" may be used when others might actually mean, "I am excited" or "I can't wait to go to school." Thinking about feelings with language helps assign language to feelings called emotions.

Activity: What are feelings? What are emotions?

Learning to Think About Emotions

Thinking with emotions requires the acquisition of concepts. Neurotypical learners acquire concepts over time. In the U.S. culture, adults use oral language to assign meaning to what a child is able to see, touch, hear, taste, and smell. These meanings enter the child's brain as sensory inputs. The inputs integrate, and the brain creates meaning. A child "feels" these sensory integrations as a bodily state. The child then learns the word that goes with the state and the behaviors that represent those meanings. For example, a newborn cries, and the baby's mother responds by picking up the baby. Within three days, (e.g., Brennan & Kirkland, 1982), a baby has learned how to make different cries for different responses by Mother. Later the child learns the language for the behavior, "cry." But the acquisition of concepts continues throughout a lifetime. So, later the baby grows into a child who learns that there are different "feelings" for crying, such as "sad" versus crying out of "joy." The behavior does not determine the feeling or the emotional language assigned to the behavior.

Activity: How do neurotypical children learn to think about feelings?

As the authors suggest, for individuals with ASD, sensory inputs do not always integrate for concept acquisition and language development (*Chapters One-Four*). Therefore, children with ASD or language learning problems or social communication disorders struggle acquiring the social-emotional concepts such as anger, happy, and sad. For example, the authors have worked with children who are able to chew off their fingers over time. The child starts to chew on the finger. The pressure is new sensory input, which the brain likes. So the child continues with the sensory input. The child does not have the conceptual development of "hurt" or "pain." The sores become infected and may lead to loss of skin tissue and even bone over time. Hurting one's body may actually "feel good" when the environment is not meaningful.

When a child's environment presents itself in a way that allows the child to construct meaning, the child is able to acquire the social-emotional concepts that society expects. Since many learners do not use the sounds of oral language for developing concepts, assigning meaning with typical oral language is not effective. Further, where visuals are otherwise often effective, visuals such as a sad face do not connect the child's feelings with the word used to represent the face in the picture. These visuals do not show the child what the child feels. Instead, individuals with ASD must be able to mentally think about what they feel and what others see so that they can connect their bodily states of feelings with expected words. The name of these concepts about feelings or language provides the connection between feelings and emotions.

Activity: How do individuals with ASD best learn about their feelings?

The idea that many learners use movement to create meaning is particularly significant to remember when it comes to self-injurious behavior. This type of behavior suggests that the environment is not providing input in a meaningful way (Arwood, 2011; Arwood & Kaulitz, 2007). Stopping self-stimulation or injurious behavior requires that the environment needs to change the input into something that is visual-motor with lots of language patters to begin to think at a higher level. For example, when individuals with ASD watch others draw and write the meaning of the behavior, the hand movements create the meaning of the shape of the hand, which creates the concepts. With self-stimulation or self-injurious behavior, higher thinking changes the meaning of the input from pressure to pain through the acquisition of the meaning of the concept "hurt" or "pain." Overlapping concepts (drawings and the writing of ideas or shapes in a language context is needed to acquire conceptual meaning such as emotions.

Activity: How do individuals with ASD learn the language of their emotional concepts?

Learning to think about concepts related to emotion is a process of acquiring the meaning of a child's world over time. This means that social-emotional concepts have developmental levels that correspond to the child's developmental level of thinking with language. The reader was introduced to those language levels in *Chapter Eight*. *Table 11.1* shows an example of the acquisition of a concept related to emotion over time. This process assumes that 1) the input is in the way the child learns concepts, such as visual-motor patterns; 2) the patterns representing the ideas overlap with assigned meaning from the adults; 3) the overlap of the patterns with the assignment of meaning creates concepts in the way the child learns; 4) the concepts are used in a variety of language contexts about "who, what, where, when, why, and how;" and 5) the learner has opportunities to use the concepts in a variety of overlapping contexts to layer the meaning of the concepts over time.

Table 11.1. *Thinking with Emotions*

UNDERSTANDING LEVEL	THINKING LEVEL	LANGUAGE OF "SAD"
Sensory responses … child does not have emotions … only feelings	Sensori-motor	Behavior is nonverbal – crying, wiggling, moving toward sound, etc.
Imitated phrases … cannot use emotional words to explain thinking or feeling for self or others	Preoperational	May use the same word for lots of different feeling… "potato is sad," "I am sad" is said while the child is laughing … Child uses the emotional words as patterns, not concepts
The child is able to associate the feeling of "sad" to self or others. The child is able to understand the cultural rules about a concept like sad and the behaviors that relate to sadness. The child does not like to be sad, so she tries to cheer up the other child who does feel sad	Concrete	Mary is crying, and Sally asks, "Why are you sad?" Mary explains her sadness, so Sally tells the teacher, "Mary is in the bathroom crying because those boys (points) called her a mean name." Later, Sally writes to Mary, "I am sorry you feel sad. Want to play on the swings?"

Table 11.1. *Continued*

UNDERSTANDING LEVEL	THINKING LEVEL	LANGUAGE OF "SAD"
Not everyone feels the same way in response to the same stimuli. Therefore, a range of emotions fit with the same behavior … frowning may mean sad, thoughtful, curious, wonder, disappointment, etc.	Formal	Instead of assuming a particular emotion, when an adult sees someone cry, the adult says "What are you feeling?" The adult does not assume the feeling that goes with the behavior … crying may represent joy, loss, frustration, anxiety, and so forth

Thinking with emotions requires language lessons that use emotional words in context to represent a variety of meanings. Learning to think with emotion and to understand the emotions of social concepts requires a lot of functional language. As illustrated in *Table 11.1*, it is not until the concrete level of language and thinking that a child is able to use the words of emotion in a rule-governed way. In fact, it is not until the formal level (typical age of 11+) that the learner is able to understand that multiple meanings are attached to behaviors such as crying. Therefore, lessons for learning words of emotion are not effective until a child has a complete language grammar with lots of vocabulary (3,000-5,000 words). This means that many special education lessons that try to teach emotions to children who do not have lots of language are not developmentally appropriate. Since the lessons are not developmentally appropriate, the children spit back patterns of words, "I am happy!" or "The boy is sad!" without conceptual understanding. Such lessons are taught over and over since the children do not truly acquire the concepts, but only memorized or taught skills of patterns. (Remember that patterns must be rehearsed or practiced. Otherwise, they are not remembered even to spit back.) Concepts are thoughts that are part of the cerebral cortex networks of the brain; and, therefore, concept learning will last a long time without practice.

Activity: At which developmental level is a person able to think the rules about feelings and the language that goes with those rules?

To be developmentally appropriate, lessons targeted to teach words like "angry" or "sad" must assume that the learner not only has lots of language and a concrete level of cognition but is also able to be compliant socially and behaviorally. In other words, to benefit from such lessons, learners must be at a concrete level of understanding. To learn social-emotional concepts, multiple lessons that incorporate these concepts into activities of thinking and language must occur. Such lessons must be presented in ways that enable learners with ASD and related disorders are able to think and learn concepts (motor access to form shapes).

Activity: How are social-emotional concepts learned through lessons?

Methods for Learning Social-Emotional Concepts

The methods offered in *Chapters Eight-Ten* may be used to teach the concepts of emotion. The following case studies provide examples of how to use the methods for matching behavior to feelings of emotion and thinking.

Case Study 1. Cassie Compton, a teacher in Washington State, provided this case study of Bert. Bert is a 7-year-old male who shows a lack of understanding of language related to emotion and behavior, which often is part of a diagnosis of ASD. Bert also has a diagnosis that includes traumatic brain injury (TBI) along with shaken baby syndrome. Bert was sexually abused by a family member as an infant and has been with foster parents since infancy. He often shows behavior that does not match his academic level of development. For example, Bert is able to read, write, and talk with lots of ideas; but adults report that he sometimes shows distressed behavior such as being upset, sad, or anxious and worried for no apparent reason. When Bert shows that he is distressed, Cassie is able to change his behavior through drawing and writing about the concepts. Bert is able to learn what pro-social behavior is appropriate through drawing the concepts and attaching the language needed to name the concepts.

Once, Bert's foster parents took a weeklong trip to Hawaii and left Bert with Peggy, a babysitter for Bert. The foster parents explained to Bert that they would be back, when they would be back, where they were going, what they were doing, and what Bert would be doing with Peggy in his own home. Bert appeared to understand these events when he was told, but he stopped eating as soon as the parents left. Peggy reported to Cassie that Bert had eaten almost nothing for two days and that his behavior showed that he was "sad."

It would have been easy to say that based on his behavior that Bert was depressed, sad, missing his parents, and so on. But the behavior does not really match the feelings. In other words, eating or not eating are not natural consequences of an emotion. Instead, there are feelings that are more likely associated with a queasy stomach related to a "loss." But the parents are not a loss – they are returning. Bert needed more information or knowledge so that he could think about the events in relationship to what he is feeling.

Activity: How is it that individuals might interpret another person's feelings incorrectly?

Cassie pulled out a paper and pencil and began to draw. She did not have a lot of time, so the picture she drew does not have complete people, only their heads, but the drawing provided Bert with what he needed to understand the events. *Figure 11.1* shows the drawing for Bert.

Figure 11.1. *Bert is able to see his parents each day on the piece of paper.*

Even though Cassie drew floating heads, Bert had enough language to be able to understand the drawings. Cassie drew out the parents explaining their love for Bert (they were in the process of adopting him), the days that the foster parents would be in Hawaii, and when they would return. *Figure 11.2* shows the language that went with the drawing.

Bert … you are staying at home with Peggy, your sitter, while your parents are in Hawaii. Before your parents climbed on a plane to fly to Hawaii, they sat down with you and told you they love you and that they would be back in seven days. While your parents are in Hawaii, they are doing many of the same things that they do when they are at home: They sleep, they wake up, they get dressed, they eat breakfast, they do tasks, they eat lunch, they do more tasks, they eat dinner, they relax, they get ready for bed, and then they go to sleep.

While your parents are in Hawaii, sleeping, eating, and doing tasks, they are thinking about you here at your home in your house, also sleeping, eating, and playing. So it is important that every day you sleep well, eat well, and play well so that you will have lots of stories to tell your parents when they fly back from Hawaii to see you on Tuesday!

Figure 11.2. *Oral language during the drawing.*

After the session, Bert immediately relaxed and ate some food. Peggy used the picture at home and Bert ate every day, always checking the calendar to "see" when his foster parents would be returning. He continued to eat. Bert's behavior showed a lack of understanding, not of emotion. Emotion is language-based. The adults interpreting his behavior have the emotions. Bert is at a developmental level of feeling that he does not have the language for. He needed language to understand the meaning of his world. Furthermore, Bert does not use spoken language for learning difficult concepts (concepts he cannot see or touch), such as the absence of foster parents. Instead, he has bodily feelings without the language of emotion. By Cassie drawing out the concepts for him, he was able to see how he fit with their behavior. He could begin to understand what he felt and how to behave appropriately. Ultimately, these types of experiences will provide Bert with the language of emotion.

Activity: How does drawing help a child learn to behave in ways that match his feelings?

Case Study 2. Gary is an 11-year-old male diagnosed with ASD when he was 3 years old. By the time he was eight, he still did not talk but his behavior was becoming more aggressive. His parents were frustrated with the behaviorist approach that left Gary with compliance but no thinking. Gary's parents asked the authors to evaluate their son and subsequently they were given language tools to begin to assign more meaning to Gary's behavior and to help him begin to see the words on a page so that writing would yield talking. The parents began writing everything to Gary: rules, actions, and daily activities. All talking was translated into writing. Three years later, at 11 years of age, Gary had developed the oral language and academics that allowed him to function in the general education classroom with some academic support provided by the special education department in his school. However, he was puzzled by some social-emotional behaviors, so the parents asked that the author again evaluate Gary.

At the time of the second evaluation, one of the first questions Gary asked was about "burning his arm." He wanted to know why the guys thought it was cool that Gary used the fire of a lighter on his arms while the girls made faces and said "gross." Gary was lighting the skin on his arm with a lighter. The burned skin would scab over and when Gary saw the scabs he would pick them off, eventually leading to infections, doctor's visits, and scars. None of the latter issues had any meaning for him. The only meaning Gary had was of what he saw – the boys intently watching as Gary burned his skin and saying, "cool," girls running away saying, "gross."

For Gary to feel the pain that others would experience in response to his skin on fire, the concepts had to be drawn and written about. By the end of the evaluation, not only could he feel the pressure from the fire on his skin as pain, but because this behavior now "hurt," Gary no longer set his skin on fire. *Figure 11.3* shows some of the drawing and writing that were provided.

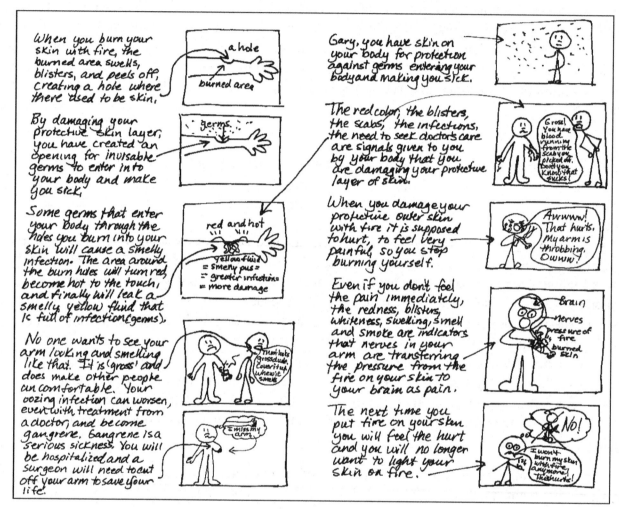

Figure 11.3. *Understanding "pain" and "hurt".*

Gary did not have the association of language to the behavior to understand the emotion with the feeling so he literally could not feel the pain. Pain was the language for the sensory feeling. Once he could understand the "pain," he could also begin to understand others' reactions.

Figure 11.4 shows the drawings to help him understand what "cool" and "gross" meant in terms of the boys' and girls' thoughts.

Figure 11.4. *Understanding "cool" and "gross"*

Learning to feel with the emotions of the language and culture requires a lot of language. Individuals with ASD and related disorders learn these concepts through the use of movement of the hand and/or mouth to create the shapes of ideas as visual thoughts.

Activity: How does feeling become painful?

Case Study 3. Learning to think with emotion necessitates learning concepts that connect behavior with societal interpretations of meaning. Adults with ASD and related disorders must use the same process of acquiring the language of emotion that Gary and Bert used: Learn to think about the meaning of feelings and then use language to represent those thoughts.

This case study is about a 37-year-old adult, Dana, diagnosed with Asperger Syndrome. Because of Dana's diagnosis and a long history of brilliance for minutia, he had managed to make it through the public school system with adults viewing his irritability, excitability, lack of flexibility, meltdowns, and verbal name calling as "eccentric" and a result of him not being able to "handle his brilliance." However, these types of behavior are not pro-social in nature and will spiral (see *Chapter Five*) into anti-social behavior that is often difficult to separate from mental illness. Unable to live independently or with others, Dana was sliding down into full disability.

The authors worked with Dana. They spent sessions writing and writing and writing, trying to connect all of the words that he could produce but had little conceptual understanding. *Figure 11.5* shows an example of how writing his spoken words gives him the opportunity to see what he says and then match it against what he understands (*Figure 11.6*)

Dana- I asked you to use a few words to characterize yourself, as a way for me to get to know you better. You described yourself as honest, responsible, thoughtful, respectful, trustworthy and dependable.

Let's put those words along with examples and definitions on to a picture dictionary page. →

You also told me that you are a husband, father, employee at a local company and a college graduate.

Presently, you say that you are feeling overwhelmed, stressed out, depressed and angry.

Two bothersome situations have arisen: 1) you are on probation at work and in jeopardy of losing your job. And, 2) your wife, Marnie, is threatening to walk away from your marriage of 15 years.

You said that yesterday was an especially bad day because of the fight you and Marnie had regarding some dry cleaning that wasn't picked up.

I am going to sketch out the details of what you told me. I want to make sure I have the details correct, and the drawings will allow us to see that. →

Figure 11.5. Writing to see words.

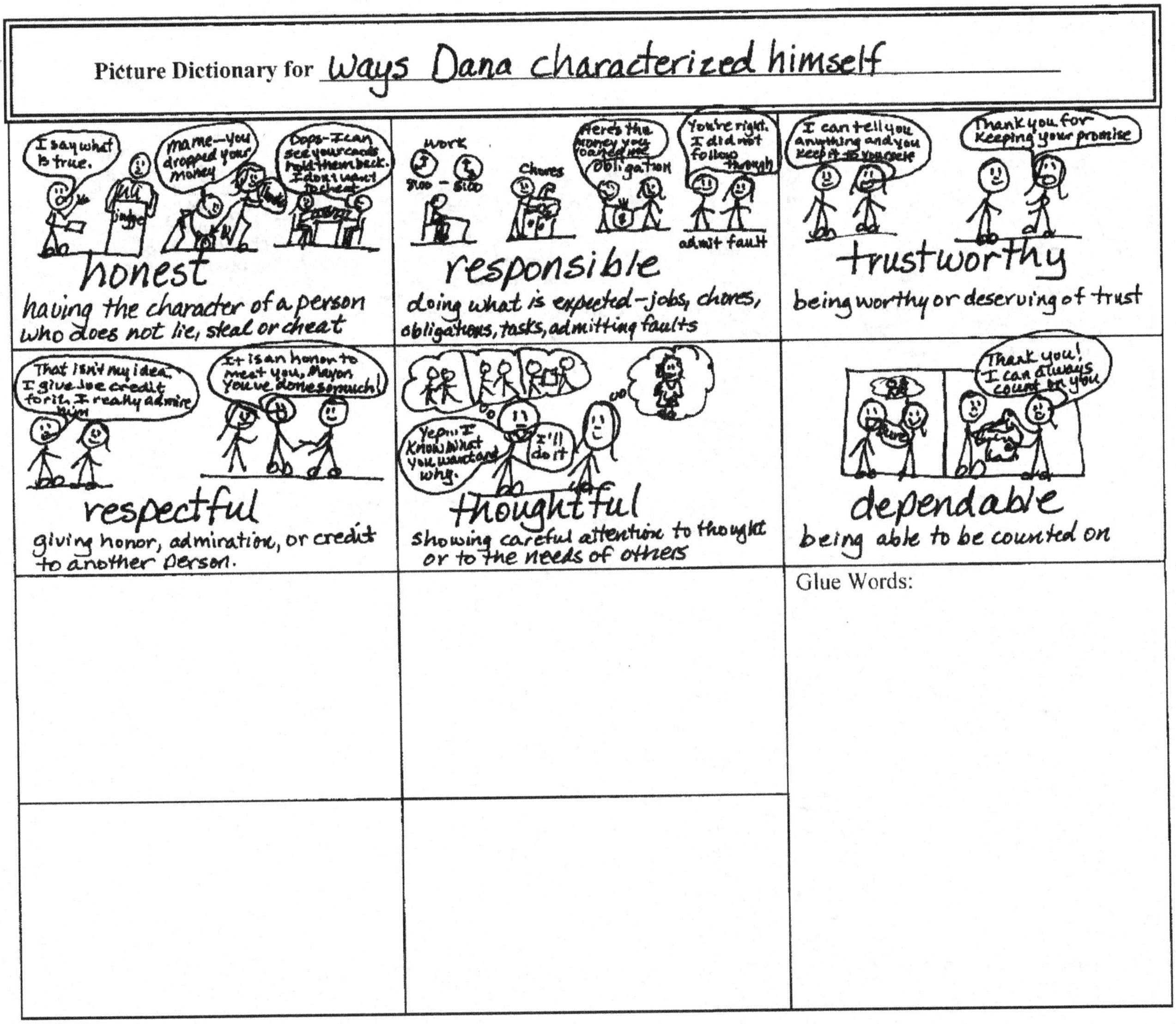

Figure 11.6. Drawing the meaning of words to understand oral language.

It is important to understand that emotion is language-based. Feelings are sensory-based. Language represents the feelings. But for individuals with ASD and related disorders, the connection between feelings and emotion often lacks the language or concepts for language to name. For Dana and many others with ASD, stress results in functioning with behavior that does not have the underlying concepts necessary to connect language with thinking.

Figure 11.7 shows how Dana could choose to use different behavior in a situation with a family member so that there is a shared understanding.

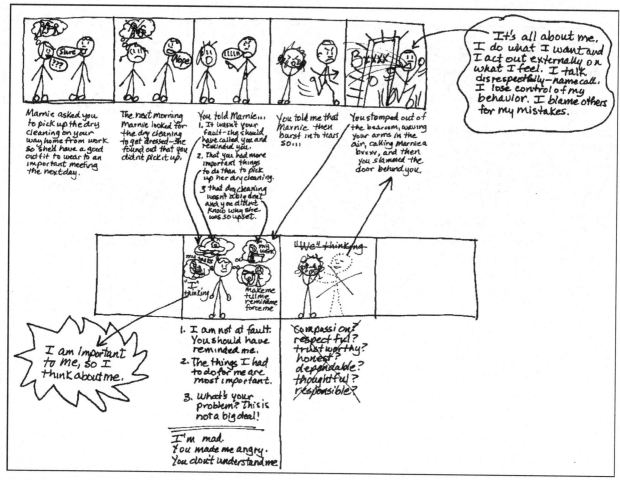

Figure 11.7. *Learning to share behavior requires conceptual thinking and language.*

Figure 11.8 shows the language that was written for Dana to see how behavior and thinking are linked and that emotion is not feelings. Feelings are sensory responses that can be interpreted with language in a variety of ways.

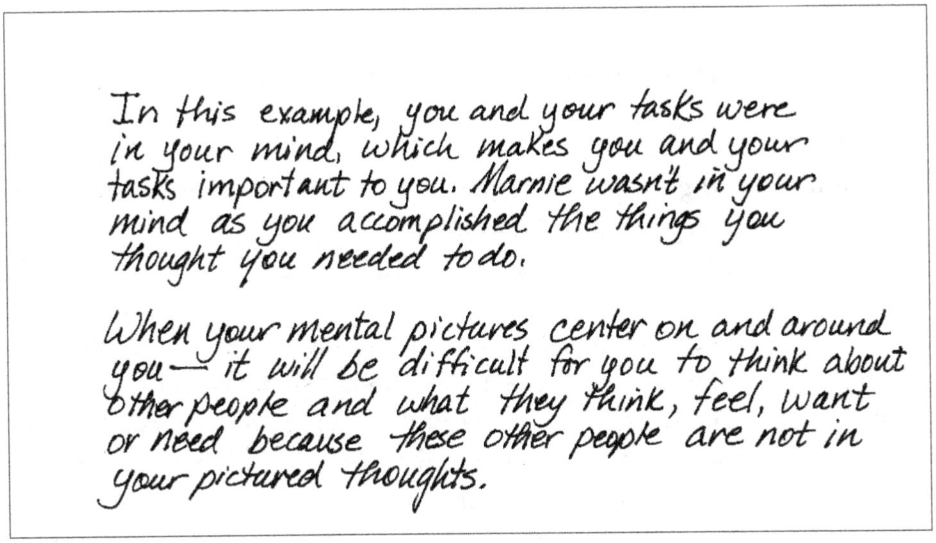

In this example, you and your tasks were in your mind, which makes you and your tasks important to you. Marnie wasn't in your mind as you accomplished the things you thought you needed to do.

When your mental pictures center on and around you — it will be difficult for you to think about other people and what they think, feel, want or need because these other people are not in your pictured thoughts.

Figure 11.8. *Learn how to make choices based on language, not feelings.*

Activity: How does language and feelings form emotions?

As individuals learn the language of emotions, they learn to behave as culture expects them. In other words, they learn that there are choices of how to assign meaning to specific feelings. And, they learn that others' behaviors also reflect different feelings and therefore different ways to name what they see. For example, they see someone with tears and learn that the tears could mean the person is happy or sad. They learn that thinking and feeling are not the same and that language names feelings (social) and thoughts (cognitive). Those with pro-social thoughts move toward social competence with each of the layers about thinking, behavior, and pro-social development.

Social Competence

The ability to initiate and maintain healthy relationships is called social competence. Most parents and educators want their children to become socially competent. Social competence is based on learning social-emotional concepts. Teaching social skills without emphasis on social and cognitive concept development will not lead the child to the development of social competence.

To create opportunities for learners to acquire social and cognitive concepts, adults must provide a match between what the learners are able to see and what they are able to do. In other words, the language of their behavior must match feel, see and think. When language about emotion is put into the equation, then the learners acquire the words that associate with the language of their behaviors. Bert, Gary, and Dana were not learning the concepts for how to match thinking and feeling into the language of behavior, separate from emotion. Through learning language, they are learning to think about what their feelings mean.

As with the previous case studies, specific language for Dana was paired with social-emotional thoughts in order to change behavior. Often the authors are amazed when they emphasize thinking and language and find that the social-emotional behavior develops without being targeted. In other words, children come to the authors with problems with reading, writing, calculating, and/or speaking and the authors work with the language for thinking. When a learner's thinking changes, the child's language and behavior often changes to represent more pro-social development.

Activity: How do learning social and cognitive concepts lead to the development of language of emotions?

Case Study 4. Erin is a 10-year-old female. She is struggling in many academic areas and, more importantly, she is starting to become aggressive – pushing other students, yelling at peers and parents, throwing pencils, and so forth. The school is referring Erin for a possible diagnosis on the autism spectrum. Erin presents herself with dirty hands, disheveled clothes, with lunch food on her face and clothes, a drooped head, slouched posture, tangled hair, and a sweater that she pulls over her head whenever anyone speaks directly to her. Furthermore, Erin is not imitating what she sees in her family.

Both her parents are professionals: One is a teacher and the other is a sheriff. Both present themselves clean and socially competent. Erin has two siblings, ages eight and six, and they too are age-appropriately clean and show pro-social age-appropriate development. So, Erin's behavior shows that she is lacking some information that the rest of the family has learned. Erin is not learning to be socially competent. She is not learning to socially think at an age-appropriate level of language development.

Given the scenario, what comes first: Erin's lack of agency, which results in bad hygiene or bad hygiene, which results in a poor concept of agency? The school is working on behavior. The parents are working on Erin's reading and writing by having her read out loud after school. Both parents help with homework as Erin rarely is able to complete her own school work. Erin refuses to do chores and fights with her parents about why she has to do chores, go to school, and come see the authors for help. Erin is moving away from social competence and into more and more anti-social behavior. Her most recent behavior has included bullying others by name calling, spitting, and threatening bodily harm. Adults around Erin say she is "angry" and parents have sought therapy for anger management. Erin refuses to go to the counselor.

The adults in Erin's life are using their emotions to interpret Erin's feelings: She is angry. She is frustrated. She is anxious so she is being belligerent. She doesn't feel good. She is bored. She is under-stimulated, and so on. But Erin is not thinking like an adult and her behavior shows that she does not have the meaning that the adults in her environment have. So how is Erin learning to behave the way she behaves when those at home and at school do not behave the way she does?

The answer is: Erin is learning to behave the way she does through the way she learns all concepts. So how does she learn concepts? Erin struggles with reading with sounds (out loud), with writing with sounds that name letters, with following the sounds of others' words in oral instructions, and with following the sound of oral language for chores or for directions. Erin does not use sound well and, therefore, must use the other sensory system receptors such as sight for learning concepts.

She is learning to think in what she sees. She cannot see mental pictures for words like "bored," so she has learned to say that phrase "I am bored" and the adults around her find something else for her to do. In fact, she does not know what boredom is. She knows how to change the task in order to get others to act differently. She pulls the sweater over her head so others think she is "shy," "afraid," or "anxious." She is learning to use these visual props as ways not to have to do what she cannot do – learn to use sound for thinking and doing.

Erin learns best with the shapes of ideas that are written so that she can see the meaning. Erin's world of adults use lots and lots of sound – they talk to her about her behavior, they teach her to read and write with sounds and letters, they explain to her about chores and hygiene with their voices, and so forth. Erin is learning how to avoid situations that she does not understand. Avoidance without the social-emotional concepts and the language tools for explaining what she can and can't do is the basis for a lot of anti-social behavior. The more the adults use sound, the more anti-social Erin becomes. Here is a list of methods for working with Erin.

1. Draw and write in cartoon form all expectations – from what Erin looks like coming to therapy to what she does for chores. This gives Erin the visual pictures for what is expected.

2. Since Erin does not see how she fits or does not fit in with others in her classroom or at home, she does not learn with visual pictures alone. Write for her about what the words mean that match the cartoon drawings. Use lots of language with the cartoons so she understands the overlap of the drawing and writing. *Figure 11.9* shows a cartoon for how Erin and the author, Brown, work together. By putting both Erin and Brown into the pictures, Erin is learning how to think about others, what others think, and what others know.

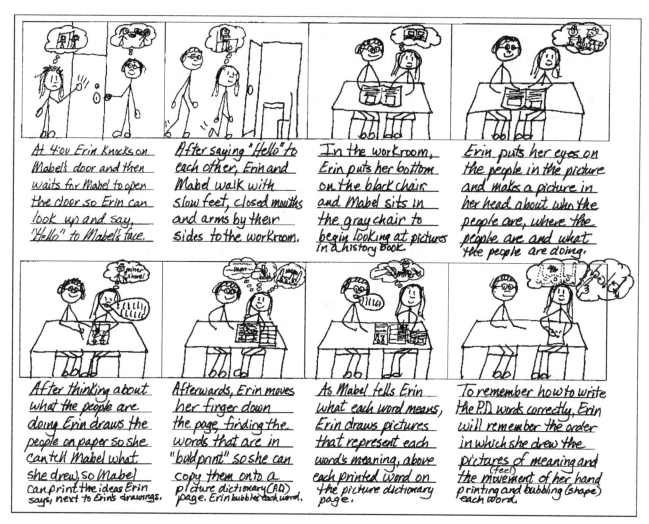

Figure 11.9a. *Thinking about learning with someone else.*

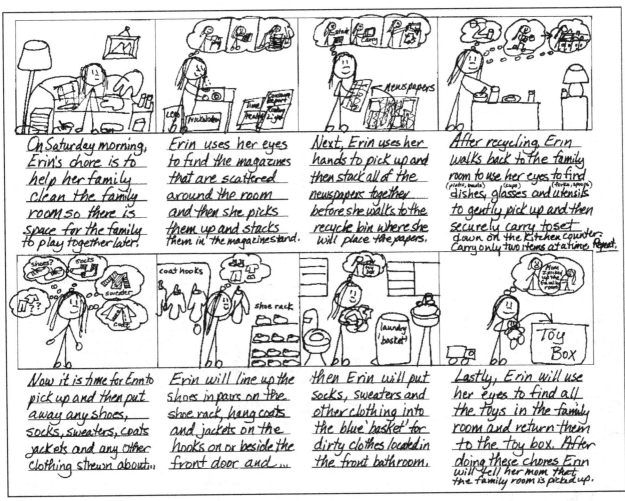

Figure 11.9b. *Thinking about choices every day.*

3. Be sure to include mental thought bubbles about what the choices of behavior are about.

   Figure 11.10 shows the thinking connected to others' spoken words.

Figure 11.10. *Erin begins to learn what behavior goes with the language of emotion.*

4. Interconnect the meaning of concepts that are related; for example, overlapping meanings such as "boredom" and "being successful" helps create different mental pictures. The learning of concepts is always relational: How do the ideas connect or relate to one another? How do the behaviors affect others? What do others think when Erin behaves a certain way? Only by learning how Erin's behavior affects others will she be able to see herself as an agent that has choices.

5. Emphasize thinking and language, not words or skills. By helping Erin learn to think about her choices and to use language as a tool for learning, she will change the way she presents herself. In fact, Erin did change. She began to walk with an assertive posture. Her face was clean and her hair was not tangled (she didn't twist it anymore). She smiled and greeted people as she began to see herself in the pictures. She also began to see how she could think to behave and

that she had control over her behavior and her thoughts by using writing to access her language. Adults in her environment asked what had been done to help Erin develop good hygiene, but no one had worked on hygiene. Erin was learning to be socially competent. She was learning that she could initiate and maintain healthy relationships through thinking and language. Brown provided Erin with lots of opportunity to increase her thinking as an agent so that she began to function as a pro-social being at more of an age-appropriate level.

Activity: How does learning to be socially competent help develop developmentally appropriate social behavior?

Language of Social Competence

Thinking about one's own self is heard as early, preoperational language: "I am bored." "I am hungry." "I am angry." Learning to think about others develops as the learner begins to see others in the learner's picture. The language of this learning sounds like this: "We are going to go play at the park. We will be back by dinner." "Do you want some help with the dishes?" As the thinking becomes more complex, room for the language of emotions becomes more likely. For example, as the seventh grader tells his mom, "We are going to go play in the park. We will be back by dinner," he realizes that his mom would worry if he did not tell her where he was and when he would be home. Emotionally, he thinks about her feelings and her language of emotion when she used to tell him to be sure to let her know where he was going so that his mom did not have to worry.

The English language is full of these types of more complex words that reflect the more complex thinking and the effects of behavior on others' thinking: "considerate," "kind," "empathy," "sympathy," "respectful," "collaborative," "responsible," "accountable," "trustworthy," and so on. To be able to use and understand these types of words, learners also must be able to understand how their behavior fits into others' lives. Furthermore, they must be able to understand how others' thinking is affected by their behavior and how their behavior, in turn, makes others feels. Complex words of emotion such as "love," "integrity," "trust," "happy," "sad," "glad," "joy," and "angry" all involve thinking about one's self in relation to others in the same picture – what others think, what others feel, what happens to others when one acts, and so on.

Practicing social skills or learning words does not develop the thinking that goes with behavior that reflects pro-social development. Pro-social development occurs in response to acting in ways that show an increase in understanding how one's behavior affects others, the thinking behind others' behavior, and the language that represents the behavior. Only with the development of such thinking, which shows this level of conceptual development, can educators or parents expect children to use adult-based emotional words that are understood.

Activity: At what level does a person understand how to think and use emotions?

Summary

Learning to use words that describe emotions requires a lot of language, language that uses a variety of vocabulary and that represents how thoughts connect with states of feelings. Language develops over time as a result of acquiring the thinking or concepts that language represents. In order to help individuals learn to think about their feelings, educational programs should focus on concept development or thinking with language. As the learner acquires more concepts and more language, the learner is better able to express feelings that others are able to understand. Over time, the learner's behavior changes to demonstrate feelings and emotions that are interconnected by appropriate language. The minimum developmental level for the use of the language of emotion is a concrete level of thinking and language use. Concrete levels of thinking are represented in shared, conversational language levels.

The opposite of learning to be pro-social is the development of anti-social behavior that often begins as bullying. *Chapter Twelve* provides the reader with an understanding of bullying.

278 | Pro-Social Language

Important Concepts in *Chapter Twelve*

Readers should be able to explain each of these behavior principles upon completion of this chapter:

1. Bullying is learned.

2. Bullying is a common form of anti-social behavior.

3. Bullying is often the result of not having an adequate pro-social development.

4. Bullying does not occur when people are socially competent.

5. Bullying is a societal problem.

6. Bullying is the lack of shared power.

7. Bullying is an attempt to control others' thoughts, beliefs, and behaviors.

8. Bullying is a form of abuse that objectifies others.

9. Social exclusion, marginalization, and name calling or labeling are examples of bullying.

10. Setting limits with language helps prevent bullying.

11. Learning to think about others through the use of language-based strategies for better conceptualization helps eliminate bullying.

CHAPTER TWELVE
Bullying

I am not a label or a can.
I am not a name or a bam!
I am who I am,
Respect me as I am.

This book emphasizes the development of cognition and language as ways to increase literacy for better problem solving, decision- making, and pro-social behavior. By increasing a learner's ability to make choices and decisions that fit in with pro-social development, the learner engages in more acceptable behavior. The emphasis in this book has continued to be on increasing pro-social development. But, all behavior affects others; so, this chapter discusses how to deal with anti-social behavior when it happens. Bullying is the most common form of anti-social behavior.

Bullying happens when one person uses his or her power to limit the power of another person. To be effective in this imbalance of power, the bully must repeatedly devalue or create unwanted, aggressive behavior that limits another person's social well-being over time. Bullying is a type of abuse. Bullying, like all anti-social behavior, does not promote or maintain healthy relationships. Since all anti-social behavior does not promote the initiation and maintenance of healthy relationships, anti-social behavior is abusive to either the person performing anti-social behavior and/or to others.

Despite programs and school wide initiatives to stop bullying, the number of those who are bullied has been steadily increasing. Thus, it is estimated by some scholars that as many as 75% of all school children report that they have been bullied or have bullied others. This percentage (75%) may seem high but when the numbers from various studies (e.g., Good, McIntosh, Gietz; 2011) are added together, the percentage of school age children who are bullied or bully others may actually be higher. Unfortunately, people who are bullied learn that bullying pays off. The bullied person feels diminished, so the bullier is victorious. And, the victims want to be successful so they too learn to bully, thus, perpetuating the anti-social, abusive aspects of bullying.

And, if you wondering if those with ASD are bullied (e.g., O'Connor, 2012), yes they are! In fact, a person who exhibits any sort of difference provides a bully with the fuel for bullying. Differences may be good, bad, or neutral, but bullies do not want others to have more power than they do. So bullies devalue those with differences to be sure that the differences are not somehow better than what they may possess themselves. In this way, the bullies retain the power. Sharing the power would suggest that the bully felt socially competent, powerful, capable of initiating and maintaining healthy relationships with others. For numerous reasons, bullies "need" to make themselves feel "better" so they devalue others to compensate for their lack of social competence. Bullying is a social problem, a societal problem! Bullying is a part of the anti-social spiral (*Chapter Five*) that may lead to more aggressive behavior against others. A high incidence of bullying means that there is a high incidence of anti-social behavior within schools as well as the work place.

With the statistics for bullying increasing, it is a small minority who are not bullied. The incidence of bullying suggests that typical behavior of U.S. society includes the anti-social behaviors associated with bullying. So why do the majority of people engage in anti-social behavior such as bullying?

There are two important issues with regard to the persistence of bullying: 1) Adults must be able to recognize anti-social behavior in order to stop bullying; and, 2) Adults must be able to set limits so as to stop the bullying once they recognize behavior as bullying. In other words, adults must know what bullying is and, therefore, not engage in bullying as well as set limits so bullying does not occur. This chapter will deal with both of these issues: recognizing bullying and setting limits to stop bullying.

Activity: What is bullying?

Recognizing Bullying

Early in this book, *Chapter Six*, a test for reasonableness was suggested as a way to know if behavior is typical in a pro-social sense or whether it is anti-social. It would be reasonable to assume that if most people say they do not bully then they do not like to be bullied. Unfortunately, many well-intentioned educators exhibit behavior that would be classified as bullying. For example, the authors have heard many educators use "put-downs" such as "John knows better; he is just being non-compliant. He doesn't want to do the task. He is being ornery." These individuals are not aware that their verbal behavior is a form of bullying. If these adults cannot see when they bully others, they cannot recognize bullying when students are engaged in bullying acts. Therefore, they also are not able to stop bullying in schools or at home.

This section of the book will highlight bullying behavior as a way to help adults learn to recognize bullying behavior.

Activity: What are the two main issues that need to be addressed to begin to curtail bullying behavior?

Verbal Devaluations. The old saying "Sticks and stones may break my bones but words will never hurt me" is not true. Sticks and stones can do physical harm that is observable; words can do physical harm that can be seen in physiological tests and in brain imaging. Neuroscientists have discovered that individuals who are verbally abused, such as called names or given putdowns, show the same lack of brain function as if they had been physically abused. In fact, even early stressors may change the brain function (e.g., Paul et al., 2008).

So what determines which words devalue a person? When a person is devalued, the person's agency is attacked. This means that comments that put down a person's agency, the person's "who," are devaluations. For example, most people view themselves as people who have a special identification, a personal name – Christy, Max, Jane, Beth, and so forth. To refer to Christy as the "smart one," or Max as the "athletic one," or Jane as the "autistic one," or Beth as the "quiet one," places meaning on characteristics about "what" these people do or "what" they look like. Any time emphasis is placed on people's attributes of "what" they look like, "what" they act like, or "what" they sound like, the value is on the "what," not the "who." Emphasizing a person's "what" takes value or meaning away from the person's "who," who he or she is as a person or agent.

Taking meaning or value away from a person's "who" results in objectifying the person. Adults who assign meaning to a child's "who" help promote agency for increases in pro-social behavior (see *Chapter Six*). But, emphasis on a person's "what's," objectifies the person which results in a loss or value of agency (Arwood & Young, 2000). Examples of such objectifications include identifying a person by the labels used for eligibility of services (the autistic boy), or naming a person based on what the person does (the flapper) or what he sounds like (the noise maker). Using these types of labels to refer to a person is "name calling." Name calling is a type of bullying and like all bullying, is a type of verbal devaluation or abuse.

Activity: Why is name calling a form of bullying?

When people are objectified with labels, they are viewed as "goods." The U.S. culture values its many material goods, and this value for objects is easily placed on people, resulting in a person's worth being valued in a similar manner as material goods. While adults may offer what they perceive as positive names – smart head, smarty, genius, cutie, sweetie, and so forth – in reality these are names that a person may not perceive as reflective of who the person thinks he or she is. It should be noted that sometimes an adult refers to all children as "sweetie," making the term an expression of endearment. But, if the label takes the place of a name specifically for a given person, it is devaluation. For example, a teacher had a private conversation with an adolescent. Realizing that this student was struggling personally with a variety of issues, the teacher said, "Good luck, sweetie" at the end of the conversation. The student turned the teacher in for calling her a name and refused to meet with the teacher again. The best policy is not to use "labels" to refer to another person. People have names as part of their "who" or agency. Using a different "name" that reflects an attribute may be abusive.

Activity: Why are labels devaluations?

Labels are not the only type of verbal devaluation. Using descriptors or adjectives that put down ideas, thoughts, beliefs, philosophies, interests, and desires also devalues a person. For example, a student asks lots and lots of questions. The teacher, a little frustrated with the number of questions, says, "Michael that is another silly question." "Silly" is a word meant to describe the question, but it is also a putdown to Michael. In other words, using "silly" to describe Michael's question is similar to saying, "Michael asks a question. The question that Michael asked is silly. Because the question is Michael's question, then Michael is silly."

Even though many people in such situations think that their descriptor ("silly") refers only to the question, not to Michael, it takes a lot of language and social development to separate out the "question" from the person. For the most part, it is better not to assign this type of descriptive language to what people do. There are plenty of examples: "stupid idea, dumb thing to do, that's not smart, that is simply idiotic; can't believe that you would do such a crazy thing," and so forth. Descriptive ways to talk about what people do or think is the same as talking about the person. Derogatory comments about what people think, believe, or feel is the same as a verbal putdown.

Activity: Why do descriptive words sometimes devalue people?

With regard to positive attributes, such as "That was a brilliant idea" or "That is so smart!" most of the time, people feel positive about these types of comments. However, the person is still being valued for what he does, not who he is. And, if a learner or thinker does not agree with the comment, he may still feel devalued. For example, the child says, "Look, look at my picture!" The adult says, "That is a beautiful picture." But the child's emphatic "look!" was over the fact that she does not like the picture because she did not have the color of crayons she wanted to use. The adult's intended positive statement is perceived by the child as devaluation because the child does not think what the adult is thinking. The child feels the adult devalued her. From a social perspective, it is better to leave the judgment up to the learner. "I see your picture. Tell me about it!" Or "I see the picture; what do you think about the picture?" Imposing values or beliefs on the person is a form of devaluation of another person's values or beliefs.

Activity: Why does valuing a person's what over the person's who devalue the person?

Some families spend a lot of time "name calling" one another, giving certain descriptive attributes to the children, creating nicknames, or even making lots of emotional judgments to what children say or do. In these families, it is difficult to identify bullying acts because the family is set up with this type of talk. Teachers who grow up in these families do not hear the children bullying each other in the classroom. Here is a conversation among some second graders put into small groups as part of a project.

Beth:	I like to color the bucket.
Ralph:	You don't color good. I will color it.
Chuck:	Yeah, you just watch.
Isaiah:	Yeah, your coloring is bad.
Beth:	I can color the bucket.
Chuck:	No, give me the paper.
Isaiah:	Go clean up.
Ralph:	(takes the picture from Chuck and colors the bucket) There.
Teacher:	It is time to clean up. (Beth has already returned the materials for her group and is sitting quietly.)
Teacher:	Beth, don't just sit there. Help the other groups clean up. (Beth gets up and puts away paper, scissors, and crayons that are left out around the room).
Teacher:	Who wants to share their group's picture?
Ralph:	I do
Teacher:	Ok, Ralph.
Ralph:	Chuck, Isaiah, and me did this story about the boy and girl at the well. Here is the bucket. Here is the well and here the boy and girl are walking.
Teacher:	You boys did a good job. Anyone else?

In this setting Beth was bullied by the boys in her group as well as by the teacher. Prior to the conversation about the bucket, the boys had not let Beth do anything she asked to do. She had been told that she could not get out the colored paper, that she could not glue the paper, and that they did not want her to write, even though Beth had the best writing skills. Furthermore, Beth was told what to do by both the boys and the teacher, which is a way of imposing the boys' and the teacher's will onto her. Beth was not given options or choices for how to remove herself from the boys nor was she allowed to help make decisions, and she was further devalued with words. She was marginalized (more about this in the next section of this chapter) or left out of the heart of the group work and told that she was being left out because she could not do what the boys could do. This means that she also was not valued as a member or agent of the group. Neither the boys nor the teacher found a way to help include Beth into the group activities.

Activity: How does leaving a person out of the mainstream of an activity result in bullying?

The next day, the teacher again chose who would be in which small groups. (This decides who works with whom.) The teacher is making the choices for the students without protecting the interactions of those with whom Beth was working. The teacher's attempt to control their behavior also did not empower students to make their own choices nor allow Beth an option for how to not be devalued. In other words, the adult's message is that the students are not able to make good choices about whom to work with. Nor was this teacher able to protect Beth from the verbal bullying.

Again, Beth was assigned to work with three boys. After 20 minutes of being told that she could not color, paste, cut, or do any of the actual paperwork, Beth sat down in a corner and just watched the classmates move around the room. Seeing Beth sitting in the corner, the teacher told her to clean up for the other groups. Beth, who never exhibited unwanted classroom behavior, said to the teacher, "I don't want to do that." At that point, the teacher walked over and told Beth that it was not a choice; the teacher was telling her to do the tasks. So Beth stood up and went around the room gathering scissors that she put away for the class. Interestingly, Beth had lots of language, and here are the two perspectives:

That night at home after school:	Back to School Night Conference with Mrs. Jorge and Mom about two weeks after these events:
Beth to her mother: I had a bad day at school These boys won't let me do any work.	**Mom:** How is Beth doing these days?
Mom: What do you mean?	**Mrs. Jorge:** She is a joy to have in the classroom, but I wish she would stand up for herself a bit.
Beth: We have to work in groups. (Beth then told the whole story about the day before and the repeat of the day's activities and how she just wanted to be left alone since she could not do the work.)	**Mom:** What do you mean?
	Mrs. Jorge: Well, the boys tell her what to do and what not to do and she takes a back seat.
Mom: So when you are left alone, what do you do?	**Mom:** Can you give me an example?
Beth: I just sat and watched. But Mrs. Jorge told me to not sit there. She said to clean up.	**Mrs. Jorge:** Yes, one day she just went over and sat in the corner. Instead of sitting in the corner, she needs to put some of the boys in their places.
Mom: Did you talk to Mrs. Jorge about how you feel?	**Mom:** Have you talked with Beth about this?
Beth: No, she tells us not to tattle-tale. I told her about Jeffrey grabbing my pencil off my desk and not returning it and she told me to "take care of it." I asked Jeffrey for my pencil and he laughed.	**Mrs. Jorge:** No, I really can't do that. I want the students to work it out. But I want you to know that if she stands up for herself and physically puts them in their place, I won't get after her.
Mom: Did you get your pencil back?	**Mom:** What? What do you mean by "physically?"
Beth: No. And Emanuel has most of my crayons.	**Mrs. Jorge:** Well you know… sometimes kids just have to let others know who is boss. I will turn a blind eye if she physically takes care of it.
Mom: So how do you feel about all of this?	**Mom:** You are giving her permission to hit another child? (Mrs. Jorge nods her head.) That is not acceptable in our family – hitting is not the solution to problems. IF she ever hits another child, I want to know immediately because that is not acceptable behavior.
Beth: I don't like school.	
Mom: You don't like school, or don't like the work with these classmates, the boys?	**Mrs. Jorge:** Well, I am not saying that she needs to get into a fight, just put the boys in their places.
Beth: I don't like to work with the boys. They are mean and hurt my feelings. I feel bad (Beth then cried).	**Mom:** That is not acceptable behavior. I will talk with Beth about using her words to let the boys know that she means business. Beth has talked to me about the boys not allowing her to contribute. I will see if I can give Beth some tools for working with the boys.
Mom: How often does this happen?	
Beth: Every day we do groups.	

Soon thereafter, Mrs. Jorge became a principal. Her school's walls were covered with signs about no tolerance for bullying even though there was plenty of evidence that bullying was taking place. Mrs. Jorge did not know that the lack of pro-social tools meant that she was tolerating bullying by the boys. Her beliefs about allowing children to marginalize one another, to devalue one another, to order one another around in an attempt to help children "work out their social development" is a form of bullying. The adult, a teacher in this case, was not using her adult social status to nurture, support, and protect children from the unskilled behavior of other children who do not have the language or cognitive social tools necessary to be pro-social.

This teacher/principal did not provide the social development that Beth or the boys needed. Furthermore, research (Eddy & Reid, 2011) shows that anti-social behavior increases over time, which means that the teacher needed to stop the boys' ways of interacting with Beth. In this case, the teacher is more responsible for the bullying than the under skilled preadolescent boys. By ignoring the boys' interactions with Beth, the teacher allowed the boys to impose their power on Beth, stripping her of her agency in this situation. In short, the teacher contributed to the boys' bullying of Beth.

Activity: How does ignoring children's interaction allow bullying to occur?

Bullying verbally also comes as threats: "If you don't do your math, you will miss recess." What is the connection between math and recess? Unless, the adult's language connects the behavior to the outcome, the language is threatening. Connecting the behavior to the consequence sounds like this: "Betty, if you do your math while everyone else is doing their math, then you will be finished with your math by the time the bell rings for recess. If you are finished with your math by the time the bell rings for recess, then you will be ready to go to recess. If you do not do your math while everyone else does their math, then your math may not be finished when the bell rings for recess. If you still have math to do when the bell rings, then you will be doing your math while everyone else goes to recess. If you want to go to recess when everyone else goes to recess, then you will want to do your math while everyone else does their math. So do your math now and you will be finished with your math when the bell rings so you will be able to enjoy recess. Is there something I can do to help you finish your math so you can go to recess when the other children go?" The adult might also want to add information about other people, such as the fact the teacher likes fresh air and wants to go outside with the other students. The teacher won't be able to do that if she stays inside with Betty so Betty is able to do her math. Of course, this connection suggests Betty likes recess. Many students do not like recess because there is sometimes more bullying during recess than at any other time of the school day since the adults stand back and watch safety without hearing what students are saying or doing. The lack of structure at recess often allows students who do not have the cognitive, language skills a greater opportunity to bully and be bullied.

Threatening language also sounds like this: "You better behave." "You will get in trouble." "I will call your mom." "You are on my last nerve." "You are going to turn out like your brother!" "You'll be sorry." "I'm watching you!" "You are going to go to jail you keep that up." "Nobody's goin' to like you!" "You should know better!" Threatening language is a form of bullying.

Activity: Why is threatening language abusive?

Language that is personally derogatory or inflammatory is also a form of bullying. This type of language sounds like this: "You are so rude." "You should know better." "Your work is not acceptable." "You are rotten." "You give me a headache." "You are unkind." "You are spoiled." "You are silly." "You are shy." "You are just like your sister." "You are so manipulative." "You're a non-reader." "You're always wiggling." "You can't know; you are not a parent." "You aren't qualified." "You're autistic."

Activity: What does derogatory language sound like?

Language that stereotypes a person is also a form of bullying. Stereotypical language sounds like this: "Andy is a non-reader." "He is one of those blonde haired, blue-eyed boys." "He is one of those Smith kids. None of them are any good." "He's autistic." "She's an aspie." "He's a squirmer." "She's one of those kids." "She's a Mark School kid." Again, this type of language labels the person in terms of the person's behavior and therefore devalues the person.

Activity: Why does stereotypical language devalue a person?

Power Plays. Any time an adult uses his power to manipulate a child's behavior into meeting the adult's needs; there is a "power play," whereby the adult takes some of the child's power for the adult's needs. Physical or sexual abuse of a child is a clear example of power play that most people recognize. But there are also emotional power plays. Emotional power plays often set the child up to try to take care of the adult's physical or emotional well-being. For example, the adult who plays with a child's emotions to get the child to take care of the adult is engaging in a power play. It might sound like this: "Jasmine, I just can't take care of your brother. You take care of him. He needs you. You are better at caring for him. He will cry if you don't hold him and care for him. I need to go out. He will be happier with you and I will love you." Jasmine is not only a parent for her brother; she is also a parent for the mother who is holding her love for Jasmine in hostage. If Jasmine does what the mother wants, then Jasmine's mother will love her.

Power play language often turns the parent-child relationship upside down or turns one parent against the other parent. Power play language sounds like this: "You just don't understand that Sarah (who has ASD) needs me (spoken to a spouse who wants some time with the other spouse.)" A parent might say this to a teacher, "You would understand if you were a parent." A teacher might say, "Make me look good for the principal, who is coming to evaluate me." Or a teacher might appeal to students to take care of her needs. "I am having trouble at home and need you all to be especially good for me."

Power plays can result in very unhealthy relationships where children must stay socially isolated and part of the adult's activities in order for the adult(s) to feel fulfilled. Unfortunately, this has serious consequences on other adult relationships. Sometimes, special educators must "keep" a child in their "control" in order to be sure the child gets what he or she needs. This type of control is also a type of power play. "Marianne is doing well in the learning resource center. She is mine." This suggests that Marianne is a material good to be bartered over. What does Marianne need? Marianne's education is about Marianne, not about the teacher's classroom or what the teacher is doing in the classroom.

Activity: What is a power play?

Social Exclusion. Social exclusion or marginalization is another form of bullying. This type of bullying occurs as a result of limiting a person's pro-social power by limiting the child's power to be with others and, therefore, to initiate and maintain healthy relationships. On one hand, children with ASD and many related social communication or learning/language disorders often seek to be alone, which makes it difficult for adults to push the isolated students to seek out being with other students. On the other hand, educators often place these same students into small groups of children who do not socially interact well. And, sometimes, adults work alone with these students, which also limit children's time to be social with others their own age.

Many of these students isolate themselves not only to be able to process their thinking but to avoid the types of anti-social situations that they find with students who do not want to sit with them, eat with them, choose them to play on their teams, and so forth. To be included with others in a social situation, students must be able to fit into a group. To "fit into a group," a student must have the tools necessary for being part of the group. These tools are language ways to interact with other students – how to ask others to play, how to use words to share ideas, how to speak about activities that are shared interests, and so forth. The language methods provided throughout the book will work for students to learn how to talk with others about shared activities.

Activity: What are the tools needed to initiate and maintain a pro-social type of inclusion with others?

Even though students sometimes do not have the socio-cognitive language tools to "think" about others and to be in the picture with others, educators are responsible for social exclusion or marginalization. Placing students in small groups of children who do not have the tools for initiating and maintaining healthy relationships means that these students, who are at risk for not being social, are being placed with others who also do not have the language, cognitive, and social tools to initiate and maintain social interactions. These types of environments limit the socio-cognitive tools that children need to be pro-social. Children need to be in supportive, caring, pro-social environments to feel included.

Activity: How does being placed with others who lack pro-social tools result in a form of seclusion or bullying?

Adults often marginalize children as a form of punishment. For example, educators will not allow children go to recess as a form of punishment for not completing work, for receiving too many warnings about class behavior, and so forth. This means that the students who are kept from being included in recess are excluded. They are being marginalized from the whole community. Sending students out of the classroom for services is also a form of marginalization. Yes, many of the services for which children receive academic support result when children are sent out to the speech-language therapist, the reading teacher, the autism specialist, or the behavior support person. But, these students are separated from the class and therefore are often marginalized from the classroom community. The more often the child is sent away to be with others, the more likely it is that the child does not find a community. (It is interesting to see how the included students handle marginalization of other students. If a student is not allowed to be at recess, the other students cannot count on this person for play, for lunch, and soon the student is also marginalized by the other students.)

Activity: How do support activities actually marginalize rather than support some students?

When students possess few opportunities to be part of the community, they will most likely do the same sort of psychological marginalization to others: "You can't be here." "You have to go to the counselor." "You aren't right." "I don't want X to be at my party." "You can't read." Students will talk about what is different about the student who is not part of the community. Soon they will use verbal putdowns. "She rides the short bus." "She is SPED"

"He's a stutterer." "He's weird. He sees this counselor."

The authors have also heard many teachers make comments such as "Never mind him, he is being tested for SPED. Or "Don't bother working with him, he can't do the task. He gets help from Title I." "She is not going anywhere; her whole family are losers." These types of comments in front of a student, or in privacy, are still forms of marginalization, a form of bullying.

Activity: Why is leaving a classroom to work with others a form of social exclusion?

One more type of social exclusion needs to be addressed, attending to deficits. Any time educators or parents draw attention to a child's differences (deficits) as a way to help the child; the child is set apart from being fully included in the child's community. For example, a teacher moves a student who has trouble focusing to the front of the classroom to help her focus. In doing so, the emphasis is on what this child can't do – focus. So the child is marginalized. However, if the classroom were set up to recognize all students as special, then one child might sit closer to the teacher to be able to see the board while another child sits on couch with a lapboard. The issue is choice! When the teacher moves one child so that one child's needs are met, that child is no longer part of the group. When the group recognizes the differences of people within the group, the group includes those with differences[28] and there is support for all learners' needs.

Even giving a child part of the work asked of other children is a form of marginalization. "Sean, you do just the first 15 problems." This means that he is not the same capable person as the others who are doing 30 problems. In order for Sean to be included or to fit in with the community, he must be able to use strategies to do all 30 problems or the classroom community is set up differently: "Class, choose which 15 problems you will do."

Activity: Why is social exclusion a form of bullying? Give some examples.

Physical Bullying. Bullying does not always take the form of verbal words or marginalization. Bullying can also be physical such as hitting, pushing, giving other students a swirly (head held in the toilet and flushed), spitting on students and so forth. Due to its visible and often vocal nature, most adults notice this physical type of bullying.

However, not all physical bullying is so aggressive. For example, any time a student is physically redirected, there is a chance that the physical act might be a form of bullying. Many of the students who are severely impacted by autism are often physically redirected because they lack the language to be able to understand and comply with adults' requests. In order for the adults to "control" such students, the adults escort, physically move the learner's body, physically aid the child to walk, and so forth. The child is manually moved to do what the adult wants him to do. When children are young (0-3) such physical redirection is easy and typical.

When children are older but do not have the necessary language or thinking to be an agent, these acts manipulate the child's body as if the child were an object. The child is not making the choice to walk, to move independently, or to be an agent. Such physical manipulation is a form of psychological objectification. These children often get bigger and a lot more aggressive. For example, a five-year-old male with autism falls down on the floor and cries and cries when the content of the curriculum is delivered with sound. He cannot use sound for speaking, reading or writing. But, at five, he can be physically helped up, rewarded for walking, and be guided into another place where the task is working with puzzles or some other visual-motor task. As he grows older, he grows bigger but he has not learned to be literate (does not speak, read, write, view or think about others). He is now 12 years old and much bigger. When he throws himself on the floor or cries and cries, his hands and feet often hit others and hurt them. So, he has to be medicated and physically restrained and even hospitalized. Because his learning needs were not met, he never was empowered to becoming an agent. The meaning assigned to him was as if he was an object to be controlled through external rewards and now he is even more physically acted upon because he hurts others. Being acted on like an object results in children learning to objectify others.

---

[28] For more information about how to set up a classroom of respect, see Arwood and Young (2000).

To avoid bullying or imposing the adults' will on a child who is not compliant, the adults must help the child develop the language necessary to behave. Previous chapters provided examples of using language tools to help children learn to think to make choices to be an agent.[29] These types of tools help empower children. As a result, they soon walk independently, point to appropriate pictures for choices, gaze at others to show agency between the child and the adults, and so forth. The following is a case example.

Case Study: Arjun

When I first started working with Arjun, she was a 14-year-old young woman significantly impacted by ASD. Although she had not been removed from the classroom or isolated from her peers in her special education placement, she required a high level of supervision to be successful at school due to the aggressive behaviors she had developed. Some of her behaviors included pulling hair, grabbing glasses, vomiting, biting, and smearing bodily fluids.

Arjun had some verbal ability, but her oral communication was monotone and difficult to understand unless the listener was familiar with her speech patterns. Arjun had some sign language ability and used signs to supplement her verbalizations, although her verbalizations did not necessarily match what she was really trying to communicate. Object pictures had been used for many years in the form of visual schedules and an augmentative communication system, but Arjun was not independent in her usage of those formal pictures and needed multiple cues to use her communication system independently, especially in various settings in school. She was more successful at home. Arjun showed significant delays in processing time, and if the adults around her did not give her the time she needed to process information, she acted out one or more of her aggressive behaviors to communicate her confusion.

Arjun had a very active IEP team, who met regularly to develop and refine behavioral support plans for both home and school. Her school and family also received regular support from independent autism specialists outside of the school system, and her behavioral support plan was extremely detailed and organized.

The staff assistant, Molly, who was working with Arjun was highly trained in multiple educational methodologies and in dealing with sensory issues surrounding autism. In addition, she was very open to new ideas to help support Arjun. But Molly reported that she noticed Arjun was getting older and the behaviors were more aggressive. It was apparent to Molly that the more she tried to physically assist Arjun, the more she acted out. Molly also functioned as Arjun's co-parent in that Molly was given court approval to act as Arjun's guardian for school activities.

Molly was introduced to using visual language and thinking for assigning meaning by Carole Kaulitz (one of the authors). Because of Molly's dedication to making sure Arjun had access to information in a way Arjun could process through drawing, hand-over-hand writing, and signing; a sophisticated communication system has been developed over the past few years for Arjun. Molly has become very skilled at drawing and writing about social events for Arjun. These drawings and writings have made a big difference in how Arjun behaves. Both stick figures and symbolic line drawings provide Arjun a visual-motor way she can use to independently meet her needs a majority of the time.

On days when Arjun needs more support to get through her day successfully, the staff assistant utilizes more hand-over-hand writing and drawing as well as physical assistance for other motor tasks, especially for transition times.

Arjun is now 20 years old. Although her aggressive behaviors have significantly decreased as she has gained more meaning, she still reverts to old behavior patterns in situations that she does not have the language to understand. However, she is able to let her caregivers know through her various communication systems what information she needs. She currently has multiple jobs with access to job coaches and with her visual supports is becoming independent in her job skills with the goal that she can eventually work without support. It is hoped that the visual communication systems will include more writing and more information about what others think in order for Arjun to develop even greater understanding for more choices and continued pro-social development.

---

[29] Also see Arwood (2011), Arwood & Kaulitz (2007), and Arwood, Kaulitz, and Brown (2009) for more methods.

This case points out the need to not try to control the behavior physically but to try to provide even those severely impacted by autism more thinking through better learning of language for communication. Remember from *Chapter One*, all behavior is a form of communication: The better the behavior, the more likely the child learns to be pro-social. Also, the more thinking and using language in the way the child learns to think, the better the child will be able to pro-socially behave.

Activity: Why does physically manipulating a child around for compliance lead to bullying?

Techno-bullying. Techno or cyber bullying is a form of controlling others through the use of technology. For example, using the many social media forms of technology provides students with many opportunities to bully others, including leaving groups within a community out of "friend" options or marginalizing peers by writing false rumors through texting about others. Individuals with ASD are affected by the technology age just like any others in our society. In fact, the authors are aware of students diagnosed with ASD who have been encouraged to write false rumors about others through texting in order to fulfill the initiators' need to "have fun." For example, one young man who wanted a girlfriend was told to send out a message about how he and she were in love and going together to the school dance. When the girl read the messages, it was projected she would want to go with him. He sent out the messages. Not surprisingly the young women did not want to go with him and was furious about the false information. She had become a victim by a young man who was the victim of some other students "having fun." Having fun at another's expense is a form of bullying.

Educators must provide students with pictures about what others think (thought bubbles) as well as the words that go with those thoughts. With this overlap of thinking ideas that match with written words, students with ASD are more likely able to understand that verbal communication is about thoughts. Thoughts are matched to words. Words, whether spoken or written, link what others think when a person texts or posts a comment or emails. Writing is a behavior, and that behavior must match thoughts of others in the same picture as the author, not wishes about others. Students need to see that writing does not make something true and that the writing is a behavior and that these behaviors do not make ideas or thoughts for someone else real. Thinking and doing need to be in the same picture with the person that is the recipient of the messages either spoken in real time or through technology.

Activity: What do individuals need to know about writing to avoid situations that bully others?

Taking Material Goods. When a person has material goods or property taken away or damaged, the person's ability to protect those goods is limited. Limiting the power of a person is a form of bullying. Some of these acts of bullying seem simple, such as the kindergarten student who brings crayons to school only to have a couple of other students take the crayons and then break or lose them. Educators have found it easier to have a large bunch of crayons in the middle of the table or in a bin rather than deal with upset students.

But such a solution lacks the language of behavior. Educators and parents can use language to set the stage for what "sharing" is all about, what "accidents" are all about, and what an apology is. For example, saying "sorry" is not an apology. An apology is an act that accomplishes a communication with a specific purpose.[30] In an apology, the person offering the apology must wait for a reply from the recipient and the recipient must be allowed to comment and share feelings. Only then is there a solution or an outcome to make "whole" the person who is experiencing the loss.

For example, Marylou brings crayons to class. She puts the crayons out to share with others. Dennis takes a black crayon and decides to test the crayon's strength by bending it and breaking it in two parts. The teacher, Mrs. Palmer, sees this happen and walks over to the students. In Mrs. Palmer's classroom, the students have learned about sharing and apologies. Marylou says, "That was my only black crayon." Dennis replies, "Well, I didn't mean to." Mrs. Palmer interjects, "What did you not mean to do Dennis?" He says, "To test how strong." Mrs. Palmer says, "Then tell Marylou that you didn't mean to break the crayon and that you will get her another black crayon from the classroom box." Dennis jumps up, goes to the classroom box of crayons, and finds a black crayon and brings it over to Marylou. "Here." Mrs. Palmer helps Dennis again, "Dennis, tell her that you hope she will accept this black crayon for the one you broke." Dennis says, "I am sorry I broke your crayon. Here is another black crayon for you. Okay?"

Marylou says, "Okay. Thanks."

Mrs. Palmer has set up her classroom as a community. She has already spoken to the students about the "classroom materials" being limited, where the supplies come from, how their parents and how the school's taxpayers have paid for the supplies. She has drawn out these relationships, and Mrs. Palmer has included in these concepts the fact that there is no more money to buy more supplies. So Mrs. Palmer will want to talk on a one-to-one basis with Dennis about the black crayon he received to replace the one he broke. In this way, Dennis begins to learn how his actions affect others, not just Marylou but the others in the class when all of the black crayons have been used. Dennis might even be asked to draw and write about what happened so he is able to see how his behavior affects others. In this way, Dennis is learning about how to take responsibility for his actions

---

Activity: How does taking, breaking, or using others' materials without permission become a form of bullying?

The previous example was a simple use of one's goods. There are more serious violations such as graffiti on the walls, spitting on other students from a loft in the school, stealing books, damaging desks, and so forth. Society has set up ways to protect students from having to be responsible for their acts such as not requiring students to sand, repair, and paint items that they break or misuse. But prevention helps. For example, if students are part of the school's decorating committee where the students design what goes on the walls and the students paint and decorate the walls, then they are less likely to damage the walls. If students are given the responsibility for acting as responsible agents, they

---

[30] These specific-purpose acts are called performatives (Arwood, 2011) in language studies. Performatives are powerful acts that accomplish a shared understanding between a speaker and hearer. Other performatives include steal, lie, marry, vow, and promise.

are less likely to destroy their own work, their own planning, and so forth. And if students have the language for understanding how their actions affect others and the language to understand how they are positive (pro-social) agents, they have no need to hurt others and will understand when their actions do hurt others.

For example, a student steals another student's backpack. The educator says, "Miguel, I saw you steal Humberto's backpack." Miguel responds, "I didn't steal anything." "Miguel, did you take Humberto's backpack?" "No, I didn't. I am not bad. I don't steal." "Miguel, did that hand (educator points to Miguel's hand) pick up that backpack (educator points to the backpack)?" Miguel watches the educator and says, "Yes."

So now, the educator must take the time to draw out what it looks like for a hand to pick up a backpack that Miguel did not bring, did not buy and, therefore, does not own. Miguel needs to learn that when someone else buys a backpack with the money that they had to work for and brings the backpack that they paid for to school and sets the backpack down, then, even if his or her hands on no longer on the backpack, the backpack belongs to the person who left it there because that person bought the backpack and, therefore, the person who left the backpack owns the backpack. WHEW! If that explanation seems like a lot of concepts and a lot of language; then, yes, there are a lot of concepts and language that go into ideas like "steal" or "respect." Concepts take a lot of language to learn (*Chapters Eight-Ten*).

There is a lot of language in this situation, but without the language Miguel believes that he did not steal the backpack. The prisons are full of people who do not believe they did crimes for which they are accused. Some of these people have created the language to fit their beliefs and, therefore, their mental pictures. Many people, like Miguel, do bad things without knowing they are doing bad things. Their environments and their lives are full of behaviors to which there is little language. Therefore, they are prey to others with more language and understanding. In turn, those who are prey learn to prey on others who do not expect to be victims. In a way, students who lack this sort of deep conceptual understanding of their behavior are also victims. They are victims of society's a lack of using enough language to help them learn the concepts.

Activity: How does language affect a person's damage of others and their goods?

Racial and Sexual Bullying. Any type of stereotyping can contribute to bullying, which is an abuse of power. The idea of isolating a group, a characteristic, or a difference is to make the other person feel less powerful so that the person or group offending is feeling superior. Name calling and marginalization fits into this category of bullying, but so does stereotyping. Language such as "those people," "they're all alike," "blondes are so ditsy," "blacks are athletic," "she's autistic," fit into the stereotyping category. Individuals who stereotype others or groups of others sometimes lose sight of people being individuals. If the thinker does not see a person who is stereotyped as an individual, the thinker is more likely to believe that racial or sexual comments are okay. For example, just shy of date rape is the pressure of telling a person that he or she won't date the person without sex or that the person has to have sex because the victim owes the bully sex, and so forth. These are power plays designed to feel more powerful through manipulating another person into behavior that makes the bully feel good.

Language that belittles a person for a person's racial background is also a form of bullying. For example, "He's an autistic Asian … got to be a genius." Or as a teacher said to one of the authors, "He's one of those Arian blondes, you know, a trouble maker." When the author looked dumbfounded, the teacher continued, "You know the type, blonde hair and blue eyes, wiry; can't sit still and won't do anything. I had three of those this year. Two are in special education and this one will be soon." That teacher began the school year with 17 children. By April, she had six children left, all dark-haired Caucasians. The neighborhood was racially diverse, but all the non-Caucasian, or blonde Caucasian children, were referred out of the general education classroom.

Activity: What is sexual and racial bullying?

Setting Limits to Stop Bullying

The biggest hurdle in stopping bullying is being able to recognize bullying, all sorts of bullying. The purpose of the previous section was to help the reader understand that words and actions result in bullying any time a child, youth, or adult is name called, marginalized, socially excluded, stereotyped, or physically/sexually or materially hindered. In order to prevent bullying, set limits with language. The following are suggestions for how to set limits.

- Get involved – Standing back does not protect a child and is, therefore, an indirect form of bullying. For example, Joe sees Will rocking while eating his sandwich. Joe walks past Will and asks if he is a retard. Joe laughs because he is uncomfortable and not used to social interaction. A teacher nearby sees the interaction and thinks, "Well, it is good that Will has a sense of humor." This is also bullying by the teacher because the teacher does not get involved. Get involved and set limits. To set limits use language.

- Use lots of language – The teacher sees Joe call Will a name, "Are you a retard?" The teacher, Mr. Robertson, walks over to Joe and says, "I heard you ask Will if he was a retard? What does that mean?" Joe giggles out of discomfort and says, "I don't know." Mr. Robertson now takes Joe to a corner and begins to draw, write, and talk about what that means, what Will thought, and why this sort of language is bullying another person. Then Joe is told that he must do something to undo the mean act, so Joe suggests that he go to Will and talk to him. Mr. Robertson tells Joe that he must draw out the scenario and change his words and his thoughts so that Will can see that Joe was trying to greet Will.

Activity: Many examples of how to draw and write were presented in previous chapters. The reader is encouraged to use the Joe and Will situation to try to cartoon and write about the situation.

- Socially connect students so they are not easy prey: Will was sitting alone when Joe passed by. Sitting alone creates an opportunity for others to pick on the lone student. So, set up a community atmosphere in the school (Arwood & Young, 2000). This type of atmosphere encourages individuals to be connected with one another. A school based on community uses ways to validate the person by inviting lone individuals to join a group. Teachers would model this type of behavior in the classroom and help students learn how to invite others to join in all sorts of community activities. Teachers don't just model the appropriate way to socially include others, but provide the language of the thinking behind including all people into groups. When students are not excluded, they are not easy prey.

- Protect, nurture, and support – These three acts are best accomplished by using language to recognize others, give credit to all contributions of all students, and show appreciation for all actions. Recognizing another person is learning to speak to the person, greeting a person, saying how you missed the person when the person is absent, or even asking the person a question about what the person likes, doesn't like, or about the person's interests, ideas, hobbies, etc. Giving credit means to use language to let others know about contributions to a community. For example, after transition, Mr. Young comments, "We need to thank Ralph for his help. Ralph saw that there were scraps of paper on the floor so he stopped and picked up the paper. Ralph, your generosity of time and effort will pay off this evening when the janitors come in. The janitors will be able to leave earlier than usual and spend more time with their families because you were willing to help them by picking up scraps of paper. Thank you!" Giving credit really encourages others to perform acts of kindness. The next day, others were also picking up scraps and Mr. Young talked about how kind the whole group functioned in their help keeping their room clean and respectful. Appreciation can be simply a thank you for your time, effort, help, etc. Or, showing appreciation can be writing a thank you note. It is amazing how often people comment about receiving a thank you note. Even in class, thank you notes can be given so that all students are shown appreciation for just being who they are. Recognizing others, giving credit, and appreciating take the place of rewarding and punishing the "what's" or the behaviors. In this way, emphasis is on agency so that children and youth understand their strengths.

- Teach meta-cognitive strategies – If students know how they learn best, they are more likely to be empowered. When a child believes she is capable, the child is more likely to stop others from bullying because the empowered student does not need to bully others to feel good. In earlier chapters, the authors explained how we learn and how most children and youth who struggle with pro-social development are learning to think in a visual-motor way, making mental pictures, shapes, movies, and so forth. Knowing that a particular way of thinking is okay and that there are ways to capitalize on the strengths of a learning system is empowering.

- Know what is okay behavior and what is not okay behavior– This is critical for adults in order to be able to set limits. When adults are confident about what behavior is okay or not okay, they are more likely to be consistent. If an adult cannot be consistent, then children are not sure about what is okay or not okay. This lack of certainty sets up an opportunity for a child to test his or her competence by devaluing others by name calling, socially excluding, and so on.

- Make pro-social development a priority – Talk about when it is appropriate to use technology and explain about how there are others who think, feel, and so on, on the other end as a way to stop cyber bullying. Talk about how to recognize others, give credit to others, and appreciate others. Talk about what others think and feel in response to specific behaviors. Model what pro-social behavior looks like by stepping in and stopping students' putdowns, name calling, and so on. Explain to students how you expect the same protection that you give to them from them for their friends. Explain friendship and what it looks like behaviorally. Use everyday activities as an opportunity for students to learn how to behave.

Activity: What are some ways to set limits on behavior so as to eliminate bullying?

Summary

Programs have been designed to stop bullying in schools and homes, yet bullying continues, and even increases. Bullying behavior represents a bully's thoughts. To change a bully's thoughts, language about behavior and the effects of behavior on others may be used. Language is a tool that can be used to represent the thinking that goes with pro-social behavior. Pro-social behavior is about initiating and maintaining healthy relationships. Bullying is anti-social behavior that does not foster healthy relationships. When children, youth, and adults are able to understand through thinking the effects of behavior, they are able to change their behavior to match their thinking. By changing anti-social thoughts to pro-social thoughts, bullying is eliminated and children develop pro-social relationships instead.

Important Concepts in *Chapter Thirteen*

Readers should be able to explain each of these behavior principles upon completion of this chapter:

1. Learning to promote thinking and language of behavior is part of a prevention program.

2. Preventing behavior problems through strategies for better learning, literacy and higher levels of problem solving improves pro-social development.

3. Learning to be pro-social prevents the development of anti-social behavior.

4. Language is a tool for prevention as well as intervention with regard to behavior.

5. Language mediates thinking and, therefore, also behavior.

6. Deciding how to think about behavior helps determine the way to assign meaning to behavior.

7. The best behavior programs include prevention measures along with tools to facilitate, pro-social development

CHAPTER THIRTEEN
Prevention—A Different Way to Think about Behavior

I see that this is different.
At school I am told "no."
At home I am told "why."
I like knowing why....

This book emphasizes developing pro-social development as a result of improved thinking for better behavior. In this sense, this book is about prevention as an approach to helping children learn the language of behavior. In other words, all behavior is a form of communication. If adults assign pro-social meaning through consistent setting of limits, the elimination or focus on "what's" such as rewards and punishers, and provide more emphasis on the use of language to develop the child's "who"; then the child is more likely to learn to be pro-social. However, even with the best prevention, there are times when intervention seems to be the only option. In the spirit of intervening while also preventing a further negative spiral of anti-social behavior, this last chapter is set up for the reader to apply the knowledge in this book to a particular child or group of children. The reader will be guided through questions and activities designed to help the reader establish an effective language approach to a specific child or group of children as a means to prevent behavior problems or to intervene when behavior problems occur. Emphasis will be on how to help children learn the language of behavior for improved pro-social development. As a way to use all tools, this chapter will highlight the methods of prevention as well as intervention from the previous chapters.

Learning to Behave
Learning to behave is a pro-social approach to learning how to initiate and maintain healthy relationships. The child is not the child's behavior. So, for adults to learn to assign pro-social meaning while separating what a child does from the child, the adult must learn to observe behavior without judgment or emotional interpretation.

1. *Use unbiased observation.* Observe a child or a small group of children. Record exactly what you see. If the child's hand moves then write down which hand moved, what direction did the hand move, and did the hand touch anything or anybody? Where did the hand touch? What did you see after the hand touched? For example, a parent is watching a child at a playground. The parent records, "John pushed Sara with his left hand." This report is not specific and does not separate John from his behavior. The report also is a judgment since the act of "pushing" cannot be seen. *Behavior is a set of acts, without language of judgment.* Here is the same report

looking at behavior only, without judgment: "John is standing next to Sara who is sitting on her bottom on the bench. John's left hand moves up into the air and then his left hand falls down on Sara's shoulder. Sara turns her head and her eyes gaze on John's face." So do you know if John hit Sara? We really don't know. It is important not to assume that John's behavior had intentionality. Hitting implies an intention and casts a judgment on John. On the other hand, if John did not know how to interact with Sara in a socially appropriate way, then he probably did not know what to do. John is not his behavior so record only the behavior not his thinking. When he learns to think about behavior then he can explain why he hit Sara or did not hit Sara. It is important to take John through a cartoon of what he looked like and what he could do depending on what John and Sara had in common. For example, maybe John was trying to get Sara's attention or maybe John wanted Sara to play or maybe he wanted to hit her for taking something of his. Drawing out what the adult saw and then adding the various scenarios and what is okay and not okay helps John learn what behaviors are okay under these conditions (*Chapter Two* also provides examples.

2. ***Decide the learning level.*** Choose what level of learning you want. All behavior is learned. What do you want your child or children to learn? Do you want them to learn the skills and patterns for imitation, copying, or regurgitation? Or, do you want them to learn to think about their choices of behavior?

Methods that use principles of operant conditioning (direct instruction, discrete trials, targeting behavior) to reinforce, chain, and successively approximate target behaviors will work well for psychomotor skills such as "doing" something. But if you want the child to socially think for problem solving and learning, then methods that focus on helping children learn how to think and use language are important.

Consider both options: 1) observe a child or children and decide which behaviors or clusters of behavior that you want to improve. If the child (children) already uses this targeted behavior or is capable of imitating a target behavior, you can increase the number of times the behavior occurs by pairing the behavior with positive reinforcement. For example, the child knows some sounds and letters but does not read fluently. You can help the child practice the sounds and letters for faster reading, but the child may still not be able to think about what the words mean. If a child can sit down, increasing the number of times a child sits on command does not improve the child's thinking. Or increasing the number of fluently read words does not improve the understanding of the story. 2) If you want the child to think, then you will want to draw the child sitting and thinking (thought bubbles) with words below the frames as well as provide a lot of language overlap in order to increase the child's choice of sitting and engaging in thinking. And, if the oral fluency is not becoming understanding, then the child does not learn concepts with sound. So, change the approach to reading. Help the child learn to read through the child's own use of language to name the child's concepts about activities the child does or can see in a shared picture.[31] Remember that all concepts are both social and cognitive. As a child learns to think at a higher level of conceptualization, the child's pro-social development will increase as long as the environment continues to assign positive meaning to the child's

---

[31] More about how to increase literacy can be found in Arwood, Kaulitz, and Brown (2009) or Arwood (2011).

agency or "who." So learning to be literate runs parallel to learning to be pro-social, given a supportive, protective, and nurturing environment.

3. *Know what behavior is okay.* It is important that as an adult you have made a decision about what behavior is okay or not okay (See *Chapter Three* about what constitutes acceptable behavior). Remember all behavior is okay; it is just when, where, and under what conditions a behavior can exist. Consistent assignment of meaning to behavior can only occur if the adults "know" what is okay. Whatever you decide, you must be able to explain why you made that decision. For example, if you want your child to sit on his bottom, then why? If you try to explain why and can't, then you need some work on your own boundaries of what is okay and not okay for children to do. Drawing out what you would like as desired behavior; then put the "who, what, where, when, how, and why" to the behavior to help establish the boundaries to behavior.

4. *Assign pro-social meaning to behavior.* Many adults think that using reinforcement or rewards is the same as assigning meaning. Assigning meaning is a commentary to help the child learn about how and why to engage in certain behaviors. For most children who struggle in an auditory culture, like the US, they need to learn the meaning of behavior through visual-motor language approaches such as cartoons. This type of assigning meaning is pro-social in nature and focuses on the development of the child as an agent, someone who is able to think about choices.

To increase a targeted or desired behavior through the use of rewards, an adult pairs the behavior the adult wants or expects with positive reinforcement. For example, you want the child to sit down, so you get the child to sit (maybe through imitation, pointing, talking, or catching the child sitting) and then you give something paired with sitting (verbal "good sitting", bean in a jar to be turned in with other beans for a prize, etc.). The trick to reinforcement is that the learner has to be able to explain if he or she finds the reinforcement to really be positive. The idea behind reinforcement is that it is supposed to increase the likelihood of a behavior occurring again. Since most children with low levels of social functioning do not have the language for this approach, it is probably best to consider another option. In other words, a child with low level language will not understand why you are pairing a behavior with a reinforcer. The behavior temporarily increases; but, the child may or may not know when to use the behavior, what the behavior means, or how to think about the behavior. The result is that the child will temporarily show changes but without an approach that focuses on the language of behavior, the child will not learn to think at a higher level. Responding to cues for compliance is learning at a pattern level. There is little thinking. The child gets bigger and bigger. *Use lots of language about behavior through writing, drawing, and refining the writing and drawing, even with non-verbal, non-readers and writers to increase their thinking.* Remember adults do not wait until babies can talk to talk to babies. Adults do not need to wait until children can say their alphabet before we can write to them. And children can tell you what they write and draw about before they can read. Assign meaning so that children can learn to be literate which means that they are learning the relationships among thinking, language, and behavior.

Activity: What level of learning is used to get a target behavior?

---

5. *Emphasize thinking.* What about getting rid of a behavior you don't want? If a behavior is not something that an adult wants, then gradually decreasing the behavior gives learners the message that the behavior is sometimes okay, a mixed message. In other words, as long as the behavior continues, even at a lower percentage, the behavior is still happening, which means it is okay. When and where and why a person chooses a behavior is a thinking issue, not a quantitative issue. It's probably better to go for eliminating the behavior so that the child knows that the behavior is not okay in the situation that the behavior is targeted.[32]

To eliminate a behavior: Since rewards are punishers and vice versa, it is probably best to try to replace unwanted behaviors with desirable behaviors. However, in the case of violence (aggressive behavior that will self-injure or hurt another person), the unwanted behavior must be prevented...that is, prevented and/or stopped. Punishment has a short-lived viability. The child starts to draw a concealed weapon and the adult immediately suppresses the child's body movement so the child cannot use the weapon. This type of "stopping" the behavior and then later adding a punisher such as expelling the student from school does not provide the reasoning behind not bringing a gun to school or drawing a concealed gun. As long as the punishment option exists, the child may not bring the gun to school but again working only with the behavior without spending time on the child's thinking does not help the child learn when and where to use a gun and why he should or should not have a gun to use. Punishment works to stop an unwanted behavior for a short time but does not really eliminate the possibility of the behavior happening again under the specific circumstances. Only changing a child's thinking is truly successful in eliminating a behavior. Increasing pro-social thinking will prevent an unwanted behavior from happening again.

6. *Empowerment is better than control.* Physical restraint is also a type of punishment that stops a behavior but does not change the thinking behind the behavior that occurred and had to be stopped such as being physically out of control. Adults must learn the law and the rules related to physical restraint. Learning to physically restrain requires special training and should occur only as a last resort. All individuals who work with individuals who are externally aggressive should have training in how to restrain in order to stop behavior that could result in someone being injured. Restraint is punishment! Restraint does not help a child learn how to replace the unwanted behavior with other behaviors that stem from better choices. Restraint focuses on the "what" of the child, not the child's who. And, in some ways, restraint is a form of objectification. In order for a child to act as an agent with pro-social behavior, the child must be able to be empowered to think as an agent. Thinking like an agent in relationship to other agents develops the child's pro-social thinking with the language of behavior. If the child is functioning as an agent in relationship to others, then physical restraint would not be needed.

7. *Emphasize being an agent.* An agent is a person who is able to function in pro-social ways to initiate and maintain healthy relationships with others. By emphasizing behavior that makes the

---

[32] Remember that all behaviors are okay...it is when and where and why the behavior occurs that is the critical issue in learning to behave.

child an agent, the child cannot perform unwanted anti-social behavior. For example, a child cannot throw a pencil if the child is writing with the pencil. An adult could choose to wait until the pencil is thrown and then punish the child; or, the adult could see the child raise the pencil and say, "I see you put your pencil on your paper so you can write your name." It is important that the assigned meaning is something the child can do. A child cannot run down the hall if the child is walking. So, drawing, in a cartoon, the child walking down the hall puts the child in the hallway. Now draw the thought bubbles of what it looks like to walk and think about where the child is going keeps the child walking, not running. Emphasizing the child and why the child is walking places the child in the child's own picture as an agent. Probably the easiest replacement of behavior occurs in the classroom where students are behaving in unwanted ways; blurting out, interrupting a speaker, walking round the room when others are sitting, sharpening pencils when listening is expected, and so forth. Since most children today use a visual way of thinking, then these children are engaging in behavior that shows how they are learning concepts. If these children are using their bodies for meaningful tasks, then they probably use a movement to create mental shapes for thinking. It is easy to provide them with a replacement behavior that supports these learners as agents. For example, primary students are sitting on a carpet. Two students are using their hands to go through the books on the shelf next to the carpeted area. One student is playing with a fan in her lap. Another student is twisting her hair. A third girl is reaching up to undo the hair twists. The boy sitting next to her tells her to not touch. Meanwhile, another student is scooting over to where he is up against another child who pushes him away. Several students are tying or untying their shoes, pulling up socks, adjusting skirts, looking at lint in pockets, etc. Hand them all child-sized white dry erase boards for drawing and writing. The dry erase boards fit into the classroom better than scooting, pushing, twisting, and untying.

All of these children needed something in their hands to do with their hands. By drawing and writing on their boards, they are acting in pro-social ways as agents. Furthermore, the adult can draw and write for the children; so, the children know what to think, what others are thinking and what they can choose to do. The teacher assigns meaning with visually rich language such as "Your job when you are sitting on the carpet is to look at the teacher's mouth move and make pictures of what the teacher says. When you have several pictures in your head, draw some of those pictures onto your dry erase board." The purpose of this language is to help the children learn to be pro-social agents who make choices based on their thinking. The teacher is using the language of behavior to help the students pro-socially behave.

Activity: Find an irritating behavior such as drumming, untying shoes, picking skin, and decide what do you want the children who are doing this disturbing behavior to really be doing and why? How can I make that child's hands productive by using language to explain what actions are expected? How do I help the child become an agent?

Learning to Think

Learning to think as an agent engaged in pro-social behavior provides opportunities for continuing to learn. For example, children who are writing, drawing, constructing a model, cartooning, coloring, speaking, viewing, listening, watching, painting, and calculating are thinking. Being agents engaged in appropriate behaviors offer additional opportunities to learn to think. So, anytime there is a choice between giving the child something to stay busy with or giving the child a form of literacy, choose the literacy. Thinking is better learning than sitting on bumpy balls or handling squishy balls. Keep in mind that the form of literacy must match the way the child learns to think. For example, asking a child to write, to stay busy, when the child has only been taught to use sounds for writing will be a punishment, if the child cannot use the sounds for learning concepts. Asking the same child to draw pictures about what the teacher is saying could be a great replacement for doing origami during class time. There are additional benefits to the writing or drawing in that the child is learning to think about what he sees cognitively as well as in the particular situation. In this way, the drawing of ideas means the child is learning concepts; the writing with shapes and drawings is helping the child to think at a higher level, and so forth. Remember, use lots of the language of behavior. For example, "John when you sit on your bottom with your feet flat on the floor, your eyes can see the print on the page better. When your eyes can see the print, then you can make pictures in your head so you can think about what you see on the page."

Learning to think with the language of behavior is to empower a learner to be an agent, thinking about others in healthy, pro-social relationships.

Thinking is unique. It is very easy to assume that a behavior occurs for the same reasons under similar circumstances. However, each person brings unique experience to a situation because no two people have the exact-same past experiences. Therefore, the thinking or cognition behind a given behavior is unique. Each person's thinking or cognition is a compilation of past ideas resulting in unique meta-cognition. No two people will draw the same idea for the same word, for example. Ask a room of educators to each draw his or her own picture of the meaning of "Respect." The educators may draw similar examples but their thinking will be different and so will their pictures. Learning to think to make choices means that learners need to know that people have different mental pictures for the same spoken or written idea.

Language names thinking. How well a person is able to make the choices that others expect depends on the person's level of language. Language names the thinking; so, it is important to use a lot of language to go with the different drawn pictures or mental pictures. Knowing a learner's level of language is important in setting up ways to help the child learn to pro-socially behave.

Select a student that you feel has a problem with a behavior and if the student is older than eight, ask the student the question, "What do you do on a typical day?" Audio record the student's words and then transcribe exactly what the student said. Look at the student's words and answer the following questions:

- Do the words connect with a variety of time based words such as "and," "then," "while," "because," "during," "also" and so forth? Or do the learner's words just create a list of activities. *Table 13.1* provides the reader with an example of the difference between language that is connected in time and language that is not time-based.

Table 13.1. Time-based vs. Non-Time-based Language

Time-Based Language	Not Time-based Language
Well, on most days, I go to work. But once I am at work, my days vary a lot. For example, this semester I teach on Wednesday and Thursday evenings but on Mondays and Fridays, I work in the schools. So a typical day is really hard to define. I guess I could sum up my typical day as some sort of work related to the university and then I try to find time for some sort of exercise followed by family time.	First, I get out of bed, usually at 7:00, do my hygiene thing, put on some clothes, walk the dog, have a cup of coffee and drive to work. I answer emails, work on some reports, teach sometimes, go home. I like to run. Walk the dog for a long time. Eat dinner. Watch some TV or play with my kids. I sort of have a typical day. You know, I do the same sort of things but not the same each day. Each day is different. Is this okay?

If the language is not time-based, then the person thinks visually so using oral language to help a person talk through the thinking behind a behavior will not be effective. If the person qualifies for special education, shows a non-time-based use of language, or limited language production, then talking about thinking will be ineffective. Therefore, to capitalize on how the person learns to think, the reader will want to use visual methods that are language-based as suggested by the Neurosemantic Language Learning Theory (Arwood, 2011) proposed in earlier chapters.

Activity: Why does therapy that emphasizes thinking require inputs to be visual for children with ASD?

Thinking in Visual Language

The majority of learners in the auditory culture of the US think with visual concepts. Language names those concepts. Neuroscience provides the basis for how most people learn concepts. The Neuro-Semantic Language Learning Theory (NLLT) (Arwood, 2011) provides not only the theory behind the neuroscience of learning but how to translate the neuroscience into cognitive and language based methods. Since most individuals with ASD and related disorders think with the shape of visual ideas (Arwood & Kaulitz, 2007), then this theory suggests that learning to behave requires the use of visual thinking strategies. This use of visual thinking works for the majority of learners (about 85%).

Use visual language. Translate the sound of words into mental visual pictures. Simple oral translations sound like this: "Look with your eyes not your hand" for "Don't touch." "Use your words not your hands" for looking at a vase. "Sit on your bottom so that your eyes can look at the paper and make pictures in your head" in place of "Sit down." "When you open your mouth, your ideas fall out and fill my space and make my pictures go away" in place of "Don't interrupt" or "Be quiet!" Pick two commands that you say over and over. First, draw out the pictures of what the words really mean. Then write the words that go with the pictures. Make sure your words match the pictures you drew, not what you often say. Use the pictures to refine your words and then write out what you really mean when you say the phrases you chose.

Use visual sequences of events. To follow instructions or directions, use a sequence of pictures like cartooning. Examples are found in several sections of the book. These cartoons are explained in detail in Arwood &Brown (1999) and Arwood, Kaulitz, &Brown (2007). Brown is the author of most of the cartoons in these books. By using the sequence of pictures, the child begins to see how behavior connects self to others. Draw out two cartoons about behavior. Use at least three frames or squares and as many as five squares for each cartoon. Make sure the person the cartoon is about is facing the same way in each frame so that the learner is able to see him or her move in one direction like a movie film. Draw a line across the bottom of each square so that the person moving in each cartoon frame is on that line (grounded). Be sure that all people are stick figures with two eyes, a nose, a mouth, and two hands and feet. Be sure that all of your square frames connect and that there are no missing pictures.

Write! Do so, even if the child does not know how to read and write. Writing shows what the language for behavior visually looks like and shows the child what the visual-motor patterns look like that match the child's thinking. Instead of drawing out pictures, write out the words to what you see as a behavior. Watch the behavior and then use written words to say exactly what you see. Connect all ideas with connective language such as "because," "during," "while," "when," "then," "also," "which," "that," "meanwhile," "even though," "although," "so," etc.

Use rich language. As Mabel Brown (one of the authors) often says, "You cannot give a child too many rules!" As Carole Kaulitz (one of the authors) says, "When it comes to language, more is better than less to help create mental movies in an individual's head." And, Ellyn Arwood (another of the authors) says, "If the person cannot read, write, and tell about the behavior; then the person does not know why he or she did the behavior." All of the authors are saying that learning to behave is a neurosemantic consequence of the learning language system so when a child or adult does not behave as expected, then the child or adult does not have the language for behaving as expected.

Use a video recorder to collect a baseline of data on how much and what type of language you use during a session with a child or adult whose behavior you want to change. Play back the recorder and transcribe your language and the learner's language. Does each learner's behavior have a language-based response from the adult with lots of connections? Do you respond to the learner's behavior with language that sets limits and explains consequences of behavior? Increase your use of rich, visual type of language for all activities. Then check to see if the behavior you want to change is changing. The more language a child has, the better the child will be behave as expected; provided that the child knows what is expected and that the expectations have been given to the child or learner the way that person learns.

Use language to set limits. A child behaves in the way that the adults allow the child to behave since the child must learn the language of how to behave. To set limits of what is okay or not okay, here is a task:

Go into a home or classroom. Look around. Do you see instructions and expectations drawn out with *added written words* explaining the pictures? Based on what you see, would you know what you are expected to do? Do you understand the daily sequence of events? Do you know what others think about behaviors? Remember the following:

- Tell children the behaviors you expect by drawing out the expectations

- Make expected behaviors into rules that are written to the drawn pictures

- Consistently follow through with the behavioral rules you establish by drawing and writing the rules

- If you have to say the expectation/rule more than twice, it suggests that the child does not understand something about the spoken words used. Instead of talking to the child, draw out the expectation/rule to show what you expect and why.

Construct Pro-Social meaning

The construction of meaning is dependent on what others in a learner's environment believe as well as the way others assign meaning to behavior. So what others assign as meaningful determines what learners often think.

Choose a behavior that is irritating or annoying such as a child fussing when it is time to take a bath and re-assign meaning. For example, a child fusses when the water touches his face and you gently laugh and say, "Oh, the water feels so funny. The water is getting your face all clean!" And, immediately add more water. The child learns to laugh in association to the water rather than to fuss. Or, a child sees the oatmeal bowl come out of the cupboard and the child lies down on the floor, tantrums, and yells "No oatmeal, too hot!" Re-assign meaning by saying, "Okay, I see you don't want that bowl, let's get another bowl and let's touch it to see how cold the bowl is." Now work the child through the next pieces of the task of heating the oatmeal, take it out of the bowl, put it in another cool bowl, etc.

Now choose a behavior that is not acceptable, such as a child urinating in a classroom trashcan. The same assignment is to reassign meaning. This low level of understanding (urinating in the trashcan) of social appropriateness of meaning tells the adult that the child does not understand what others see or think about the behavior. Draw out the scenario so that the child can see where he should go to urinate, how to ask to get to a bathroom, etc. And, especially draw out what others think when they see him urinate in the trashcan and how their thoughts will affect the way they interact with the student in the future.

Constructing meaning is a neurobiological process. Based on the notion that the child's learning system is the origin of all learned behavior, then all learning is neurosemantic and, therefore, chemical and biophysical in nature. This means that some children or adults may not be able to learn the pro-social way to behave in the way that society expects.

There are some simple biophysical interventions that the reader might consider in the process of looking at a child's behavior especially related to diet and exercise. For the best advice in this area, discuss options with physicians (medical doctors and naturopathic doctors); nutritionists; and other health professionals. The authors often find simple changes to diets such as eliminating red dye colors and sugar helps with irritability but does not develop thinking without emphasis on language development. Some children are able to focus for better processing when gluten or dairy are eliminated, not as a cure, but to help with the child's overall health. The healthier a child feels, the better the child is able to perceive the child's world. And, perceptions form concepts. Concepts are named through language. The language of behavior helps a child learn to become pro-socially interdependent.

This chapter has provided an overview of the chapters in this book: *Language of Behavior: A Way to Pro-Socially Think.* Here are some frequently asked questions and answers.

FAQ

QUESTION: Neil was out of control, what do I do?

ANSWER: Any time a child's or an adult's behavior is "out of control," then the learner is functioning at the sensori-motor level. At this level, the learner is responding to sensory input … so change the sensory input. Put a piece of paper in front of the learner's eyes and start drawing and writing in a calm manner. If the behavior will hurt the learner or someone else, then try to physically get as close as possible where the learner cannot "run away" and draw quickly in front of the learner's eyes. Functioning at the sensori-motor level means the learner will not have "thinking" to remember what happens during the event. So having a paper copy that you can refer back to later actually helps scaffold the concepts so that the learner has other choices of behavior based on better thinking in future situations. Also when a learner is out of control, the environment was not providing what the learner needed. Rethink what you were doing just before the learner's behavior deteriorated. Maybe it was math and the learner cannot do the math the way the math is being taught. Maybe there was not enough structure (for example recess) so the learner did not have anything to think about.

QUESTION: Nancy is always picking at her face. It makes the other students cringe and it is so unsanitary.

ANSWER: When a learner does a behavior that others do not like, the first thing to remember is that the learner does not know what impact her behavior has on others. Repetitive motor behaviors such as picking often suggests the individual is learning concepts with motor access to visual thoughts; so begin with writing out what others see: "Nancy, when you put your hand on your face, then others see you put your hand on your face. When the fingers on your hand scratch and pick the skin on your face, then the other boys and girls can see your scratch and pick. When you scratch and pick your skin on your face, then your skin begins to bleed. Other boys and girls can see your face bleed. Sara sees your face bleed. Mark sees your face bleed. Mrs. Smith sees your face bleed. When your face bleeds, you fingers touch the blood. The blood runs under your nails on your fingers. Your fingers and nails have blood on them. Then you touch your books and papers. You touch desks, door handles, pencils and the other boys and girls do not want to touch the same desks, door handles, pencils because blood can sometimes carry diseases and so forth." The more language the learner is given about why picking skin is not liked by the others in the classroom, the better the learner is able to think about the behavior and make other choices. Also, be sure to focus on how picking affects Nancy. Once the writing is started, then draw some of the people thinking about these ideas. Be sure to put thought bubbles over their heads and make the faces match the thinking.

QUESTION: **My student doesn't talk, read or write. I can't use all of the drawing and writing. What can I do?**

ANSWER: Learning to think requires language acquisition. Language is learned first as patterns, then as concepts, then as a representation of thinking. When babies are born, adults talk to the babies even though the babies cannot talk. The same logic holds for writing and drawing. Even though the child does not use sound for reading, writing, or speaking, the child is still able to learn the patterns of how the hand moves during drawing and writing. These visual-motor patterns provide the same overlap of input for learning to think in a visual way, just like the oral language provides the patterns for babies to learn to speak and read/write with sound. Adults do not wait for children to talk in order to talk with them. And, there is no reason to wait to write to children who think visually. Visual-motor patterns do not need sound to learn. These visual-motor patterns create shapes, which form ideas (reading) that can help a child learn to think in those shapes so that she can learn to say what she sees (speaking). Many severely impacted children learn to speak by learning to see what the visual-motor patterns mean. Write and draw as early as you want and as often as possible, especially for those children who do not have the language or literacy to choose to draw and write. Their learning to pro-socially think will come from the meaning of the visual-motor shapes of written and drawn ideas on a page.

QUESTION: **My school uses a system of rewards and punishers. I have to use that system. How can I not punish students while giving rewards?**

ANSWER: Instead of giving rewards, give gifts. Use the concepts of recognition, credit, support, and nurturance as the foundation for honoring all students as experts and specialists in one or two acts. For example, Sharon blurts out. Thank her in front of the class for her desire to share with one another and for her ideas. This recognizes her and gives her credit for her abilities. Then, Mark raises his hand and the teacher thanks Mark for waiting for Sharon to share her ideas and supports him by saying how it helps the teacher know that Mark is waiting to share so that everyone is able to hear him by raising his hand.

If there are tokens to trade in, then hand out the tokens as gifts. "I know you are all working to contribute your work to the success of our class." Quietly walk by and leave a handful of tokens on each student's desk. This recognizes all of the students as contributors to the class. Give the tokens as gifts to everyone for each person's contribution (being in class), for recognition that each has a strength (recognition), for "credit" for what each provides to the well-being of the classroom, and for helping each person feel like an agent (expert) in order to nurture the development of each person's "who."

QUESTION: **I've tried the drawing and writing and John's behavior is still bad. What can I do besides drawing and writing?**

ANSWER: It is not the magic of the drawing and writing that makes a difference. The effectiveness of providing visual-motor ways to think, for pro-social behavior, has to do with the following factors. 1) What is the developmental level of John's language? In other words, what does he understand? 2) What is the developmental level of the adult's drawing and writing? In other words, is the adult providing the drawing and writing at John's developmental language level? 3) Is the adult providing enough overlapping information in the drawing and writing to create the visual motor patterns in the way the John learns so that John is actually acquiring more conceptual meaning? The modality of drawing and writing is not effective by itself without consideration for the level of drawing and writing matched to John's level of understanding, which is then layered for concept learning.

Given the neurosemantic language learning system, there are not a lot of choices of how to provide the information (eyes, ears, nose, smell, and taste) but there are many ways to create overlapping visual-motor patterns so as to create better thinking: Are you using hand-over-hand methods? Are you using an overlap of mouth movements with hand movements? Are you having John do his own drawing and writing so that his brain is activated in the learning process? Are you adding details to your drawings along with thought bubbles of John in each frame of each picture? Are you sure you are providing an overlap of the type of patterns with the right level of language needed for John?

QUESTION: **My child doesn't sit. How can I expect to use some type of reading and writing if he won't sit down?**

ANSWER: Kaulitz, one of the authors, has a video of a 19-year-old who never sat down to work. An occupational therapist colleague, Lorraine Little, who had never worked with this student before, was asked to evaluate him and wanted the youth to sit down to work on some tasks using his hands. First she tells him what to do, then she points to the chair, points to his hands, repeats the words with different phrasing, shakes the materials she wants him to use, points again to his hands, restates the desired behavior using different words indicating with gestural signs that she wants him to sit so he can use his hands to fill the sacks. Finally, she picks up an individual dry-erase board and talks the youth through the task that she has drawn out. The youth is looking around the room. She takes his hand and hand-over-hand draws him as a stick figure with big hands putting things in the sacks while she overlaps the drawing, pointing, and hand-over-hand pointing with her oral language. Then she takes his hand and restates what he is to do while she hand-over-hand points to the pictures and to the picture of him. He immediately pulls out his chair and sits down. The whole process took about 1-1/2 minutes. Everyone was shocked; he sat down! And, he worked. He was able to do the tasks. He has consistently made progress since that day. Remember that people do not see themselves; only their hands and feet. To see what a person looks like, he has to see himself and drawing him into a picture with a label provides that information.

QUESTION: **We've tried everything. Milani is aggressive. She kicks, bites, and throws objects. Her mother doesn't know what to do with her. She is afraid of Milani. We have tried all sorts of behavior programs but the behaviors just change and Milani gets older and bigger.**

ANSWER: Milani's behavior tells us that Milani is functioning at the sensori-motor level and, therefore, does not have enough thinking and language to be able to make choices of her behavior. Forget working on the behavior and start working on increasing the thinking or cognition to develop language. Use motor access tools such as hand-over-hand drawing and writing to the drawings so Milani can learn what she looks like, what others think, and what she is expected to do. As Milani's cognition increases, her language will also increase. With an increase in cognition, Milani will also show a higher level of behavior that uses more conventional language such as words rather than aggressive behavior. Don't forget to use very rich language with Milani. Most programs ask adults to limit what is said. So, if you have used a number of programs to work on Milani's behavior, the chances are that your language is not rich but rather restricted. Your language must match the cartooned pictures. So, draw out the entire day for Milani as cartoon strips and then write all of the words that go with each drawing of each frame of the cartoon. This exercise will help you to begin to use richer language. For example, "Sit down! Be Quiet!" is visually seen by a child, like Milani, as "visually big eyes, big-open mouths." But, this language offers ways for Milani to learn to be pro-social, not just controlled: "Milani, I need to see you sit in your seat so that the bus can take you to your house. When you see your house, you will see your mother. Your mother will walk you from the bus to your house. When you walk into your house, you will hang up your coat and backpack and walk into the kitchen. When you walk into the kitchen, sit down on the stool so you can eat your snack." Milani has more language of behavior to know how to pro-socially act.

QUESTION: **Jack is very smart; but he is so smart that he manipulates everybody. Nobody wants to play with him. Even his teacher said that he never stops wheeling and dealing. What can we do to get Jack to stop the manipulation?**

ANSWER: Manipulation is an anti-social way to get one's needs met. As long as Jack is feeling that his behavior pays off, he will continue with the behavior, so two simultaneous goals are needed: 1) Help Jack learn to use his expertise in pro-social ways; and 2) Help Jack understand how others think of him when he is wheeling and dealing. For the first goal, give Jack credit for his strengths: "Jack, I see that you were able to find a baseball when all of the baseballs were already checked out. How were you able to do this?" Jack will tell you that Mark said he would give him the baseball. Now it is time to get the two boys together, each with paper and pencil and find out what each boy draws as what the event really was, what each boy thinks about the situation, and how each boy feels. At the end, it appears that Mark gave the baseball to Jack to use because Jack promised a half of his sandwich; but Jack has no sandwich to give as he is having hot lunch. When Mark finds out that Jack cannot give him a sandwich, then Mark is upset. Still using paper and pencil draw out how Mark feels and what he thinks. Mark does not see Jack as a friend, does not trust Jack, and does not want to play with Jack ever again. All of these concepts will need to be drawn for Jack so that he learns how to think differently about how to make friends and maintain healthy relationships. The authors remind the reader that all of this drawing will have to happen several times for several situations before Jack learns sufficient concepts to make better behavioral choices. In essence,

Jack needs to see his own agency develop so as to become pro-social. His wheeling and dealing is actually anti-social in nature.

QUESTION: I am not visual. I cannot draw. Besides, my students have lots of language and don't need pictures.

ANSWER: Be assured that none of the three authors of this book thinks in pictures or any other visual meta-cognition. However, almost all of the drawings in this book, as well as the other Arwood-referenced books were completed by the authors, and are about real situations with real students. The bottom-line is that drawing is not about the parent or the educator; drawing is about providing the learner a form of thinking that the learner needs. Furthermore, many professionals use all sorts of graphics (pictures, drawings, video clips, diagrams, cartoons, and flowcharts) to help explain complex ideas. Many college professors "draw out" concepts and students take visual notes (Arwood & Brown; 2001; Arwood & Kaakinen, 2004; Arwood & Kaakinen, 2009; Arwood, Kaakinen, & Wynne, 2002; Fallon & Brown, 2010). Finally, please note that individuals with ASD and related disorders may have a lot of language structures or patterns without conceptual understanding. If a person thinks in a visual meta-cognition, then visual representations provide the most meaning to learn conceptually.

QUESTION: My district requires us to use evidence-based practices. I don't see where the methods in this book meet the research requirement.

ANSWER: All of the methods suggested in this book are cognitive strategies, which are suggested to be an effective evidence-based researched method (Mitchell, 2008). Furthermore, the Neurosemantic Language Learning Theory (Arwood, 2011) is based on the translation of neuroscience. Neuroscience research is well regulated and documented in referenced journals. The research in neuroscience is often funded by grant processes, which also are based on research and must show evidence to maintain funding. What is not regulated is the educational type of data collection that uses data as a form of research. Collecting data does not tell the educator the quality of the data, only the number. For example, it is never okay to hit someone; therefore, reducing the number of hits by a child is not an acceptable goal. Only replacing the hit with better use of behavior based on thinking and learning is acceptable. Working on behavior goals, separate from the child's development as a person, does not provide the child with an increased ability to function with higher order thinking and problem solving. Using neuroscience along with the use of language literature and cognitive psychology for neuroeducation applications will show self-evident data….if it works, the learner needs it.

Summary

The authors recommend a pro-social way to handle behavior. Behavior is a product of the learning system. Therefore, increasing thinking through learning higher-order cognitive functions of language provides learners with improved abilities to make decisions, solve problems, and, therefore, learning more pro-social ways to behave. This language-based approach to behavior is both preventive in nature and a form of intervention designed to work with all levels of severity of behavior problems and all levels of cognition.

GLOSSARY

Acts – Individual movements that build up into an overall behavior. For example, arms moving and legs moving with a scrunched up face and tears is called crying. These individual movements or acts form clusters of behavior, for example, a tantrum consists of kicking, hitting, crying, and so forth.

Agent – Someone who does something. This concept of "agency" develops across ages and stages of learning processes.

Antecedents – Specific behaviors or stimuli result in specific responses or behaviors. The antecedent is the behavior or stimulus that occurs before a target or unwanted behavior.

Anti-social behavior – The way a child moves away from initiating and maintaining healthy relationships toward more aggressive, societally unacceptable behaviors.

Assign meaning –The act of interpreting behavior through actions, verbal comments, and nonverbal responses.

Behavior – Made up of a series of recognizable movements or acts to which someone assigns meaning. The child's arm moves toward an adult who interprets the behavior as hitting.

Behavior disorders – A term used to describe behavior that is socially unacceptable to multiple people who observe the behavior occurring across multiple settings, across time, and to the determent of others or the person engaging in the behavior.

Behavioral consequences – Refer to behavior that is a result of some type of input.

Behaviorism – A theory based on B. F. Skinner's approach to learning behavior through a system of rewards and punishers.

Biophysical model – Behavior as the result of physical changes within the neurobiological system often remedied through medical interventions.

Boundaries – Refer to the limit of individuals within a culture, family, or group in terms of what is personal and what is the norm.

Bubbling – A procedure whereby the configuration of a word is shaped so that the learner is able to see how the idea creates a visual pattern.

Bullying – The result of behavior that limits the power of another person through attacking another person's social well-being or agency.

Choices – Are part of decision-making or problem solving where an individual learns to think about options (see Options).

Classical conditioning – Refers to behavior that is paired with a natural consequence such as the smell of food paired with salivating.

Communication – People assign meaning to behavior so that all behavior shows what others think the behavior means or communicates.

Consequences – A behavior leads to a payoff, a reward, or an effect on someone else. The outcomes of a behavior are the consequences. Consequences are often considered in classical conditioning where there is a naturally occurring behavior; for example, a child touches a hot stove and immediately the hand jerks away from the heat. Being burned is a natural consequence.

Context – People (agents) share actions with each other and their objects in a recognizable place, which creates a story or event. See event.

Contract – Two or more people enter into an agreed-upon set of rules that benefit both parties when the agreement is executed.

Control – The use of any force or power necessary to limit another person's actions regardless of what the person thinks, believes, or wants.

Discrete trial training – A method of teaching new skills consisting of a series of distinct repeated lessons or trials taught one-to-one through manipulation of antecedent and consequences, to include direct instruction (specific stimuli elicit specific or target responses), prompting (stimuli or cues are used to define target responses), and reinforcing, followed with attention to intervals.

Displacement – A language principle that refers to how far away an idea is from its physical referent. For example, the term "dog" refers to an animal that can be touched so there is little distance between the animal and the language term "dog" used to name the animal. But, the expression "dog days of summer" refers to how hot the day is, not a dog. This expression shows a lot of displacement since the listener cannot touch or even see to what the speaker is referring.

Disturbing behavior – Behavior is labeled "disturbing" when a person does not "like" a particular behavior, or finds a particular behavior annoying or irritating.

Ecological theory – This theory is associated with Bronfenbrenner who set up behavior as a result of a set of systems that alter the meaning and motivation of behavior.

Efficiency – Occurs in language function when a thinker is able to quickly analyze options and respond with the behavior that a reasonable person would produce.

Emotions – Refer to the language for concepts of bodily states of thinking and feeling.

Empowerment – Refers to the ability to think as a socially competent person who is capable of being interdependent (see Interdependence).

Event – When people (agents) interact (actions) in a shared activity, they create a story or event.

Feelings – Refers to the sensory responses of input, such as touch, taste, smell, hearing, and sight.

Flexibility – The ability to think about others and, therefore, have more choices and opportunities to behave in a variety of ways. Linguistic flexibility refers to the ability to understand ideas from many different perspectives.

Functional behavior assessment (FBA) – A systematic way to determine the present level of performance (PLOP) of behavior including antecedents and consequences, in order to determine a schedule of reinforcement that is effective for a particular set of target behaviors.

Generalize – Practicing behavior through a stimulus-reward system in a variety of settings and conditions that result in the behavior occurring in non-rewarded situations.

Hand-over-hand (HoH) – The educator or parent using his or her hand on top of a learner's hand to help him learn the shape of the patterns of moving the hand to do an activity of daily living such as eating or brushing teeth or for patterns related to academic tasks such as writing.

Indicators – Behaviors, gestures, and/or words that tell a person what to do. For example, a mother looks at the clothes hamper and the teenage daughter picks it up, walks to the laundry room, and begins to wash the clothes in the hamper. In this case, the mother's look serves as an indicator.

Inhibition – The recognition of incoming stimuli or neurological messages as old messages so that there is more opportunity for new information to be acted on. Neurological inhibition occurs as cells either have already fired or are prevented from firing because of neurotransmitter activity. Observers see inhibition as a change in behavior that shows that the input is recognized as meaningful.

Integrate (integration) – The neurobiological ability to overlap sensory patterns to form concepts.

Interdependence – The ability to be independent functionally while recognizing the needs of others and considering others' perspectives.

Layers of learning – Occur as a result of complex neurological integration and inhibition of sensory input that forms patterns creating interconnected circuits of neurosemantic meaning.

Learning – A process that is defined differently. Some believe that learning is a two-tier model of input and output where output is imitated, copied, memorized, and produced. Others view learning as a series of layers of acquiring meaning at four tiers or levels as the result of a neurobiological set of processes that result in the acquisition of neurosemantic concepts represented by language, referred to as the neurosemantic language learning theory (Arwood, 2011).

Limits – The behaviors that the adult interprets as okay or not okay within the expectations of others in the context. Limits are often set through rules that we impose on a child so that the child will eventually learn how to govern his own behavior.

Marginalized – Being left out of the flow of information, activities, or decision-making.

Mixed messages – Result when a thinker cannot resolve a conflict in meaning from multiple inputs about what behavior is okay or not okay.

Natural consequences – Responses to sensation without having language or thought about the meaning of the behavior such as withdrawing the hand from the hot element of a stove.

Neurosemantic language learning theory – Consists of four levels of meaningful (semantic feature) acquisition: sensory input, perceptual patterns, concepts, and language. Each of these levels parallels neurobiological function.

Objectification – Occurs in abusive types of relationships or relationships in which the person has little, if any, control over his life – others make all decisions about what he is able to do.

Operant conditioning. This process refers to controlling the conditions under which a target behavior is paired with a reward to increase the likelihood of a behavior occurring again under similar conditions. Increasing the likelihood of the behavior occurring again is called reinforcing the behavior.

Options – refers to the choices that are real, as opposed to choices that are not acceptable or appropriate. For example, an adult is in an abusive situation and a friend tells the adult that it is her choice to stay or leave. But the adult in the abusive situation does not see how to leave the situation; therefore the choice is not a real option. .

Overlapping – Refers to the way that multiple sets of neurons and circuits of neurons interconnect to form more complex behavior.

Personal limits – What a person considers acceptable or not acceptable, especially as it relates to social norms or behavior.

Perspective – A person's mental view of relationships, ideas, and facts.

Power – The ability to make choices based on knowledge.

Problem solving – The process of making a decision based on knowledge of choices.

Productivity – The ability to use language in a variety of ways to communicate complex ideas.

Proprioceptive – Feedback from the nerves to the muscles that inform the body where it is in space.

Pro-social behavior –The way that we initiate and maintain healthy relationships with others.

Psychomotor social skills –The ability to do a behavior pattern. Therefore, psychomotor social skills refers to the ability to imitate a behavior that is related to social patterns such as etiquette rules like saying "thank you."

Psychodynamic theory – A theory, often associated with Sigmund Freud, which views behavior as a result of thinking developed in the family system.

Punishment (punishers) – Temporarily suppresses or stops a behavior from occurring.

Reductionism – Refers to breaking down a skill or task into its parts and then teaching the parts with the expectation that the parts will equal the whole.

Reinforcement – Increases the likelihood of a targeted behavior occurring again.

Rewards – Refers to tangible and non-tangible items that are paired with a targeted behavior based on the assumption that they will increase the likelihood of a behavior occurring in the future.

Rich language – Consists of ideas that are expanded in structure, extended to include multiple meanings, and modulated in grammar to address the constituent of who, what, where, when, why, and how questions.

Schedule of reinforcement – The ratio of behavior to rewards. Intermittent schedules that over time require more behavior for fewer rewards are most effective for long-term learning.

Self – Refers to the development of a person's "who" such as self-esteem, self-concept, self-image, self-awareness, and so forth. Self develops from becoming an agent (see agent).

Semanticity – The ability to acquire depth of meaning in concepts. The depth of meaning occurs through adding layers of meaning.

Social – Learning to be "social" refers to using appropriate behaviors to initiate and maintain healthy relationships with self and others. This is based on being able to use the typical environmental input for becoming an agent.

Social competence- Refers to the ability to initiate and maintain healthy positive (pro-social) relationships.

Social constructivism – Seeing behavior as an intentional development of meaning from the models in the child's environment.

Social development – Refers to the various levels of conceptual learning and is about how to initiate and maintain healthy relationships with others. The child's ability to fit into a variety of settings, to understand others' perspectives, and to initiate and maintain healthy relationships are all part of socializing. Social development stems from the acquisition of meaning about being an agent so as to develop the "self" or concept of "who". Social concepts are learned over time through the use of thinking with language.

Social skills – The acquisition of patterns of behavior, but without the underlying conceptual meaning of those skills. Skills are acquired through imitation, practice, and reward.

Successive approximation – The use of rewards to shape a behavior that is not exactly what is wanted into a better behavior, one that is wanted. For example, speech sounds or productions such as blowing bubbles are often rewarded with input to improve the productions to form words. The steps of moving from sound to words are successive and more closely approximate the target the closer to the wanted word or behavior.

Task analysis – Taking a complex behavior such as reading apart into its smaller units such as letters and sounds.

Target behavior – Behaviors that are selected to be paired with a reward; to be negatively or positively reinforced, or to be increased in similar situations or to be extinguished.

Transfer – A behavior term that refers to skills or behaviors that are reinforced so as to occur in similar settings or under similar stimulus controls.

Values – Positive or negative judgments or interpretations about beliefs, interests, desires, and needs.

Viewing – How a person sees others based on his own thinking or past learning about who the person is.

REFERENCES

Association for Positive Behavior Support (2008) www.apbs.org

Arwood, E. (1985). *APRICOT I kit.* Portland, OR: APRICOT Inc.

Arwood, E. (1991). *Semantic and pragmatic language disorders* (2nd ed.). Gaithersburg, MD: Aspen Publishers Inc.

Arwood, E. (2010). Developing the hand and the mind through language of the brain. Presentation at symposium on the hand, University of Portland.

Arwood, E. L. (2011). *Language function: An introduction to pragmatic assessment and intervention for higher order thinking and better literacy.* London, UK: Jessica Kingsley Publications.

Arwood, E. & Brown, M. (1999). *A guide to cartooning and flowcharting.* Portland, OR: APRICOT Inc.

Arwood, E. L. & Brown, M. (2001). *A guide to visual strategies for young adults.* Portland, OR: APRICOT Inc.

Arwood, E. & Kaakinen, J. (2004). Visual language strategies for innovative teaching of science. *Journal of Science Education for Students with Disabilities*, 10, 27-36.

Arwood, E. L. & Kaakinen, J. R. (2009). SIMulation Based on Language and Learning (SIMBaLL): The Model. *International Journal for Nursing Education Scholarship*, 6(1), article 9. Retrieved from www.bepress.com/ijnes/vol.6/issi/art9/

Arwood, E. L. & Kaakinen, J. R. (2010). Using language successfully in the college classroom. In S. C. Brown & M. A. Fallon (Eds.), *Teaching inclusively in higher education* (pp. 95-112). Charlotte, NC: Information Age Publishing.

Arwood, E., Kaakinen, J., & Wynne, A. (2002). *Nurse educators: Using visual language.* Portland, OR: APRICOT Inc.

Arwood, E. & Kaulitz, C. (2007). *Learning with a visual brain in an auditory world: Language strategies for individuals with autism spectrum disorders.* Shawnee Mission, KS: AAPC Publishing.

Arwood, E., Kaulitz, C., & Brown, M. (2009). *Visual thinking strategies for individuals with autism spectrum disorders: The language of pictures.* Shawnee Mission, KS: AAPC Publishing.

Arwood, E. L. & Young, E. (2000). *The Language of RESPECT: The right of each student to participate in an environment of communicative thoughtfulness.* Portland, OR: APRICOT Inc.

Bandura, A. (1968). Social learning interpretation of psychological dysfunctions. In P. London & D. Rosenhan (Eds.), *Foundation of abnormal psychology*. New York, NY: Holt, Rinehart, & Winston.

Baars, B. J. & Gage, N.M. (2010). *Cognition, brain, and consciousness* (2nd ed.). Elsevier/Academic Press.

Brennan, M. & Kirkland, J. (1982). Classification of infant cries using descriptive scales. *Infant behavior and development*, 5, 2–4, 341–346.doi.org/10.1016/S0163-6383(82)80044-1.

Briers, S. (2009). *Brilliant Cognitive Behavioural Therapy: How to Use CBT to Improve Your Mind and Your Life*. Harlow, England: Pearson Prentice Hall.

Bookheimer, S. (2004). Overview on learning and memory: Insights from functional brain imaging. *Learning Brain Expo Conference Proceedings*. San Diego, CA: Brain Store.

Bronfenbrenner, U. (1979). *The ecology of human development: Experiments by nature and design*. Cambridge, MA: Harvard University Press.

Bronfenbrenner, U. (1993). The ecology of cognitive development: Research models and fugitive findings. In R. H. Wozniak & K. W. Fischer (Eds.), *Development in context* (pp. 3-44). Hillsdale, NJ: Lawrence Erlbaum.

Bruner, J. S. (1983). *Child's talk: Learning to use language*. New York, NY: Norton.

Cooper, J. D. (2006). *Literacy: Helping children construct meaning*. Burlington, MA: Houghton Mifflin.

Eddy, J. M. & Reid, J. B. (2001). *The anti-social behavior of the adolescent children of incarcerated parents: A developmental perspective*. Oregon Social Learning Center. http://aspe.hhs.gov/hsp/prison2home02/eddy.htm

Fallon, M. & Brown. S. (2010). *Teaching inclusively in higher education*. Charlotte, NC: Information Age Publishing.

Freud, S. (1957). Mourning and melancholia. In J. Strachey (Ed. & Trans.), *The standard edition of the complete psychological works of Sigmund Freud*, 14. London, UK: Hogard Press. (Original work published in 1917.)

Garfinkle, A. N. & Schwartz, I. S. (2002). Peer Imitation Increasing Social Interactions in Children with Autism and Other Developmental Disabilities in Inclusive Preschool Classrooms. *Topics in Early Childhood Special Education*, 22, 1, 26-38 doi: 10.1177/027112140202200103.

Good, C. P., McIntosh, K., & Gietz, C. (2011). Integrating bullying prevention into schoolwide positive behavior support. *Teaching Exceptional Children*, 44(3), 48-56.

Grandin, T. & Johnson, C. (2005). *Animals in translation*. Orlando, FL: A Harvest Book/Harcourt Inc.

Grandin, T. & Panek, R. (2013). *The Autistic Brain: Thinking Across the Spectrum*. New York, NY: Houghton Mifflin Harcourt.

Hubel, D. (1988). *Eye, brain, and vision.* New York, NY: Scientific American Library: Distributed by W. H. Freeman.

Kelly, G. A. (1955). *The psychology of personal constructs.* New York, NY: Norton.

Merzenich, M. M., Saunders, G., Jenkins, W. M., Miller, S., Peterson, B., & Tallal, P. (1999). Pervasive developmental disorders: Listening training and language abilities. In S. H. Broman & J. M. Fletcher (Eds.), *The changing nervous system: Neurobehavioral consequences of early brain disorders* (pp. 365-385). New York, NY: Oxford University Press.

Merzenich, M. M., Tallal, P., Peterson, B., Miller, S. L., & Jenkins, W. M. (1998). Some neurological principles relevant to the origins of and the cortical plasticity based remediation of language learning impairments. In J. Grafman & Y. Christen (Eds.), *Neuroplasticity: Building a bridge from the laboratory to the clinic* (pp. 169-187). Amsterdam, Netherlands: Elsevier.

Mitchell, D. (2008). *What really works in special and inclusive education: Using evidence-based teaching strategies.* London, UK: Routledge.

O'Connor, A. (2012). *School bullies prey on children with autism.* NewYorkTimes.Com., September 3.

Osgood, C. E. (1956). *Method and Theory in Experimental Psychology*, Oxford University Press.

Patterson, G. R., DeBaryshe, & Ramsey, E. (1990). A developmental perspective on anti-social behavior. *American Psychologist*, 44, 329-335. Reprinted in: Gauvin, M. & Cole, M. (Eds.), *Readings on the development of children*, 2nd Ed. (1993, pp. 263-271). NY: Freeman.

Paul, R., Henry, L., Grieve, S. M., Guilmette, T. J., Niaura, R., Bryant, R., Bruce, S., Williams, L. M., Richard, C. C., Cohen, R. A., & Gordon, E. (2008). The relationship between early life stress and microstructural integrity of the corpus callosum in a non-clinical population. *Journal of Neuropsychiatric Disease and Treatment*, 4(1), 193-201.

Piaget, J. (1952). (Translated by M. Cook). *The origins of intelligence in children.* New York, NY: International Universities Press Inc.

Pulvermuller, F. (2003). *The neuroscience of language: Brain circuits of words and serial order.* Cambridge, MA: Cambridge University Press.

Sadato, N. (1996). In breakthroughs. *Discover*, 17, 27-28.

Skinner, B. F. (1953). *Science and human behavior.* New York, NY: Macmillan.

U.S. Department of Education. (2004). *Individuals with disabilities education act (IDEA).* IDEA.ed.gov.

Youth Violence Project. http://youthviolence.edschool.virginia.edu/bullying/bullying-middle-school-research.html; youthviolence.edschool.virginia.edu

Vygotsky, L. S. (1962). *Thought and language.* Cambridge, MA: MIT Press. (Originally published, 1934).

Walker, H. M., Ramsey, E., & Gresham, F. M. (2004). *Anti-social behavior in school: Evidence-based practices* (2nd ed.). Belmont, CA: Wadsworth/Thomson Learning.

Webber, J. & Plotts, C. (2008). *Emotional and behavioral disorders: Theory and Practice* (5th Ed.), New York: Pearson Education.

Winner, M. G. (2002). *Inside out: What makes a person with social cognitive deficits tick?* San Jose, CA: Think Social Publishing Inc.

Winner, M. G. (2007). *Thinking about you, thinking about me* (2nd ed.). San Jose, CA: Think Social Publishing Inc.

Winner, M. G. & Crooke, P. (2011). *Social thinking at work: Why should I care?* Great Barrington, MA: Think Social Publishing Inc. & The North River Press Publishing Company.